SECRETS
of
EVE

Understanding the Mystery of Female Sexuality

SECRETS
of
EVE

Understanding the Mystery of Female Sexuality

Archibald D. Hart, Ph.D.
Catherine Hart Weber, Ph.D.
Debra Taylor, M.A.

WORD PUBLISHING
Nashville • London • Vancouver • Melbourne

WORD PUBLISHING
Nashville, Tennessee

Unless otherwise marked, all Scripture quotations are from the King James Version of the Holy Bible.

Verses marked NIV are taken from the HOLY BIBLE, NEW INTERNATIONAL VERSION. Copyright © 1973, 1978, 1984 by the International Bible Society. Used by permission of Zondervan Publishing House. All rights reserved.

Verses marked NKJV are taken from the NEW KING JAMES VERSION, © 1979, 1980, 1982 by Thomas Nelson Publishers.

Book design by Kandi Shepherd

Library of Congress Cataloging-in-Publication Data

Hart, Archibald D.
    Secrets of Eve: understanding the mystery of female sexuality/
  Archibald D. Hart, Catherine Hart Weber, Debra Taylor.
      p. cm.
    Includes bibliographical references (p. 261) and index.
    ISBN 0-8499-1340-3
    1. Women—Sexual behavior. 2. Sex (Psychology). 3. Sex—Religious aspects—Christianity. 4. Sexual behavior surveys. I. Weber, Catherine Hart, 1957–   . II. Taylor, Debra, 1955–   . III. Title.
HQ29.H375 1998
306.7'082—dc21

                                    97–44364
                                        CIP

Printed in the United States of America
8 9 0 1 2 3 4 5 6 BVG 9 8 7 6 5 4 3 2 1

We dedicate this book to our spouses:
Kathleen, Rick, and Kent

Contents

List of Figures

Acknowledgments

So many have helped to make this book possible that it is difficult to know where to begin in expressing our appreciation. Foremost, however, is Dr. Kent Taylor, Debra's husband, who has been the mainstay of our statistical analyses. Dr. Taylor's background is in teaching biology and genetics, but he now works primarily as a research molecular biologist in the area of the genetics of diseases. His work in research may at first glance seem to be far removed from our topic here, but he is no stranger to the field of sexuality. He has taught college biology and co-taught with Debra on many aspects of sexuality, so he brings a wealth of background on this topic, not just his research expertise. He assisted us in many ways. He advised us on research design, wrote the data entry programs, and then did most of the data analysis. Above all, he helped us to remain scientifically honest. Without his help this project could easily have taken many years to complete!

Naomi Beard, the Director of Women's Ministry at The Church on the Way, Van Nuys, California, was particularly key in conceptualizing this project. An outstanding speaker and leader, she is nationally recognized as an expert in women's ministries. Not only did she launch us in the right direction, she enthusiastically distributed surveys wherever she traveled. Naomi, you are greatly valued for your help in this study.

Many friends and family covered this project with prayer and encouraging support. In particular we thank Debra's prayer group: Gretchen, Christine, Linda, Pam, Julie, Lisa, and Kristy; Catherine's friend Debra Montana, her sisters Sharon and Sylvia, her mother Kathleen, and the prayer ministry at The Church on the Way.

Assisting us in data entry were three stalwarts: Dr. Hart's secretary, Linda Rojas, Tim Jacklitch, and Jim Chapman. Jim carried the main responsibility for data entry, and with meticulous care he ensured that there were no errors to be reckoned with. He also provided helpful feedback on much of the data.

We are also indebted to the wonderful people of Nelson/Word who encouraged our work all along the way. Ernie Owen, Kip Jordan (who, regrettably, passed away while we were finishing this manuscript), Nelson Keener, Senior Editor Ami McConnell, and the other staff never flagged in their support. It is a great privilege to work with such tremendously competent professionals in the publishing field.

But the greatest appreciation of all goes to our three spouses, Rick, Kent, and Kathleen. We owe them a very special expression of our gratitude. Not only do they epitomize what it means to be an ideal partner, but also, without the full measure of what they contribute to the healing of our own sexuality, we would not have had the courage or the insights to tackle a topic as delicate as this one. Thank you for your patience and support.

Special thanks to Debra's children, Anna and Michael, and Catherine's girls, Nicole and Caitlan, who have prayed, forgiven, and sacrificed to love their moms through it all.

Archibald D. Hart
Catherine Hart Weber
Debra Taylor

Preface

This book and its underlying study are the convergence of two separate developments. The first development came shortly after the publication of Dr. Archibald Hart's book *The Sexual Man*.[1] Dr. Hart received many letters from readers. Christian men wrote to express their appreciation for the help the book had given them in understanding their sexuality. But the letters were not all from men. *The Sexual Man* contained a message to women, also, so their many letters were eagerly devoured.

These women praised Dr. Hart for helping them understand the perpetual "testosterone fog" that clung to their partners. Many reported that one of the benefits of the book was that it opened up conversations with their husbands. Previously, they had found it almost impossible to engage their partners in any serious dialogue about sexual matters. One lady wrote:

> *"My husband would never talk seriously with me about sex, even though we were having problems. I bought your book, took it home, and left it on the coffee table hoping that he would see it. Sure thing, he did! Next thing I knew he was carrying it around, reading it, and quoting to me from it. I didn't stop him. From there we were able to open up some real communication about how different we were. Finally, he accepted that I really did want to understand him."*

Then came her punch line: *"But when do I get to tell my story? When will I have something to share with him about how I feel?"* The book had prompted its women readers to want a book about women's sexuality.

The second development began in spring 1995 when Debra Taylor, a marriage and family counselor and certified sex therapist, and Dr. Catherine Hart Weber (Dr. Hart's daughter) sat in a restaurant discussing an upcoming seminar with Naomi Beard, the director of women's ministries at The Church on the Way. Naomi asked Debra and Catherine to put together a seminar on women's sexuality.

The more they talked, the more they realized how little was known about the sexuality of Christian women. During the discussion, Dr. Hart's study on male sexuality and his book *The Sexual Man* kept coming up. Naomi had heard Dr. Hart discuss his book on Dr. Dobson's *Focus on the Family* radio program. She was convinced of the need for a similar study and the need for a book on the sexuality of Christian women. So they approached Dr. Hart about the possibility of such a study.

Dr. Hart's Response

How could I, a male, have the gall to embark on a female research project, similar to the male study and write a book on the topic of female sexuality? Intuitively I knew that female sexuality was far more complex.

How could I ever convince anyone that I, a male, could even begin to understand where women were coming from? The male "testosterone fog" is one thing, but female estrogen/progesterone hormones are entirely another!

My eldest daughter, Catherine, a Ph.D. graduate in marital and family therapy, and Debra, one of her closest friends, boldly approached me in my vacillating uncertainty. They were convinced that women need to understand themselves better. More important, men need to understand women better. They have to stop seeing women and sex just through the male perspective. Catherine and Debra encouraged me to proceed.

It was then that I had a brilliant idea. I promptly pressed the two of them to join me on the project as coinvestigators and authors. And what a marvelous team they have proven to be! Without these two wonderful and talented collaborators I never would have considered undertaking this enormous task. Needless to say I have relied heavily on their guidance, both in the design and in the carrying out of the study that undergirds our work here. Their assistance has been indispensable in the writing of this book.

But God had also made another wonderful provision. We needed the help of a competent statistician because we did not want to trust our own expertise in this important study. Kent, Debra's husband, graciously offered to assist. His expertise as a researcher in medical biology proved to be invaluable, and right from the beginning he helped us avoid many pitfalls. The statistics and charts presented in this book are all his competent handiwork. Without his dedicated assistance we never would have survived the project, let alone finished it.

Together we launched the National Study on the Sexuality of Christian Women in early 1996 with our first questionnaire and set about recruiting participants from all around the United States. Over the next eighteen months we tried to reach all ethnic and age-groups. We were not interested only in married women but wanted to hear from single, divorced, remarried, and widowed women as well. Most important, we wanted to include as many church groups as possible. The end result is a sample of over two thousand Christian women from around the United States who represent the mainstream women in our churches today.

What follows is *crucial* information. This book is the story of many women. It is a story *that must be told*. We hope our contribution will correct myths about sexuality and encourage and reassure Christian women today.

Archibald D. Hart
Catherine Hart Weber
Debra Taylor

Chapter One

Female Sexuality—The Untold Story

"I am the rose of Sharon, and the lily of the valleys."
—*Song of Solomon 2:1*

This book is the story of two thousand women who yearn to tell their story—they deserve to be heard. It is a story about their sexuality.

These women come from all walks of life. Among them are the single, married, divorced, remarried, and widowed. They are professionals, and they are homemakers. They are at the beginning of their married lives, and they are widowed. They are mothers and grandmothers, and even a few are great-grandmothers. Some have chosen a celibate lifestyle; others await the time when they will meet the "right man" and fulfill their sexual desires.

They are by no means homogeneous. The woman who wrote the following note at the end of her questionnaire represents the sexual feelings of quite a few.

"It wouldn't bother me one little bit if I never have sex again in my life. Sex is not important to me, although I realize I am still a sexual being. I have suffered for years at the hands of a man obsessed with sex. I'm glad to be done with it all."

Yet another, far more representative of the women we studied, wrote:

"Sex is now the most beautiful thing in my marriage. It wasn't always so. It took my husband and me a long time to work out our incompatibility, but it was worth the wait. I wouldn't ever want to be without this wonderful gift from God. Sex does more to bring our marriage together than almost anything else."

Each and every one of these stories is worth telling. We knew it the moment we read the comments on the first questionnaires that came back to us. Some spoke of joy, others of pain. Many could not help contrasting their sexuality with that of their husbands. One wrote:

"I am sure we all have ups and downs in our desire levels. We can still make love even if we are not fully in the mood. But I draw the line when my husband doesn't treat me with respect. He doesn't seem to get the point that quality time in bed depends on quality time outside of bed. Until he understands this we will remain poles apart in our sexuality."

Stories like this don't just speak for the one telling it. They speak for many women.

While each story is unique, taken together they tell a compelling and universal story. We were amazed by the consistency of the themes in the stories; themes that help deepen our understanding of the bewildering sexual differences between men and women. Female sexuality is a mystery to men. But it is also a mystery to many women. Understanding our differences is without a doubt the key to achieving greater marital harmony.

These women's stories remind us of how *delicate the formation of female sexuality is* and how important it is that girls be taught *healthy attitudes toward sex*. These stories can also guide us through the changes that women go through and highlight particular challenges. As in almost everything human, prevention is better than cure. But it is especially important when it comes to the formation of healthy sexuality.

What Is Your Current Level of Sexual Interest?

Before we look too closely at the results of our study, examine your current level of sexual interest. You may want to take this test now and then repeat it after you have completed the book. You may wish to write your answers on a separate sheet of paper.

1. Do you feel sexually responsive when the circumstances are right?

    Often / Usually / Sometimes / Rarely / Never

2. Do you have pleasurable thoughts about sex one to several times a week?

    Often / Usually / Sometimes / Rarely / Never

3. Do you find it easy to get into the mood for sex?

    Often / Usually / Sometimes / Rarely / Never

4. Do you find it easy to initiate lovemaking?

    Often / Usually / Sometimes / Rarely / Never

5. Do you respond favorably to your partner's sexual advances?

    Often / Usually / Sometimes / Rarely / Never

6. Do you miss sex if you haven't made love for a while?

    Often / Usually / Sometimes / Rarely / Never

If you answered "Often" to most of the questions, your current interest in sex is very strong. If you answered "Usually," your interest is strong, and if "Sometimes," your interest is normal. If you answered most of these questions with "Rarely," your interest level is on the low side, and if "Never," you are clearly not interested in anything sexual.

If at some time in your past you would have answered these questions with a higher level of interest, then something has happened to diminish your drive. Hopefully, this book will help you to discover the reason.

The Complexity of Female Sexuality

One major difference between male and female sexuality is in complexity. Listen to what some of the women had to say in their written comments:

"I think that some of my problems with sex drive come from the fact that we only knew each other for two months before marriage—I

was pregnant right away. We never got used to each other and our sexual preferences before the baby arrived. Before the pregnancy my sex drive was good, but it has not seemed to bounce back after the baby. He is now 2 1/2 and we just learned that I'm pregnant again."

"My sexual responsiveness is strongly affected by the degree of privacy, what else is on the schedule and my emotional status, so usually I know if I will respond sexually or not. Yet I respect his needs and my lesser needs. My partner would spend time trying to arouse me if I wanted him to, but since frustration at not becoming aroused is annoying, I let him know it's not necessary."

"I've recently begun menopause. My sexual drive and response has decreased in all areas—physically and in my thoughts."

The factors that work together to shape female sexuality are mind-boggling. These range from the benefits of being raised in a Christian home and the value of an honest, forthright, and complete sex education, to the trauma of early sexual abuse. Hormonal fluctuations due to PMS, menopause, pregnancy, and childbirth can cause dramatic changes in sexual interest and responsiveness. Add to this the fact that many medications can disrupt sexual functioning. The result is an array of significant influences that impact every woman's sexuality to some degree.

By comparison, male sexuality is piffling—a drop in the cosmic puddle! (Obviously we are exaggerating.) Make no mistake about it, male sexuality is *powerful*. It is a strong, driving force, often reckless and difficult to control. Sex dominates and *controls* the male more than it does the average female. But it is not bothered or disrupted by as many factors as female sexuality. There is no menstruation, hormonal fluctuations, or pregnancy to adjust to. The fact is that it could take several books to really say all that needs to be said about female sexuality.

To illustrate this complexity, allow Dr. Hart to share about his first encounter with female research collaborators. When we first met to design the questionnaire used in this study he was quite insistent that we should follow the same approach as he did in the male study. After all, he had used a New York consultant who was an expert in the design of questionnaires. The consultant advised Dr. Hart to keep the questionnaire as short as possible. Reason? Men hate long questionnaires. They prefer the short answer, not the roundabout, intricate, detailed one. They probably wouldn't answer a questionnaire that took too long to fill out.

> **The factors that work together to shape female sexuality is mind-boggling.**

When he suggested this same principle for the female study, he was unanimously shot down. "Women will want to tell the whole story, or no story at all," he was told. "If they feel shortchanged they will refuse to answer the whole questionnaire."

So he listened and checked in with some of the other women around him—wife, daughters, and colleagues—professionals and the like. They all agreed that completeness takes precedence over shortness. So as complete a questionnaire as possible was what we aimed for. Dr. Hart had received his first major lesson in how the female's sexuality differs from the male's at very subtle levels. And the real study hadn't started yet!

Why Is This Study Important?

One of the most crucial problems facing modern society is the area of sex and love. The modern sexual revolution of the last three decades has produced a dramatic and harmful effect on the sexual behavior of our culture. It has fostered the wholesale loosening of sexual morals and the abandonment of marriage as the focus of sexual expression.

But the influence of this so-called modern sexual revolution not only has impacted the secular world of which we are all a part but also has infected our Christian world as well. In fact, we believe that one of the most critical issues facing the church as we enter the twenty-first century is the whole issue of sexuality. We need to come to grips with our culture's portrayal of what constitutes normal human sexuality. Notice, we did not just say it was a problem of sex, but of *sexuality*. We also have to open up a dialog in our churches about sexuality.

> **We believe that one of the most critical issues facing the church as we enter the twenty-first century is the whole issue of sexuality.**

What is the difference between our focus on "sexuality" and the more specific topic of "sex"? By the term *sexuality* we mean more than just sex. The word *sex* can mean many things, from gender to intercourse or other genital contact. *Sexuality* is a much broader term that embraces ALL that it means to be sexual. It includes how we feel about our bodies, men, intercourse, and sexual gratification. It encompasses our beliefs and attitudes about everything sexual including whether we like and desire sex or are repelled by it.

All sexuality is shaped by the context in which people are placed, namely their culture. Culture, with its mores and attitudes, is a powerful controller of sexuality. But there are also subcultures that have their influence. Of interest to us is the fact that these two influences, the dominant American culture and the subculture of Christianity, can combine to create a conflicted sexuality.

Other Sexual Studies

Until recent times very few studies have focused exclusively on the sexual behavior of women, let alone Christian women. The HIV/AIDS crisis has, of necessity, been society's primary focus most recently and has somewhat consumed our energy and resources. Unfortunately, those studies that have looked at female sexuality have done so in response to the loosening of values within the sexual arena generally. More and more, sex is coming to be seen as a recreational activity that has no connection to marriage or family commitment. And so research has followed suit.

Secular studies have moved from "how to enhance the sexual side of marriage," to "how to cope with multiple partners" or "sex without responsibility." The study of the sexuality of normal, heterosexual, morally sensitive and responsible women has been neglected. As a result, much of what is pedaled as "sexual wisdom" has little relevance for Christian, mainstream monogamous women. Furthermore, most studies of sexuality have contributed very little to our Christian subculture. If anything, secular studies have given the impression that they were antireligious.

Against this backdrop our study has one major advantage. It explores the sexuality of Christian women from *within*. For good or bad, we are a part of the very group we are studying. What this means is that we understand this group better than pure scientists who try to understand it from without. We will make every effort not to let our biases contaminate our findings.

The *Sex in America* report, conducted by a team of researchers from the University of Chicago, gives about the most balanced picture of what sexuality in America is like today. Just consider some of their key findings: Americans fall into three groups. One-third have sex at least twice a week, one-third a few times a month, and one-third a few times a year.[1] Americans are largely monogamous, with more than 80% having had only one or zero sex partners a year.[2] Adultery is the exception, not the rule. There are a lot fewer homosexuals than the 10% Kinsey reported. Three percent of adults have never had sex. And most Americans don't go for the kinky stuff. Not a bad picture at all.

These findings came as a great relief because they confirm the experience of the majority. They help reassure many that there is nothing wrong with them. We have sought to replicate some of these findings in our study, mainly for control purposes and for validating our sampling approach. If we are in the same ballpark as they are when we ask the same questions, then our sample must also be a fairly representative one.

We were pleasantly surprised how close we came to their very expensive study on common points. They used a sample of nearly thirty-five hundred men and women; we used a sample of over two thousand women. They were able to conduct personal interviews; we used a standardized questionnaire.

If their study is so good, why did we conduct ours? Simply because they looked at secular sexual practices. We were interested in sexuality, which goes way beyond what you DO in sex. Also, while the *Sex in America* study gave us some insights into how religion impacts sexuality, the way they categorized religious groups didn't accurately measure evangelicals. Evangelicals, who believe Scripture to be the authority in all matters of faith and conduct, are a unique group. They are frequently

---

The Most Significant Findings from Our Study

Let us present here the most significant findings of our study. These are not necessarily the most contentious or bothersome issues facing women today, but from a statistical perspective they are the most outstanding discoveries. This will help you get a feel for how important research such as this is. Later in the book, we will expand on these relationships in more detail.

• A very strong association exists between marital happiness and sexual satisfaction. (See chapter 8.)

• Sexual satisfaction is strongly associated with sexual desire. (See chapter 4.)

• Sexual satisfaction is strongly associated with duration of sex. Orgasm is associated with duration. The longer the duration of sex, up to 30 minutes, the greater your likelihood of orgasm. (See chapter 5.)

• Sexual satisfaction is strongly associated with the frequency of thinking about sex. This is perhaps the strongest statistical finding in our study. (See chapter 4.)

• Sexual satisfaction is associated with frequency of intercourse. (See chapter 8.)

• Nearly 45% of married women reported having difficulty finding the energy for sex. Women with children at home reported the greatest difficulty. (See chapter 6.)

• The most frequently reported health concern affecting women's sexuality is premenstrual syndrome (PMS); next was menopause. (See chapter 7.)

---

misrepresented as constrictive and narrow-minded. Our study explores this stereotype to see if it is true to any extent.

Another weakness in the *Sex in America* study is that it looked more at sexual *behavior between the sexes*, not at the *sexuality of the sexes*.

The sexuality of Christian women is what our study is about. It makes no attempt to draw comparisons with other groups of women, merely to describe itself to its own constituency. In this respect, our report is unique. It seeks to redress the imbalance and distortions that other reports have perpetuated.

The Church and Christian Sexuality

Given the audience for whom this book is written, some comments need to be made about the church's role in the formation of Christian sexuality. Why? Here is an example of one woman's viewpoint:

> *"The church is behind the times in many respects. Certainly, it has not helped to educate its adherents to a healthy and biblically acceptable form of sexuality. The church needs to counter hundreds of years of 'shame based' theology connected with sexuality. I want my daughters to have a healthier view of sexuality than I grew up with."*

Now let's be fair. Not every church or group of churches is this damaging to sexual formation. The church, more than any other social system, has kept our society's nose to the grindstone when it comes to sexual morals and family values. There has been a recent resurgence of interest around issues of family life. The importance of the family, the welfare of children, responsible parenthood, teenage pregnancy, and many other concerns have languished in our culture, and only the church has stayed on course. Yes, it does "take a village" to raise a family, and we are thankful for this emphasis. But it also takes godly, loving, and well-adjusted parents—and a healthy church.

But even a healthy church will not suffice. Ignorance can cause damage even where good intentions prevail. Often it is what is not talked about in healthy churches that is destructive, not what is. And it is our silence in matters of sexuality that represents the greatest threat of all to our Christian families. Our children are being left to their own devices because by and large we as Christians find sexuality too difficult to deal with openly.

> **The church, more than any other social system, has kept our society's nose to the grindstone when it comes to sexual morals and family values.**

The result? Sexual distortions. We saw it in many returned questionnaires, especially in the comments women wrote to us. Myth and confusion abound. We found unequivocal evidence that the main source of information available to our children, both boys and girls, comes from outside the family, from the tainted world of secular, nonmoral sources.

In much of the media there is a gutter view of sexuality, fed by secular research that has tended to explore the fringe behaviors of sexuality, not its core goodness. Often the agenda has been to discredit religious influences. This comes from those who have their own agendas, who want to shape a "morally free" sexuality, without constraints or inhibitions. And when Christian parents and the church are silent about the topic of sexuality, the consequences are far-reaching and damaging to our children, and to our grandchildren.

What the statistical tables and charts of all these studies have ignored is the intention of God's creative work in human sexuality. Does the Bible not have something to say? We believe it does. It is not outdated, nor are its circumstances entirely different from our own.

We are determined to present our findings in the context of a biblical perspective. There is a Christian way to be fully sexual and at the same time fully spiritual. It is imperative in these days that we lift up a balanced, biblical model of sexuality. Knowing what God intended is imperative. We would be lost without it!

Can Religion Distort Sexuality?

Let us not be too idealistic about the modern church. Religion can distort sexuality. Not all religion, only that which has been distorted. Such distorted religion has been labeled quite appropriately as *toxic*. It is a result of idiosyncratic, highly selective forms of biblical interpretation. Sometimes it is not the product of incorrect Bible interpretation but of unhealthy minds.

What has all this got to do with female sexuality? Clearly, toxic religion has the potential for harming sexuality. Males seem to be better able to override the negative views of sex perpetrated by a toxic religion. This was very clear from the findings in Dr. Hart's study of male sexuality reported in *The Sexual Man*. Women are more vulnerable because they are usually left with the effects from male sexuality when it is out of control.

The following are a few comments we received from participants in our study that help to make our point about the sexual effects of toxic religious influences:

> *"I don't know why I have the problems I have about sex. I was raised in a strongly religious home and made to feel guilty about everything sexual. I know my parents thought they were protecting me from the boys in my life, but they went overboard in labeling everything sexual as 'dirty.' Is this what God intended? How will I be able to undo this damage? (My husband prompted me to ask this question.)"*

> *"How can I get rid of the old tapes in my head from my childhood about how defiled sex is? They make me feel inhibited every time I have sex. I feel like a prostitute!"*

"More than anything else I want to abandon myself to my husband when we make love. He is kind and gentle, and very patient with me. But something inside tells me I'm doing bad things. What's wrong with me? My husband keeps assuring me that we are married and all that, but after two years of marriage I still feel like I'm sinning."

While we quote these to show how a strict and toxic religious upbringing can distort a woman's sexuality, we were pleasantly surprised to discover that although distortion happens, it wasn't prevalent in our sample. Also, nonreligious parents with hang-ups can be just as destructive to sexual attitudes in their children. If anything, the majority of respondents reported quite the opposite. They believed that their religious parents helped shape a healthier sexuality.

An honest evaluation of where Christian women are today, in light of a healthy biblical perspective, will be a valuable resource for the church. Sex is part of God's created order. He gave us sex as a way to express love, become one, and give and receive pleasure. It is also the way He has designed us to reproduce. Ignorance of God's intentions can result in distortions.

While in this study we will be ruthless in our quest for facts, we do not think that a survey such as ours that reports on the present state of affairs defines what should be normal or healthy. Something may be very common, but not healthy. The fact that everyone is doing it doesn't mean that it becomes the standard by which we judge the morality or desirability of a behavior. Whether it is right or wrong must be judged by other standards. Common sense must sometimes override statistics and facts, and you can be assured we will use caution in interpreting what we conclude from the facts. Only honesty and a matching ruthlessness in our quest for biblical truth can provide us with a balanced and healthy sexuality—male or female.

> **Only honesty and a matching ruthlessness in our quest for biblical truth can provide us with a balanced and healthy sexuality—male or female.**

Why Study Christian Women?

We purposely focused our study on a particular subgroup of women in our society: Women who identify themselves as Christians. Clearly, the women who responded to our survey fit this subgroup. Ninety-six percent consider themselves committed Christians, 90% attend church at least once per week. No doubt, some readers will be inquisitive as to why we have singled out Christian women for study. Is there anything special about this group? We believe there is.

First, these women have never been studied in any depth. Their religious feelings and influences have often been distorted or misjudged. Second, there is another and more important reason: We believe that this group of women represents the mainstream of women in our society today. They are the largest of any single sociologically defined group and are most likely to have the strongest moral convictions. In other words, if one were to select a group who would most represent the ideal of sexual behavior in our society, this would be the group.

While many of them would not claim to always have lived a sexually pure life, they would say that their desire is to live a moral life now. These women are churchgoing and committed to marriage and family values. They probably work harder at making their marriages work than any other group and have partners with very similar commitments. They represent, after all, the majority of the women in our society today.

Does such a sample leave out a significant number of other women? Of course it does. But the sexuality of the larger population has already been well studied. The *Sex in America* report was quite comprehensive.

Does excluding nontraditional groups of women, such as those who prefer sex with other women, distort our findings? Yes it does. It means that we cannot generalize to the total population. But we don't intend to. We intentionally avoided nontraditional sexuality for the simple reason that it does not represent the mainstream of women in the church today. The study of nontraditional female sexuality is a separate project and not undertaken here. We are neither passing moral judgment nor implying that they are not worthy of study. This group is simply not the focus of this study, which is confined to heterosexual women.

The Real Stories Behind Female Sexuality

While this book is based on a scientific study of a sample of women, facts and figures don't always tell the whole truth. Often they can be downright misleading. We will use every caution in our interpretation of the facts not to allow our bias to mislead or distort. We certainly do not believe that just because a certain sexual behavior is extremely common it is normal. Time and time again, we will try to interpret the data in light of what we consider to be biblical sexuality.

Charts and statistics will be presented where they are appropriate, but we want to tell a more personal story. So we will use the written comments of our participants. A few participants asked not to be quoted, and we did not quote them. If by chance you are one of those participants and something you read seems awfully familiar, please be assured that it comes from someone else and not you. Also, to avoid embarrassment, any illustrative material provided has been modified to prevent personal identification.

The Importance of This Study to All Women

This book tries to tell the whole story of female sexuality as it exists in our Christian subculture today. It is not a book about sexual technique. We believe it informs technique, but it deals with something more important than the practice of sex. It is about *sexuality*.

So this book tells the story of feelings, fears, desires, disappointments, ecstasy, and confusion. These all undergird and shape our sexual practices. It also explores the deeper *causes* of our sexual problems, not just the sexual problems themselves. We will try to identify how sexuality can be distorted early in life, as well as what can devastate it later.

We will not be able to report on everything we have discovered in this study. Some findings will have to await publication in professional journals. After all, when over two thousand Christian women speak, the world should listen. We will focus on the discoveries that appeared to be most important to Christian women.

Not all the women in our study were currently sexually active whether or not they were married. Some are in marital circumstances where sexual intercourse is no longer possible. Some are widowed after years of sexual contentedness. Some are divorced and either would like to get back into a sexual relationship or are glad to be free of sexual obligations. But whether sexually active or not, their sexuality remains intact. Sexual desire may be minimal or even nonexistent, but they will always be sexual beings.

This point is important to emphasize because it means that this study is important to all women—sexually active or not. We have avoided being sidetracked to issues of sexual technique. It is where women come from, the deeper origins of their sexual feelings and reactions, that concerns us. In this respect, this study is unique!

The Importance of This Study to Marriages

So, if this book is not about technique, of what value is it to married couples or to those planning on marriage? We believe that a really good sexual relationship, not just the performance of good sex, is the product of a strong marriage based on healthy sexual development. A bad marriage will eventually result in an unsatisfactory sex life. We hope to be able to address these deeper issues in this book.

Our study seeks to reveal what women are thinking and feeling, their frustrations and desires, needs and wants, and candid comments about sex. Our goal is to hold up a giant mirror to the church so that we can see the whole picture of Christian female sexuality.

But our goal goes beyond this. We want women to know that they are normal. Where there are problems with their sexuality, to discover the path to wholeness. We want to expose the myths that prevail in our culture. We hope that our study will help to open up a more direct and honest discussion of all matters pertaining to sexuality.

Finally, we want to help women reclaim biblical sexuality. To understand that we, women and men, can be fully human and sexual and at the same time deeply spiritual and pure. This is what redeemed sexuality is all about.

Points to Remember

1. Two thousand women courageously shared their inner-most sexual feelings and experiences, making it possible for us to realistically discuss Christian female sexuality.

2. Many factors work together to form female sexuality, and it is influenced by many more conditions than male sexuality. Men need a more complete understanding of this complexity.

3. Sexual myths, distortions, and confusions are due to our culture's view of sex and the church's lack of response in openly addressing these issues.

Chapter Two

Am I Normal?

"Behold, you are fair, my love! Behold, you are fair!"
—*Song of Solomon 4:1 NKJV*

Sarah and Jim knew their marriage was in trouble a few months after Sarah gave birth to their first son, Matthew. Until then they had experienced a mutual and very satisfying sexual relationship. Little did they know a dramatic turnaround was about to occur. They had stopped having sex toward the end of the pregnancy for fear it might harm the baby but thought that all would return to normal once Sarah recovered from the process of childbirth.

Neither had dated in earnest previously, so to discover the phenomenal passion they felt for each other was very promising. They were headed, they thought, for marital bliss. As committed Christians they decided to "save themselves for each other" until they married. And while several of their friends had warned them not to be too disappointed with sex once they married, they experienced no such disappointment—only joy in their sexual union.

For the next three years, Sarah and Jim grew closer together, and as they came to know each other more intimately their sexual satisfaction grew stronger. When Sarah discovered she was pregnant they were thrilled. During the early stages of the pregnancy, little changed sexually. Two months before she was to deliver, Sarah noticed she no longer felt as passionate. She had no interest in being fondled, and orgasm became a chore. She and Jim

17

believed it was caused by the late pregnancy stage and optimistically looked forward to things getting better.

It didn't. After the delivery Sarah felt depressed and, to her dismay, lost all interest in sex. The months rolled by, and even though her depression passed, her desire for sex seemed to have vanished into thin air. Finally, Sarah and Jim decided they needed to get help. The prospect of living the rest of their lives in a sexual desert frightened both of them.

Sarah's first words, after initial introductions with their therapist, were: "I'm here to find out if I am normal!" This is one of the most common concerns that therapists who deal with sexual problems are confronted with—the concern that one's sexual desire is not normal. Nothing is more alarming to someone like Sarah than to discover that her desire seems to have died, when she knows that she is capable of deep, passionate sexual feelings.

It is not surprising, therefore, that in response to our open-ended question "What would you like to know about female sexuality?" the question "Am I normal?" kept surfacing. Women wrote it in the comment section of our questionnaire, they scribbled it in the margins, and they elaborated on it in notes to us. It was the single most repeated query.

Sometimes it took the form: "Am I normal in how I *feel?*" Other times it was: "Do other Christians *think* the same as I do?" Also, there was concern about the acceptability of certain *behaviors.*

In the process of therapy that followed, Sarah discovered just how normal it is to temporarily lose sexual desire when hormones become unbalanced. Her sexual desire would soon return. Not all women are that fortunate! The tough years of child raising that lie ahead can threaten sexual desire, and there may be many times in her future when she will wonder, "Am I normal?"

Our Confusing Sexual World

All women are concerned about what is and isn't "normal." They have a need to know how they compare with others because they get so many conflicting messages about sexuality from our culture. Our culture has conditioned us to believe that passion belongs to the young, so as women age they wonder if their sexual years are over. Younger women worry because they don't feel as passionate as the media portrays them to be. Many resort to all sorts of excesses to try and light their fire.

A natural consequence of the distorted views of sexuality depicted in movies, television, and magazines is that we wonder if we are normal sexually. By and large the sexual messages from the media are misleading and false. Or are they? Maybe everybody else really *is* jumping from

> **A natural consequence of the distorted views of sexuality depicted in movies, television, and magazines is that we wonder if we are normal sexually.**

bed to bed, sculpting their bodies through surgery to be "sexy," and making love far more often than us.

There have been few sexual studies of a moral, much less Christian, sample of the population. We are left with the only information available to us courtesy of the Kinsey, Janus, or Hite reports. And if this is the only perspective we have about sexual behavior we *do* have reasons to be concerned!

Why Do Christian Women Wonder If They Are Normal?

We read all two thousand questionnaires in our study and looked at every question women asked. Several questions were asked over and over again, indicating that they were of particular concern. Each of these will be covered in greater detail in the chapters that follow. In this chapter we want to provide a summary of the most commonly asked questions posed to us by Christian women. Hopefully our brief discussion will provide some reassurance to those who fear that they are out of step. But first we need to discuss the whole concept of *normal.* If you don't have a clear understanding of this concept you cannot put your mind to rest over the "Am I normal?" question.

Why do Christian women ask, "Am I normal?" While all of us wonder about how we match up to others, Christian women have concerns that go beyond comparisons. Women in general may well ask, "Am I normal?" out of curiosity about whether they are missing out on something or matching up to the standards of others. Christian women, on the other hand, ask it out of concern that their sexual feelings or behaviors may be violating their integrity as a Christian woman. They want to know whether their behavior, or even their basic level of desire, is morally and biblically normal. Their concern comes out of a longing to be fully spiritual in their sexuality.

While the questions took many forms, they seemed to cluster around two themes: The first is, "Am I okay?" The second goes beyond this to, "How do I compare with others?" The first asks: Are my behaviors and thoughts typical and acceptable? The second asks: How much different am I than other Christian women?

Here are some examples of the "Am I okay?" question:

"Is it normal for me to need manual stimulation in reaching orgasm or is there something wrong with me? Why is it so difficult? Why does it take so long?"

"My sex drive is nowhere near that of my husband's. Where does a woman's sex drive go when she gets married? Am I unusual in this respect?"

Examples of the "How different am I?" question include:

"Do other women have difficulty with their husbands understanding and responding to their needs? How can I communicate to my husband that my needs, desires, and turn-ons are very different? Is my fear of offending my husband different from other women?"

"Are there other women who find more fulfillment in the closeness, touching, holding, and affection from lovemaking than the

actual act of intercourse and orgasm? The physical act seems more important to men—and the emotional closeness to women. Am I right?"

"Am I the only woman on earth who doesn't enjoy having her breasts squeezed, twisted, pushed, and bitten?"

Almost every question women asked us could be answered with a resounding, "Yes, you are normal!" But the whole issue of "what is normal?" is filled with problems, as we will see in the next section.

How Well Do You Understand Female Sexuality?

This quiz is designed to test your knowledge of female sexuality before we proceed further in the presentation of our findings. Male readers, particularly, might find this quiz challenging, but all readers may be surprised to discover how little they really know about this complex subject.

Circle T for True, or F for False for each of the following statements. You will find the answers at the end.

1. The most common sexual complaint among women is "lack of sexual desire." T/F
2. When women fantasize, it is not usually about sexual acts but scenes that are romantic, pleasant, and relaxing. T/F
3. The women who have sex the most and enjoy it more are young, attractive, and single. T/F
4. At least 50% of married women have been unfaithful to their husbands. T/F
5. Being religious has a harmful effect on a woman's sexuality. T/F
6. For a woman, good sex is spontaneous, with no talking, planning, or forethought. T/F
7. For a woman, a satisfying sexual experience always requires that she have an orgasm. T/F
8. All women are capable of multiple orgasms. T/F
9. Most women can reach orgasm through intercourse alone, without manual stimulation. T/F
10. Women are more likely than men to have contracted at least one sexually transmitted disease at some time in their lives. T/F

Answer Key:
1. True. See chapter 4.   **2.** True. See chapter 3.   **3.** False. See chapter 8.   **4.** False. See chapter 8.
5. False. See Appendix 2.   **6.** False. See chapter 3.   **7.** False. See chapter 5.   **8.** Possibly. See chapter 5.   **9.** False. See chapter 5.   **10.** True. See chapter 9.

What Is Normal?

In the previous section we mentioned that it was important that our readers understand the concept of normal. One of the problems with the question "Am I normal?" is that all sexual behaviors fall along a *continuum*. This means that one behavior or experience blends into the next without clear boundaries. There is no one category that is normal.

For example, some women are extremely orgasmic. Others are mildly so, or not at all. Who, then, is normal? The truth is that all are. There is a continuity that blends one category into the next, so you cannot always say, "This is normal" or, "That is abnormal." We wish the concept of normal were simpler, but it is not.

This means that many of us worry about whether or not we are normal when we merely differ a little from those next to us. For instance, you might feel cold whenever the temperature drops below 65 degrees (Fahrenheit, of course—for our European readers). So if someone turns up the cooling even more you will begin to shiver—and complain. Others feel hot when the room is 70 degrees and begin to sweat just at the point you are beginning to feel comfortable. They complain that the room is too warm. You complain that the room is too cold. Which of you is normal? You? Them? Obviously, you are both normal. It's just that your body thermostat is set a little higher than theirs. You're both on a continuum of comfort for room temperature. In sexuality, this type of continuum also applies.

Now this doesn't mean that there are no extremes that can be considered abnormal or beyond the bounds of the normal range. If someone is sweating when the room temperature is 50 degrees (or lower), something is wrong. Her body's heat thermostat needs medical help. So, a continuum has its limits, but only when something is outside these limits would we call it abnormal.

Furthermore, we are all a little different. Just as no two humans who have ever lived have the identical fingerprints or DNA code, so no two people show the identical set of experiences or feelings in the realm of their sexuality. You do yourself a great injustice if you condemn yourself just because you are a little different from someone else.

But we are not all that different. While we may be different in some respects, we are very much alike in others. One of the fascinating things about being a psychotherapist is that you discover just how much alike we are as humans. The human brain, and the whole body for that matter, is remarkably the same wherever you go. People everywhere hunger for love and respect. They have the same aspirations, with only minor variations. And the same sex hormones are at work in Central Africa or Central America as in central Los Angeles or New York. So, in many respects, we are not all that different.

How, then, are we to conceptualize normal and find out where the boundaries are? The most common way is statistically. We can count the number of people in a certain group who do this or that, compute the averages, and then say whether or not a particular person is normal. In this case normal means that this person is close to the *average* for the group; what the majority does or doesn't do defines normal.

As Christians, there are problems with this way of defining normal. If everyone is doing something, that behavior is common but not necessarily healthy or desirable. This is one of the reasons we conducted this study on Christian women. If you are going to judge yourself (and

> **If you think everyone is doing or feeling something that you are not, you are likely to judge yourself on the basis of faulty information.**

we wish you wouldn't), at least do so by comparing yourself with other Christian women.

There is a real danger if you don't have accurate information. If you think everyone is doing or feeling something that you are not, you are likely to judge yourself on the basis of faulty information. One of our survey respondents put it this way:

"I am depressed a lot of the time, and I think it is because I look around me and think everyone else is having a better time sexually than I am. The problem is I don't really know whether everyone else is having a better time than me because nobody ever talks about these matters. It leaves me very confused."

We can understand why she feels confused. She has no accurate information with which to compare herself. Furthermore, she has no one to talk to about how she feels so there is no "reality check" available to her. Many other Christian women also expressed this dilemma.

And this raises a further very important point. Finding out what is average or common is a good starting point in studying human sexuality, but we must go beyond this and ask the question: Is it *healthy*? Is it what God expects of us?

So, for us as Christians, the question "Is it normal?" has to go way beyond how common a certain behavior or feeling is. The fact that everyone else is doing it doesn't make it right or healthy. We will certainly be asking the "Is it right?" and "Is it healthy?" questions as we proceed through our findings. And we make no apology for insisting that our sexuality must conform to biblical standards of morality.

The Bell Curve

In the whole discussion of "what is normal," there is one further statistical concept so important that without it we could never reconcile the apparent contradiction that we are all different, yet alike. Whenever you plot a curve showing the distribution of human characteristics, things like height, weight, intelligence, and so on, what you get is a bell-shaped curve.

Take height, for instance. On the left you get those few who represent the shorter end of the continuum of height, in the middle you get the majority who are of average height, and on the right fewer again who represent the tallest. So if someone were to ask, "Am I normal in height?" the answer is that if you fit on the bell curve, you are normal! Now you may not be located in the tall section, nor in the middle where the majority are located, but on the left with those who are shorter. But you are on the bell curve!

Does this mean that everyone is normal? No it doesn't. Some people are so extremely short or tall and fall so far outside of the accepted range of human characteristics depicted on the bell curve that they would be considered abnormal. In the area of sexuality, for instance, pedophiles or rapists don't fit on the curve. Our concern is not with these extremes, but with the wide variation of normal experiences that cause women to feel that they must be the ones out of sync.

To summarize, the majority of Christian women who are bothered about whether or not they are normal are really concerned about where they fit on the bell curve of normality. Many feel abnormal when, in fact, they may be at the center of the curve where most women are anyway. A few are bothered because they are to the left or right, or because they don't know where they fit. Quite honestly, until we completed this study on the sexuality of Christian women, there was no measurement to compare ourselves to.

Being to the left of what is the normal range of experience does not make you "less" normal, just as being more to the right does not make you "more" normal. If you are to the left or right it just means that there are fewer women like you. You may see this as a blessing or a curse, depending on how you adjust to being uniquely yourself.

How can you tell whether you are to the left, the center, or the right of the curve of normal sexual experience? How can you be assured that your sexuality is normal? We hope that the discussion that follows, in which we try to address the most common questions women asked us, will help you to see where you fit.

The Eight Most Frequently Asked Questions

1. *What is normal sex drive for women? In general, do women have less desire for sex than men?*

The most common question we received was about how normal a particular level of sexual desire is. Women are particularly concerned about low sexual desire, especially after having previously experienced a higher level. They also made frequent references to how their drive differed from their partner's.

As you will see in chapter 4 where we discuss the whole topic of sexual drive or desire in more detail, there can be a huge difference between the sex drives of women and men. In Dr. Hart's book *The Sexual Man,* the majority of men reported that their sex drive was strong. Next came those who said it was moderate. Most men are driven by a strong need for sex, much stronger than what we see in the majority of women.

> **Women are particularly concerned about low sexual desire, especially after having previously experienced a higher level.**

What do women report in answer to the identical question that was put to Christian men? The majority of the women in our study reported that their sex drive was moderate, one step down from men. Next they reported low desire, and then strong desire.

Perhaps the best comparison to be made is at the low end of the spectrum. Whereas 26% of women (about one in four) said their sexual drive was low, only 3% of men (about one in thirty-three) described their sexual drive as low.

This difference also shows up in how often the sexes think about sex. Men think about sex far more frequently than women—at least once a day. Women, on the other hand, most often think about sex on a weekly basis. About half as many women as men reported thinking about sex daily. The frequency with which women think about sex is connected with how often they actually have sex. Also those who think about it more often are more likely to be sexually satisfied.

Factors such as age, marital happiness, health, and stage of life will all play a part in influencing sexual desire, as we will see in chapter 4.

2. How often do other Christian women (couples) have sex while raising kids? What do husbands expect?

This adds a special dimension to the "Am I normal?" questions—the whole matter of child raising and its impact on sexual energy—for both husband and wife.

The most common frequency of having sex is once per week. But this, alone, doesn't tell the whole story because the range of the bell curve (we told you this was an important concept) goes from once per day to once per year. Fifty-three percent of the women in our study said they were satisfied with their current frequency of sex. Reasons for dissatisfaction went from wanting sex more often to wanting it less or not at all.

Many women, however, believed their partners wanted more sex. We have no way of confirming this with their partners, but we have no reason to believe that this isn't accurate. It is a fact of life that in the majority of marriages, men would prefer sex more often. However, this does not have to be a serious hindrance to marital happiness.

Does the frequency of sex change over time? Surprisingly, not all that much. The percentages hold true over the entire life cycle. Looking at each age decade beginning with the twenties, the frequency of sex for the majority of married women remained fairly constant at between once and three times per week with only a slight downward trend with age. It appears that most couples settle into a frequency that is comfortable for them.

Having children at home is definitely a complicating factor, not so much in the frequency of sex as in the struggle to find the

> **Having children at home is definitely a complicating factor, not so much in the frequency of sex as in the struggle to find the energy and time for it.**

energy and time for it. We compared couples with children at home to couples without children, and they have sex with approximately the same frequency. Even though women with children report greater difficulty finding the energy for sex, they seem to be finding a way around their difficulties!

Of those women with children at home at least 50% of the time, 38% reported having sex once per week, and 32% still maintain the two to three times per week frequency. Of those women without children at home, 35% reported they had sex once per week, and 24% said two to three times per week. It could be, of course, that these frequencies are not set by the wife's level of desire, but by the husband's needs, which is why it remains so constant.

These figures don't adequately reflect the struggle that many women wrote to us about regarding lack of energy for sex. Many women posed questions or made comments regarding the struggle they have to balance their husband's sexual needs against the energy-sapping demands of children and their own work exhaustion. Several indicated that they barely had time even to think about sex, let alone have it. Raising children is clearly a very challenging period of a woman's life, and we explore this topic in greater depth in chapter 6.

3. What normal sexual changes can one expect as one ages, especially after menopause?

Our bodies are designed to participate in and enjoy sexuality throughout life. The ability to produce children comes and then goes, but sex is a lifetime experience. Our bodies change with age, but these changes do not necessarily restrict sexual fulfillment. Aging may change the characteristics of the stages of sexual response (See chapter 5). Menopause can mean a new freedom to engage in sex with more abandon—mainly because the risk of becoming pregnant is now over. Sexuality can be a positive force throughout life, especially if we are respectful of our bodies.

If you abuse your body in your earlier years you may not have as positive an outlook. For instance, hypertension, smoking, excessive alcohol consumption, obesity, and certain medications can all affect your body's ability to enjoy sex. In particular, any disease or medication that compromises blood circulation will impact sexual functioning as you age. A healthy flow of blood is essential to the sex organs.

Menopause, with its accompanying decrease in estrogen, can cause the tissues of the vulva and vaginal walls to grow thin and become fragile. While many women report that their sexual enjoyment actually increases after menopause, decreased vaginal lubrication and the loss of tissue flexibility can cause intercourse to be painful. Special lubricants, topical estrogen creams, or estrogen replacement therapy can help to remedy this problem.

Some women report a loss of sexual desire as they approach menopause. It is not clear if this is caused by menopause itself, or if painful or uncomfortable intercourse associated with these changes leads to this loss of desire. Women who participate in regular sexual relations during

> **Aging may change the characteristics of the stages of sexual response, but menopause can mean a new freedom to engage in sex with more abandon.**

the years leading up to and after menopause don't experience as much loss of vaginal flexibility or sexual responsiveness as those who don't.

What can you do to accommodate these natural changes of aging? Since both men and women require more time to reach maximum pleasure as they get older, they may need to set aside more time for lovemaking. Here are some suggestions:

1. Don't rush. Find out what your best time of day is for love-making (early morning, lunchtime, early evening, after a nap) and make the most of this time together.

For instance, erection problems can be overcome by having sex when an erection naturally occurs. Many elderly men continue to have erections in the early hours of the morning. This is caused by a reflex triggered by a full bladder. Couples can take advantage of these times. Late evening is usually the worst time of day for aging couples to try to make love.

2. Exercise. A well-toned body not only makes you look and feel better but also is important for good sexual functioning. Aerobic activity and weight lifting help to keep muscles, veins, and arteries healthy, as well as to increase energy.

3. Know your prescription medications. Ask your doctor about the sexual side effects that you can expect from any medications you are taking. Don't be embarrassed by what seems to be a simple question! Your sexuality is a part of who you are, and you have the right and responsibility to know what your options are when a medication is prescribed. Ask questions. Ask until you get thorough answers.

4. Deal with your depression. Depression is a widespread problem among the aging. Some gerontologists estimate that 30 to 50% of dementia, senility, and early Alzheimer's may be misdiagnosed—depression may be the real problem. When someone sleeps a lot of the time, is unable to think or concentrate, and has no interest in sex—these could just as easily be symptoms of depression as any of the more serious problems associated with aging. Depression *is treatable.*

5. Avoid the "sex busters." Other factors such as alcohol, stress, worry, and fatigue can work against you as you age even more than when you were younger. Learn to relax. Take your worries to the Lord, talk them over with your partner or a friend, or find a good counselor. Don't expect good sex when you are exhausted or pushed beyond your limits. Understand how your body works, and use this knowledge to your advantage!

4. Do other women have difficulty balancing the roles of mother and lover? Where do they get enough energy for both?

Yes, all women struggle to find enough energy and time for all the roles they have to play. If someone could invent an energy pill that wouldn't harm you in the long run, they would have a ready market in overextended mothers and wives!

We asked the women in our study to select their area of greatest sexual difficulty out of a list we provided. Finding the energy for sex was the most frequently chosen difficulty. Those with children living at home were particularly vulnerable. Fifty-five percent reported having difficulty finding the energy for sex, compared to 33% of those who did not have children at home.

Finding energy for sex is not just a problem of youth either. Women in every stage of life reported that finding energy for sex was a problem. Over 42% of women between ages thirty and forty-nine reported this problem. By age fifty-five to fifty-nine, when most children are gone, half as many women were still reporting "finding energy" as a problem.

This is an especially complex issue for those women who work outside the home, raise children, and try to be a wife and lover. Women wrote comments to us expressing their exhaustion, frustration, and despair over all of the conflicting needs that pulled at them. Many women feel that their husbands don't understand why they are so overwhelmed by trying to balance their many demanding roles.

> **Many women feel that their husbands don't understand why they are so overwhelmed by trying to balance their many demanding roles.**

In addition to overextension, there are many other reasons for fatigue. One of the biggest reasons, often overlooked, is simply not getting enough sleep. Most people need seven to nine hours of sleep per night. Even seven hours of sleep is on the low side and can leave you perpetually tired. Sleep disturbances can also be the cause. One in three Americans suffers from some form of insomnia, and one in ten Americans has chronic insomnia.[1]

Another source of low energy is unresolved grief. All of us suffer significant losses at one time or another: divorce, job loss, illness, death of a parent, death of a spouse, death of a child, a good friend moving away. All loss requires that we grieve. But most of us expect a period of grieving to be shorter than it actually is. A major loss takes from one to five years to grieve. Even when you get past the initial period of grieving, you will still have anniversary dates to get through, and these can bring on some of the original symptoms such as fatigue.

Fatigue can also be caused by depression. Depression is very common. About 24% of women and 15% of men can expect to suffer one or more episodes of clinical depression during their lives.[2] Depressed women tend to have sleep disturbances. They also may have difficulty concentrating, may have trouble remembering things, and have a struggle in decision making. All of which adds to their low energy!

Undiagnosed illness, thyroid problems, recovery from surgery, sleep apnea, chronic fatigue syndrome, and anemia also cause fatigue. In most cases, however, the cause of fatigue is our schedule and unrealistic expectations for what we truly can accomplish in a day or a week. We tend to put sleep low on our list of priorities, and then we are surprised when we drag around, feel lousy, and have little interest or energy for sex.

5. Is it normal to need manual stimulation to reach orgasm— or is there something wrong with me?

Most women *must* have some direct stimulation of the clitoris in order to reach orgasm. In our study 59% of the women said they could not reach orgasm by intercourse alone. Other researchers have estimated that as many as 66% (about two out of three) of women cannot reach orgasm solely through intercourse. So our sample is very close to these other findings.

Just as a man needs to have his penis stimulated, so a woman's clitoris, which is physiologically analogous to the man's penis, needs stimulation. The clitoris is the "trigger" of female orgasm. It is rich in nerve endings and becomes engorged with blood when a woman becomes sexually aroused. In some positions and because of the physical location of the clitoris in women, intercourse itself does not stimulate the clitoris directly, so orgasm is not possible. Manual stimulation before, during, and after intercourse may be necessary to achieve orgasm.

How much stimulation is needed to reach orgasm? In our sample, the highest rate of orgasmic response was found in those women who engaged in at least fifteen minutes of sexual stimulation with their partner.

In our clinical practices we find many women who refuse to stimulate themselves to orgasm during intercourse because they equate stimulation with masturbation. Because they have a negative view of masturbation, they won't allow anything but penile thrusting. This is most unfortunate, especially since it is due to a misunderstanding of terms. We do

> **Most women *must* have some direct stimulation of the clitoris in order to reach orgasm.**

not equate manual stimulation during intercourse with the commonly accepted understanding of masturbation. Manual stimulation as a part of the sex act is perfectly normal and acceptable.

Some decline to touch or allow themselves to be touched because they have been conditioned to think of the genitals as dirty. There is nothing dirty about our sex organs if they are kept clean. Like any other part of the body—hands, neck, armpits—they require cleansing. Naturally, you should shower and be fresh for lovemaking. When you are clean there is no hygienic reason to avoid touching, kissing, or caressing, and this includes almost every part of the body. The only truly "dirty" system in the human body is the anus, which produces waste and is full of bacteria. Most health professionals recommend avoiding touching, and especially kissing or penetrating, the anus. The reason is more for good health than morality.[3]

6. Is it unusual for a woman to masturbate? I never even heard about it when I was a teenager and never discovered it for myself until I was an adult. Is this unusual?

Masturbation is a fact of life. Ignoring it won't make it go away. Many women suffer an enormous amount of shame and confusion over masturbation. They are especially confused about whether and how it fits into a healthy and spiritually balanced life.

Masturbation is a highly controversial subject, and Christian leaders differ widely in their opinions about it. We want to respect these different opinions because none of us has the monopoly on truth. The discussion by Dr. James Dobson in his book *Solid Answers* about teenagers and masturbation is most helpful (see question 276).[4]

How common is masturbation? One of the intriguing surprises from the *Sex in America* study was that it debunked the myth that people are more likely to masturbate if they don't have a sex partner. What they found was that the people who masturbate the most were more likely to be the ones who had the most sex. They also found that nearly 60% of American women do not masturbate.

How does this compare with the Christian women in our study? This was difficult information to get. Over 43% of our respondents did not answer our questions about masturbation. We found that 20% of those currently married masturbate once per month or more, 49% of previously married singles masturbate once a month or more, and 38% of never married singles masturbate once a month or more. The range of frequency of masturbation was from never to 45 times per month. The most common frequency was once a month or less.

Married women masturbated the least. This contrasts quite starkly with the frequency for married men, where 61% admit masturbating to some extent. Of these men, 81% masturbated at least five times a month.

The most common reason why both men and women masturbate is that they "merely enjoy it" or there is "no other outlet" for their sexual feelings. Seven percent of women said that they had "strong sex drives" and 6% that their "spouse was not interested in sex." In the case of men, 23% said they masturbated because their sex drive was strong, 22% because they enjoyed it, and 21% because no sex

> **Many women refuse to stimulate themselves to orgasm during intercourse because they equate stimulation with masturbation.**

was available to them.[5] However, many men would continue to masturbate no matter how much sex was available to them. They have become addicted to it, and it is a habit often associated with pornography. We found no evidence that this was true for women.

Now, while we see no reason to view masturbation as a problem, please don't misunderstand us. We are *not* opening a door on unbridled masturbation. There are other factors to consider, including sexual responsibility to your partner, the risk of sexual addiction, and the possibility that masturbation as a secretive activity can distort your sexuality. Also, masturbation is often accompanied by the questionable practices of sexual fantasy or pornography. The three conditions under which we view masturbation as destructive are:

1. When it is used to avoid sexual intimacy or to punish a partner by satisfying oneself.

2. When it is used to fulfill an addictive urge.

3. When it is used to foster lust or a desire for someone other than your partner.

7. *What are the effects of childhood sexual abuse on sexuality? Do other women have difficulty learning to enjoy sex after being sexually abused?*

Sexual abuse can have a devastating effect on sexuality. Women who have been sexually abused experience a variety of symptoms, including: promiscuity, avoidance of sexual contact, strong negative feelings (disgust, anger, guilt) when touched sexually, difficulty becoming aroused, pain with intercourse, intrusive sexual thoughts, and numbing or "checking out" during sex. These consequences of sexual abuse don't usually just heal by themselves. The victims need help.

Our study verified that most women who have been sexually abused have experienced difficulty enjoying sex at one time or another. For them, sex is associated with pain and trauma, and it takes effort to break these connections. It doesn't mean you *can't* break the connections, just that it takes work!

Some women go through a period of seemingly "normal" sexual functioning and then gradually, or suddenly, begin to exhibit the symptoms mentioned above. Some have these problems throughout their adolescence and into adulthood. Few, if any, walk away from sexual abuse without negative side effects. So if you were sexually abused and you struggle with enjoying sex, you are very normal, and you have a lot of company with you on your journey to wholeness.

We want to make clear, however, that there is healing from sexual abuse. Many victims can attest to the redeeming power of Jesus Christ in their sexual lives. One of the women in our study wrote:

> *"I believe that God has healed the damage caused by sexual molestation by my stepfather when I was a young girl. This healing has come through my relationship with Jesus as a child, and reading His Word at ages twelve and thirteen. By His grace He has kept me from giving in to premarital sex. I believe I have a healthy view of sex and will enjoy sex very much when the time comes."*

Many survivors and therapists have attested to the fact that despite the struggle there is hope for healing. Survivors do grow beyond victimization and can thrive in life and in their sexuality!

8. Does being a Christian mean I need to view sex differently from the world? What is normal? How does a married, godly woman celebrate sexuality?

This is a wonderful question, and we can barely begin to scratch the surface in answering it!

Yes, Christians need to view sex differently from the world. Sex is not just an accident of evolution. God created it for us. He created it as a gift for us to enjoy. However, He also gave us specific boundaries, and this is where we part ways from the world.

God's intention that we enjoy sex is evident in reading the descriptive passion, delight, and celebration expressed in that great book of the Bible, Song of Solomon. You will notice that we have used quotations from this book at the beginning of each chapter. You might find it most illuminating if you and your partner read the whole book together (it is only eight chapters).

> God's intention that we enjoy sex is evident in reading the descriptive passion, delight, and celebration expressed in that great book of the Bible, Song of Solomon.

The dictionary definition of *celebrate* is "to praise or honor widely, to commemorate an event with festivities, to have a merry time." So celebrating sex includes joyfulness, approval, admiration, and thankfulness. It means that when we talk, think, or participate in sex we are to treat it with deep respect, honoring and esteeming God's high regard for His gift to us.

God intends for us to enjoy sex in many ways. It can be serious or fun, short or long, spontaneous or planned. Often couples fall into the trap of thinking that sex must always be the same, and any deviation from the rut is viewed with suspicion. Or they get so rushed that they don't devote the time it takes to build an enjoyable sexual ambience. Instead, give time to sex, keep exploring, and enjoy this wonderful gift that God has given us!

Because sex is such a powerful force it can easily be misused. For instance, you can withhold sex as a way of hurting your partner or you can demand sex out of selfish need. This violates God's intention for this beautiful gift. *Never* use sex to punish or manipulate your partner.

Conclusion

These eight questions, then, are the ones most frequently raised in one form or another by the women in our study. We have only touched on them briefly in this chapter. Many are explored in greater depth in the chapters to follow.

If you are still wondering if you are normal, read on. We believe that hearing what other women have to say will help you to accept and enjoy your sexuality more fully. And if in parts of this book you find that you are "a little different," we hope you will either celebrate your uniqueness or examine opportunities for growth and change.

Points to Remember

1. Most Christian women are bothered by the question "Am I normal?" Some want to know how they compare with others, others want to know whether they are okay.

2. Defining what is normal is not as easy as it seems. Just finding out how common something is does not define *normal*. As Christians, behavior also has to be healthy and moral.

3. We all fall along a continuous line called a bell curve. Some of us are in the minority, some in the majority, but unless we are way outside the curve we are still considered normal.

4. Eight of the most frequently asked questions regarding female sexuality are explored to clarify to the readers where they fit within the limits of normality.

Chapter Three

What Do Women Really Want from Sex?

"He brought me to the banqueting house, and his banner over me was love. Sustain me with cakes of raisins, refresh me with apples, for I am lovesick."

—*Song of Solomon 2:4–5 NKJV*

What do women really want from sex? It is a very basic question, but it goes to the heart of where many women are. Women don't feel that their needs are appreciated. Their sexuality isn't validated because male sexuality dominates much of our culture's thinking. Here are just a few comments from women to help set the stage for the topic of this chapter:

"Sexual intercourse is almost at the bottom of my list: #1 is talking; #2 is holding; #3 is sharing; #4 is sexual love."

"I like to sit next to my husband and cuddle, and most of the time that would be enough."

"Sex is extremely important to me. It is the one time I have my husband totally to myself. It is a precious time to me."

The mismatch of sex drive between the sexes is often so immense that women, quite rightly, complain that men don't readily and cheerfully comprehend their deepest needs. They feel that men unfairly project their own sexual expectations onto them with extremely unfavorable results.

This chapter is offered in the spirit of helping men and women understand and respect their individual sexualities. We invite men to "walk a mile in their partner's shoes" as a way to become more understanding of women's sexuality.

It may seem that this chapter is more informative for men than for women. However, it is our observation that women are not always confident to assert their own needs. Many women do not feel that what they desire is within the realm of what other "normal" women desire, hence the frequent question, "Am I normal?" Our purpose is not only to help men understand the real needs of women but also to affirm women for their distinctiveness.

Further, we encountered quite a few women who make the mistake of judging their sexuality by their husband's sexuality. They made comments like, "Why am I not ready for sex as often as my husband is?" Such a comparison violates God's intention in making us different. While we are sure He understands the frustration that lies behind such comparisons, this is how He made us! You may be different from your husband, but this difference is by design. Besides, too much preoccupation with how different you are will only cause overwhelming frustration. As you read this chapter, identify yourself rather with the experiences of other women, and celebrate with us the wonder of God's creation.

To find out what women really want from sex we carefully reviewed the responses to our focused questions as well as the open-ended narrative responses (see Figure 3.1). We found seven dominant themes that captured what it was that women really want. They are: closeness, time together, time for talking, time for romance, to be able to say "Not now," to be appreciated for more than sex, and to please their husbands.

WHAT MARRIED WOMEN LIKE MOST ABOUT SEX
Figure 3.1

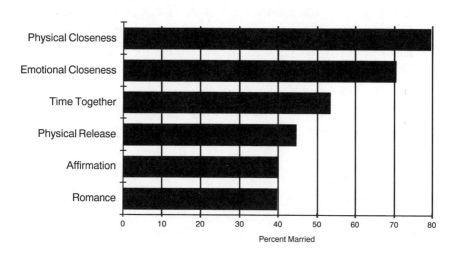

1. *Women want to be close.*

The women in our study overwhelmingly wanted closeness. When asked what they like most about having sex, 90% chose physical closeness and/or emotional closeness.

As one woman wrote:

> *"Sex is important to me because it's an expression of our love. It makes me feel close to my partner. . . ."*

Another wrote:

> *"I love the physical closeness."*

This need for closeness was also indicated in their answers to how women preferred to express love *to* their partners. Of the eight choices offered, the most frequent was "give a hug" (71%). Their next preference? One closely allied to hugging: "lie down with their arms around their partner" (37%).

Such findings do not surprise women, but the few men we have mentioned it to were quite taken by surprise. What is special about physical and emotional closeness? It cuts right to the intimacy issue, as do some of the other needs we will present. In women, intimacy is the catalyst for sexual desire.

This is one of the key areas where men and women differ. "To a woman, intimacy is a connection of hearts more than a connection of bodies."[1] To most men, intimacy means a connection of bodies. Men often use sex to express, and even feel, the emotions of love and affection. Sadly, when sex is not on the agenda their ability (not their desire) to achieve intimacy can be inhibited. Women, on the other hand, want to talk, touch, and feel love, then (maybe) express it by having sex.

> **In women, intimacy is the catalyst for sexual desire.**

This difference in priority is evident in how low on their list "making love" is as their preference for expressing love to their partner: Less than one-third (28%) chose "making love" and 22% chose "going out for a romantic evening." And remember, to a woman a romantic evening may or may not include sex.

2. *Women want to spend time with their partners.*

The second most frequent response women gave to the question of what they really wanted most was time together with their partner.

Time together, of course, can mean many things. Most often mentioned were: a romantic dinner, a vacation alone with their partner, spending time together for the sheer pleasure of being together, taking a walk together, exercising together, taking a bike ride together, taking a bubble bath together, sitting in a Jacuzzi together, dancing, sailing, swimming, and of course, a lot of conversation.

The list was lengthy and the women who responded were very creative. It seems that the specific nature of the time together was less important than the togetherness. However, we would speculate that if the time together is spent doing something that *both* enjoy, the meaningfulness of the experience would be significantly enhanced.

3. Women want time for talking.

How important is talking? Fifteen percent of our sample specifically mentioned this as a part of an "ideal sexual experience." Imagine this, men. Women want conversation as a part of the sexual experience.

In referring to the ideal sexual experience, one sixty-five-year-old woman expressed it beautifully as follows:

> *"We talk first and enjoy each other's company . . . possibly go out for a nice romantic dinner . . . alone. He talks to me about anything, past, present, future. He makes me feel necessary in his life, not just for sex."*

Another told us:

> *"Talking and connecting intimately is what I miss and want more of."*

Holly Phillips, in her book *What Does She WANT from Me, Anyway?* writes: "Most guys I know are more comfortable showing than telling. Given a choice they pick actions over words. They'd rather do something than talk about almost anything."[2]

Women want to talk *and* they want to be listened to. Quite apart from sex, one of the highest relationship needs of women is conversation. A forty-nine-year-old woman wrote this about her ideal sexual experience:

> *"He would talk to me about my feelings, really showing interest in me. I'd laugh some and cry some. He would share his feelings with me and about me. He would affirm me. . . ."*

Again and again in our work with couples, we hear one or both spouses complain: "We never talk," "You never listen to me," or "You never talk to me." This desire for communication deeply impacts both a couple's general *and* sexual relationship. Many of the women in our study mentioned desiring connection, pleasant talk, affirming words, and conversation when writing about what they long to have prior to and during sex.

> **The desire for communication deeply impacts both a couple's general *and* sexual relationship.**

While a detailed treatment of the topic of communication is beyond the scope of this book, here are a few suggestions on how to improve your communication.

1. A Chinese proverb says: "Married couples . . . tell each other a thousand things without talking." What this really means is that communication is MORE than just talking. More than half of human communication is nonverbal. Smiling at your partner across the room at a public gathering, for example, is a profound statement that no words can communicate. Try it and see! Taking your partner's hand while you are waiting frustratedly for a taxi, holding hands when you go to sleep, good and consistent eye contact, unexpected letters, love notes in his (or her) briefcase that will be discovered mid-morning when all hell has broken loose in the office, and even the old standby, flowers (yes we mean for him, too), all speak volumes, and not a spoken word has been uttered. Use your creativity.

2. Separate out those problem- or conflict-solving conversations from your more personal times of intimate talking. Men, unfortunately and without malice, often get trapped into thinking that talking is the same as problem solving. Some reeducation would help tremendously. Set the example.

During the times you are trying to have personal communication don't talk about the kids, the job, the dishwasher that needs fixing, that little accident you had with the car while taking the kids to school, or the letter from your mother. Leave these for another business time. In fact, be clear about what type of talking you want to have.

3. Learn, then model for your partner, how to be an active listener. Active listening is nothing more than the receiver of the message helping the sender feel heard and acknowledged. It is a priceless gift, worth its weight in gold. Listen carefully, then test out what you think you've heard. Listen for feelings, then validate these feelings. "You have a right to feel angry," as a response, does not imply that what has happened deserves an angry response. It merely validates that anger is appropriate *if your perception is correct*. Then, and then only, explore whether the facts are accurate and the interpretation is correct.

4. Place a higher value on listening than on talking yourself. Does this mean you may not give priority to expressing your own feelings? No, it doesn't. All it means is that if you feel as if you are doing more listening than talking, you've probably struck the right balance. And even if it means that you actually listen more than you talk, so be it. We have never heard a spouse complain that his or her partner "listens too much"! We've heard many say, "If only he (she) would stop talking, I'd be glad to say something."

4. Women want romance.

Romance is difficult to define because it means different things to different people. In our culture it is symbolized in flowers, chocolates, balloons, a candle, and love songs. In other cultures a cow, or goat, or a necklace made of beads does the trick. And to them, candles are for light, not romance. They'd gladly embrace the electric light for romance!

Romantic novels haven't exactly helped either. They have idealized a certain expression of romanticism that is almost impossible to live up to throughout a long relationship. Dictionary definitions help us to see why getting our romantic needs filled can be so elusive:

> Romance: *Having no basis in fact: imaginary; impractical in conception or plan: visionary; marked by the imaginative or emotional appeal of the heroic, adventurous, remote, mysterious, or idealized; ardent, fervent; marked by or constituting passionate love.*[3]

Our longing for and attraction to romance creates an impossible dilemma. What we want is overidealized, impractical, and subjective. Real life just can't deliver the goods consistently, at least not over the long haul!

HOW ARE MARRIED WOMEN'S ROMANTIC NEEDS MET?
Figure 3.2

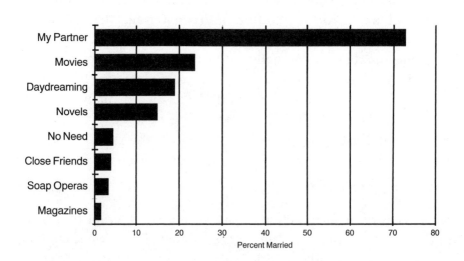

How do married women have their romantic needs met? Figure 3.2 shows the results. "My partner" is the most common way. Only 4% of married women said they "had no romantic needs." Most married women need romance. About 20% get their romantic needs met through movies, novels, or daydreaming. Among single women, 6% said they had no need for romance.

Those women who reported that they were sexually satisfied and happily married said that their partner met their romantic needs. In unhappy marriages where women reported being sexually unsatisfied, more women said they turned to soap operas and close friends to get some of their romantic needs met.

> **In unhappy marriages where women reported being sexually unsatisfied, more women turned to soap operas and close friends to get their romantic needs met.**

When we asked women to describe their ideal sexual experience, they often wrote about romantic settings and circumstances: candles, music, giving massages, a nice dinner out, wine or champagne, a fire in the fireplace, vacations, clean sheets, being completely alone with their partner, intimate conversation, cuddling, dancing, the beach, staying at a hotel, room service, the mountains, talking about feelings, and surprise gifts.

It is common knowledge that most women are more romantic than men. A better way of understanding this is to see that the romance languages of the sexes are different. For men, romance does not have to be a part of sex. Women, however, really appreciate romance, and it enhances the sexual experience.

Of the women who wrote to us about their "ideal sexual experience," 22% explicitly cited romance as an essential ingredient while others described a romantic setting. Yet when asked what they liked most about sex, "romance" was selected less often than physical closeness, emotional closeness, time together, affirmation, or physical release. This might be because in their current sexual relationship, they do not receive the romance they desire from sex. It could also be that women see romance as the precursor to sex, not as "sex" itself. (See Figure 3.1.)

Encouraging an Unromantic Partner

The unromantic partner can be a real killjoy to love and sex. He (or she) needs to be encouraged to become more romantic.

• Always express your appreciation for the smallest attempt at being romantic. Remember the behavioral principle: Desired behavior can be increased if it is reinforced. The strongest reinforcers are acknowledgment of the act and expressions of appreciation (making a fuss over it). Start by reinforcing the slightest gesture of romance, even if you really have to stretch your definition of it.

• Never reject romantic gestures. Rejection will extinguish the romantic behavior. Receive it for what it is—a gift of love.

• Never criticize your partner for not being romantic or initiating romance. Nagging never increases the behavior of romance because it makes it feel as though it is being forced.

• Romance begets romance. In order to get you have to be willing to give, and give generously. Learn what your partner considers romantic, so you are giving what he likes to receive. Let him know what is romantic to you.

• Don't be afraid to ask for romantic gestures. Don't make it sound like criticizing or nagging. Use plain language like: "You know what, honey? I would really appreciate it if tonight I didn't have to cook and we go out to a dinner by ourselves." Partners are not mind readers. Both of you will benefit from straightforward, nonthreatening requests.

• Express your appreciation for every romantic effort. *Never* let it go by without appreciation. Consistency will pay off!

---

5. Women want to be able to say, "Not now."

Women also want to be able to say to their partners: "This isn't a good time for me to make love." Many women wrote comments like:

> *"My ideal sexual experience would involve time to relax. Not having to worry about getting the children to a sitter, rushing around, etc."*

Another asked:

> *"I'd like to know how other women feel about being supermom and still having to be great in bed! I'm exhausted!"*

We will devote an entire chapter to the energy crisis, but there are several points we would like to highlight. Almost one half of women reported that finding the energy for sex was a difficulty for them. And 10% of the women who wrote comments specifically mentioned their need to be rested and to be able to relax. Some even associated napping or sleeping with good sex.

Timing for sex is more than just a low energy issue. Many men view their partners' lack of enthusiasm toward having sex as personal rejection. What may be a very important bit of information for men, then, is this: In most cases, it is not that your partner is *disinterested* in you or in sex in general but that she is just not interested in sex *at that moment.*

> **In most cases, it is not that a wife is *disinterested* in you or sex in general, but that she is just not interested in sex *at that moment.***

There may be many reasons for this disinterest. In our study we found the most common to be overload. One woman described it as follows:

> *"How do I create an exciting sexual experience with a busy work schedule and raising children?"*

A complicated, overloaded life with many distractions does not enhance the intimate mood. It interferes by robbing time or energy needed for sex.

Another woman commented:

> *"I've finally come to understand that men and women are completely different. I don't need the 'act of sex' the same way my adoring husband does . . . and he so lovingly understands that it has*

*nothing to do with him. It's just that our drives and makeup are
so different. That is how God made us, and we appreciate that."*

This is a commendable and wise conclusion! We wish more
couples would come to understand and accept their differences in
just this way.

But what about when the wife is the one with the strong desire
and the husband isn't interested? One woman described her needs
as follows:

> *"Sex is very important to me. I need the acceptance and inti-
> macy it provides. I am a sexual person, and by not being seen
> and addressed in a sensuous, sexual manner by my husband, I
> feel a sense of rejection."*

How often does her desire outstrip his? The *Sex in America* study
found that roughly one in six men lacked interest in sex for at least
one of the previous twelve months. For women it was one in three.[4]
While we will discuss desire in more detail in the next chapter,
let us emphasize that maintaining matching sexual interest over a
long period of time takes work and understanding. Over a long-
term marriage, both partners will experience a decrease in sexual
desire for some period of time. It is during these times of fluctu-
ating interest that your investment in communication, intimacy,
and solid friendship will come in handy!

6. *Women want to be appreciated for more than sex.*

One of the deep longings of the human heart is to be valued not for
what you do but for who you are. Feeling that you are valued only
for your sexual qualities is most demeaning. This is very evident in
the comments of the women in our study:

> *"I wish men could understand that if they took more time for
> emotional intimacy women would initiate physical intimacy*

more. Then we would know that we are really wanted for who we are—not just as a release valve!"

"I'd like to have a partner who listens and is not just interested in my body and sex!"

Women need to be valued and appreciated outside of the sexual arena, and they long to be told that they are cherished and shown that they are valued and appreciated. How can a caring partner do this?

• Try being more attentive at those times when you know sex isn't on the agenda. A great time to be superadoring and attentive is immediately after sex, when your motive can't be challenged.

• Focus on giving in your relationship more than getting. When giving is your focus, the message is clear: "You are very precious to me!"

• Make sure your partner knows when your attentiveness is not about sex on your mind. Most women are conditioned to interpret all loving gestures as meaning one thing only!

• Take careful note of what gestures, gifts, or comments are particularly appreciated. Make sure you surprise your partner with these often.

• You cannot fail if you remember this biological fact: Affection that doesn't immediately lead to sex enhances sexual desire through hormonal pathways. This means that hugs, kisses, and cuddles performed outside of sex will do more to enhance your sexual relationship than any known or yet-to-be-discovered aphrodisiac. The brain is still your best ally.

7. Women want to please their husbands.

One of the many pleasant surprises uncovered by our study is how often we heard women say that they had sex to please their husbands. They *wanted* to please their husbands! What is even more

> **It is when this spirit of unselfishness prevails in both partners that one creates the greatest potential for a deeply satisfying sexual relationship.**

surprising was how often we heard that women frequently have sex with their husbands, not for themselves or their own needs, but because they enjoy seeing their husbands sexually fulfilled.

It seems to us that this is a unique characteristic of female sexuality that is little understood. It leads to the essence of bonding—of being united as one. It also leads to the issue of true passion where the well-being of the other is always of greater concern than one's own well-being. To put it in a nutshell, such a spirit embodies all that love is about—one is extravagantly generous in unselfishness.

But shouldn't such a spirit also characterize the male? We think it should. Is he exempt from magnanimity? No, he isn't. Women seem to have a God-given unselfishness and an uncanny ability to derive pleasure from the pleasure they give, and we're not just talking about sex. It is when this spirit of unselfishness prevails in both partners that the greatest potential for a deeply satisfying sexual relationship is created.

Or, to put it another way, seeking the well-being of the other is what true friendship is all about. And in the final analysis, the greatest passion of all, the sort of passion that lasts a lifetime, comes when couples are not only lovers but also friends. Couples who deeply enjoy each other outside of sex not only have higher levels of interest in sex, they achieve a higher level of marital satisfaction.

What Women Like Least About Sex

And lest we overlook one closing point—there are some aspects of sex that women don't like! Other studies have not explored these. Most people assume that if you like sex then you like everything about it. We didn't think this was true, and it turns out it isn't.

Figure 3.3 shows what married women like least about sex. Topping the list is the mess of sex (30% of married women). Many wrote about the mess of contraceptive jelly, but others wrote about the mess of body fluids, both their own and their partner's. Some were embarrassed by the amount of vaginal lubrication they produce and wondered if this is normal. The pain of intercourse bothered about 8% of women. Six percent of the women wrote specific comments about tiredness. Our favorite was: "We wait to have sex until it's too late at night and I'm so tired I could die." Their partner's smell bothered 6%. From what these women told us, it seems that quite a few husbands need to improve their personal hygiene if they are going to help their sex lives. The partner's language (dirty words or suggestions) bothered 3% of women.

WHAT MARRIED WOMEN LIKE LEAST ABOUT SEX
Figure 3.3

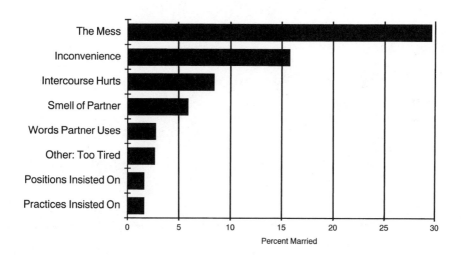

Many women wanted us to understand that while they reported these things as what they like least, very few judged them as major obstacles to their sex lives.

Six percent of the women wrote specific comments about tiredness. Our favorite was: "We wait to have sex until it's too late at night and I'm so tired I could die!"

Points to Remember

1. What women want from sex is different from what men want. More than anything else, women want closeness, both physical and emotional. To a woman, intimacy is a connection of hearts, not just bodies.

2. Women want to communicate. This includes: talking, hugging, holding, appreciating, and showing respect.

3. While there is much about romance that is overidealized, women look for, and respond to, romantic gestures.

4. Women want to be appreciated for more than being sexual. They want to be told and shown they are cherished.

Chapter Four

Sexual Desire

"I am my beloved's, and his desire is toward me."

—Song of Solomon 7:10

It is not an exaggeration to say that most women are puzzled by the fluctuations in their sexual desire. At one moment their sexual feelings can be warm, tender, and receptive, and the next moment desire is gone, snuffed out by some unknown culprit. It's like an ethereal cloud that forms when it is so inclined and then vanishes with the slightest hint of a breeze, or so it seems. Sexual desire does not appear to be consistent or predictable. It doesn't follow any logic or common sense. For many, their sexual responsiveness is as unpredictable as the weather.

Listen to what these women had to say:

"Sometimes I can become aroused in just a moment by the way I am touched or something tender my husband says to me. At other times it takes a long time for me to become aroused."

"I think I am finally figuring out why my sexual desire is so up and down, more often down than up. When we were going together, he was after me constantly. His desire for me sexually was all-consuming. Knowing his desire was wrong, I resisted, but I didn't know how to deal with it. I gave in to keep him from getting angry. This pattern lasted all the time we were dating,

and now the pattern of resisting is still with me. It doesn't make any sense."

"Presently sex is very low on my list of priorities. Other things are more important. For one thing, I find that my desire is not just a matter of my cycle. I think it is much more a matter of what is going on in my marriage."

Sometimes desire comes on strong and stays around for a while. Sometimes it vanishes and stays away for a seeming eternity. This chapter, and the chapter on the influence of hormones on sexuality, will explore the reasons for this unpredictability.

> **Sometimes desire comes on strong and stays around for a while. Sometimes it vanishes and stays away for a seeming eternity.**

The rhythm of female sexual desire is shaped by hormones and by life circumstances, by stage of life and by setting. Or, to put it another way, a candlelight dinner without a telephone in sight, no kids within a screaming mile, and the full attention of an adoring and undistracted husband is a powerful aphrodisiac. Love is the most powerful aphrodisiac!

What influences the cycle of sexual desire? Is there anything a woman can do to enhance her desire? These questions are the focus of this chapter.

The Importance of Sexual Desire

"I wish I was more sexual—more needy of sex—like my husband. I don't make love nearly as much as he'd like, and I hate that. At times it becomes such a chore. He feels bad, too—it gets in the way a lot. I wish there were other ways for men to be sexually satisfied. It shouldn't have to be such hard work to do such a natural thing."

"I just don't have any sexual desire anymore. I love my husband very much, but I don't enjoy making love until I am practically

forced or bugged to. After we have begun foreplay then I get aroused. I wish I had sexual feelings more often. My husband is always ready to make love."

"I enjoy sex once we're ten to fifteen minutes into foreplay—and I say to myself: 'Wow! We should do this more often!' But during the week I hardly ever think about it. Sometimes when my husband suggests it, I think: 'No—not that.' I think: 'I'm just too tired, and I want to be left alone.' I have a two-and-a-half-year-old and an eleven-month-old who is nursing, so sometimes it's hard for me to feel like anything but a mother. I wish I felt more sexual than I do because I enjoy the closeness it brings. What can I do to feel more sexual?"

"I don't ever initiate sex—it's never something I desire. I 'give in' because I know how important it is to my husband. As I give in, I usually enjoy it. I wish I could look forward to it and be more receptive to him. He is so patient and grateful for the 'crumbs' I give him. I really feel disgusted with myself. I pray and pray, and I've read tons of great books. But so far my desire hasn't changed!"

Almost one in three of the women in our study told us that low sexual desire was a difficulty to them. (See Figure 4.1.) And many, as the quotes above suggest, wished they possessed "more desire."

Helen Singer Kaplan, one of the first researchers to write about sexual desire, defined desire as a person's appetite "to seek out, or become receptive to, sexual experiences." When this appetite is activated, a person "may feel genital sensations, or may feel vaguely sexy, interested in sex, open to sex, or even just restless."[1]

Just as hunger prompts us to eat, so sexual desire prompts us to have sex. Your hunger pangs may be mild, ravenous, or suppressed because you have just eaten. Sexual appetite (sexual desire or sexual drive), like appetite for food, ranges along a spectrum from almost nonexistent to very high.

AREAS OF SEXUAL DIFFICULTY FOR MARRIED WOMEN
Figure 4.1

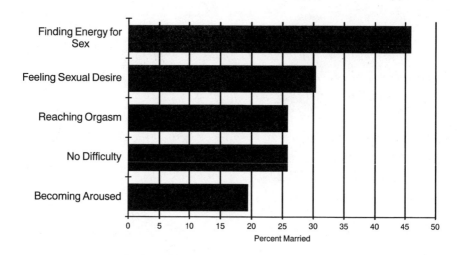

One of the major goals of our study was to find out just how much desire Christian women experienced. If you believe the secular research, Christians are supposed to be inhibited by their religious beliefs, a stereotype that has been around a long time. We analyzed the sexual drive of the women in our sample, and the results are depicted in Figure 4.2. There is absolutely no evidence whatsoever to support such a stereotype.

Only 4% of Christian women in our study said they experienced no sexual desire whatsoever. While a little over one quarter of the women said their sexual desire was low, most women (42%) reported a moderate amount of drive. Twenty-eight percent reported that their sexual drive was either strong or very strong.

How does this compare to men? Figure 4.3 shows the comparison with the male sample taken from Dr. Hart's study published in *The Sexual Man.*[2] Not surprisingly, the chart shows that there are great differences between men and women. Men generally report a higher sex drive than women, a cliché that seems to have some validity. Most men (47%) reported a strong drive, while 22% of women reported a strong drive. Women, however, exceed men at the moderate level of drive. While women and men report roughly

SEX DRIVE OF WOMEN
Figure 4.2

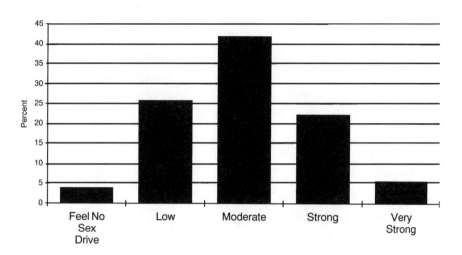

SEX DRIVE OF WOMEN AND MEN
Figure 4.3

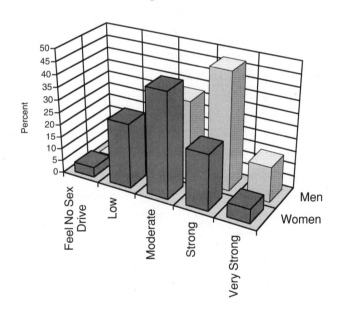

the same pattern of desire, the level of desire in the women's curve peaks one notch lower (moderate for women versus strong in the men's graph).

men's graph).

How Often Do Women Think About Sex?

One of the important indicators of sexual desire is the frequency with which one thinks about sex. When hungry, we think more about food. A similar phenomenon exists in sex. So we compared the reported drive with how often women thought about sex, and the results are shown in Figure 4.4.

The pattern here is very clear. Those women with very strong and strong sexual drives think about sex more often than those with low and no sexual drive. *This relationship between level of sexual desire and frequency of sexual thoughts is one of the strongest findings of our study.* For a woman with low sexual desire, a week can easily slip by without thinking about sex. (The frustrated husband sitting back with arms folded, waiting for the moment when his wife will think about sex, may be waiting a long time.)

When it comes to thinking about sex, how do women compare with men? Figure 4.5 shows that women think about sex less often than men. Surprised? In general, the majority of women (43%) tend to think about sex once a week, about as often or a little more frequently than they actually have sex. Men tend to think about sex on a daily basis, usually much more frequently than they have sex.

> **In general, the majority of women tend to think about sex once a week, about as often or a little more frequently than they actually have sex.**

The Link Between Sexual Frequency and Sexual Desire

Frequency of sexual relations is another measure of sexual desire. Most sex therapists and researchers are quick to back away from proclaiming what frequency is normal, and what is abnormal. On the one hand this is probably good since we tend to compare our-

HOW OFTEN DO WOMEN THINK ABOUT SEX?
Figure 4.4

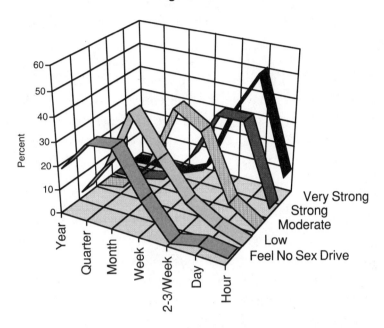

HOW OFTEN DO WOMEN AND MEN THINK ABOUT SEX?
Figure 4.5

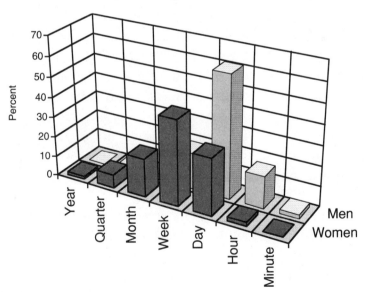

selves with others. We so desperately want to be normal. (See chapter 3.) On the other hand, not having accurate information on how frequently other women have sex can be frustrating to a couple trying to figure out what a healthy range might be.

Lack of information can leave us vulnerable to the cultural myths portrayed on billboards, in television, in magazines, and now on the Internet. Myths like "All young, healthy Americans are having a great deal of sex." Or the one that says "Everyone is having more sex, and better sex than me. There's something wrong with me." Or the one that says, "Older people aren't interested in sex and certainly don't have sex."

Normal sexual frequency is actually lower than most people seem to think. Both our study and the *Sex in America* study agree on this. "The data we will present," says the *Sex in America* study, "seem to support an extraordinarily conventional view of love, sex, and marriage."[3] We agree. Our sample, as expected, was extraordinarily conventional in its view of sex and marriage. We would have been alarmed if it was not.

But how frequent is average for our sample? To find this out we had to make a decision. We decided that it wouldn't be fair to include single women in this calculation. It would be mixing apples and oranges. We deal with the sexual patterns of singles in a separate chapter devoted to them. Christian singles, as compared with secular singles, may have different sexual standards.

So, in examining only married and remarried women, we find that the most common frequency of sex for women is once a week (38%). But the *range* of frequencies is more informative than just the average. According to most studies on sexual functioning, if you are having sex with your partner between three times per week and once or twice per month, you are within the most common range. At least two out of every three married women report that they fall within this range of frequency.

But is this really what you should compare yourself to? Sex therapists are quick to point out that it doesn't matter if "everyone else" is having sex more frequently (or less frequently) than you. The real issue is: Are you and your partner satisfied with your frequency? Do you agree that your needs as a couple are being met? Do you share affection that doesn't have to end with sex? If you can answer yes to these questions, it really doesn't matter what your sexual intercourse frequency is. Why try to compete with the national average? Set your own norms!

It is also important to remember that frequency is a measure of behavior, not necessarily desire—especially since many women report that they have sex not necessarily because they desire it but to please their partners. As one respondent wrote:

"I want to please him by giving myself to him sexually; however, I have little pleasure in sex or I lose interest quickly."

Another woman wrote:

"It is only important to me because it is important to him. It makes me happy because it gives him so much pleasure."

The Link Between Sexual Desire and Sexual Satisfaction

Sexual desire is a prerequisite to becoming sexually aroused. Arousal is required in order to reach orgasm. If you begin a sexual experience with no desire, it will take you longer to progress through the stages of sexual response until reaching orgasm. The likelihood of experiencing sexual satisfaction is much less than if you had begun the process with some level of sexual desire right at the beginning. From this understanding of the stages of the sexual response cycle, it is easy to see how sexual desire and sexual satisfaction are linked. This association was confirmed by our data.

Of those women who expressed themselves as having moderate desire, 74% rated themselves as sexually satisfied. Of those who reported very strong sexual desire, 80% rated themselves as sexually satisfied, which is only slightly higher. However, of those women who rated themselves as having low sexual desire, only

49% rated themselves as sexually satisfied, a substantial drop. Clearly, sexual desire and sexual satisfaction influence each other.

What Influences Sexual Desire?

Sexual desire is not a fixed experience in each of us. It naturally waxes and wanes, rises and falls, like the temperature in your home to which your air-conditioner thermostat responds. The temperature is determined by a combination of internal factors (the condition of your air-conditioning or how much insulation you have) and external factors (like the temperature outside, the position of the sun, and the number of open windows).

> **Sexual desire is set in the brain, which, in turn, is influenced also by both internal and external factors.**

Sexual desire is set in the brain, which, in turn, is influenced also by both internal and external factors. Internal factors include your menstrual cycle, how you view your physical body, your energy level, and your health. External factors include the habits of your partner (many women complained about how unpleasant it was when their husbands didn't bathe before sex), the number of children running around in the room next door, whether the setting is romantic, and how you've been treated lately.

Your brain is smart, and it knows how to compute all of these together before it says "go" or "no go." The sum total of all these factors sets your level of sexual desire. It can range from none to high, or anywhere in between.

Sexual desire can actually be thought of as a continuum with hyperactive sexual desire (compulsive sexuality) at one end, and sexual aversion (sexual phobia) at the other. There are six categories of desire: hyperactive sexual desire; normal-high sexual desire; normal-low sexual desire; mild-low sexual desire; severe-low sexual desire; and sexual aversion. (See Figure 4.6.)

It is important to note that so-called normal sexual desire can

SEXUAL DESIRE CENTER IN THE BRAIN
Figure 4.6

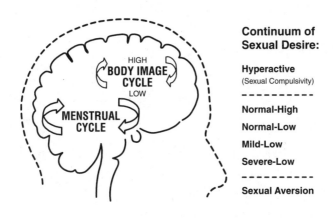

**Continuum of
Sexual Desire:**

Hyperactive
(Sexual Compulsivity)
- - - - - - - - -
Normal-High

Normal-Low

Mild-Low

Severe-Low
- - - - - - - - -
Sexual Aversion

ACCELERATORS:

Love
Romance
Physical and/or
    Emotional Closeness
Imagination
    (Daydreaming/Fantasy)
Attractive Partner
Testosterone
Erotic Stimulation
Husband's Praise of
    Wife's Body

BRAKES:
Fatigue
Depression
Stress & Anger
Body Image
Negative Thoughts
Unattractive Partner
Criticism
Medication with Sexual
    Side Effects
Pain/Illness
Previous Sexual Trauma

be normal-high or normal-low. This helps explain why many couples coming to sex therapists distressed and conflicted about their frequency of sex can *both* have normal drives. They are merely at opposite ends of the same room, not in different rooms! One is normal-high and the other is normal-low. Neither has a desire disorder, but as a couple they have *desire discrepancy.*

Desire discrepancy is very common. Here are some suggestions to help you with this:

- How has this desire discrepancy become a conflict? Explore possible causes. Look for communication problems, lack of opportunity to be intimate, trust issues, insecurity, unresolved jealousy, unresolved anger, or lack of compassion.

- Consider physical causes such as diabetes, stress, depression, infections, chronic fatigue, pain, grief, or hormonal fluctuations.

- Increase non-demanding affection. You and your partner need to experience pleasure from each other without it leading to sex.

- Decrease behaviors that are a turnoff. Bad breath, body odor, unpleasant surroundings, dirty language, use of pornography, and distasteful sexual practices can all be turnoffs and need to be corrected.

Chronic Low Sexual Desire

Chronic low sexual desire is, of course, a more serious problem usually requiring professional help.

According to a 1992 lead article in *U.S. News and World Report,* sexual desire is the number one complaint bringing clients to sex therapists.[4] On the average, about one-third of patients seeking help at American and European sex therapy clinics in the eighties had problems concerning low sexual desire.[5] Most sexual desire problems have to do with *low* sexual desire. Very few women complain about their sexual desire being too high.

Psychotherapists report that low sexual desire appears to be about twice as prevalent in women as in men. The *Sex in America* study reported similar figures: "One out of three women said they were uninterested in sex, but just one out of six men said they lacked interest" (at least in one of the past twelve months).[6] In our study, of those women who stated they had sexual difficulty, feeling sexual desire ranked second (31% of the women). The leading complaint? Finding energy for sex. And often the two go together. (See Figure 4.1.)

In 1995, Kaplan updated her pioneering work on sexual desire.[7] She reviewed the cases of 5,580 patients evaluated and/or treated by her medical group between 1972 and 1992. Thirty-eight percent of patients (2,120 people, ranging in age from eighteen to ninety-two) were diagnosed with "sexual desire disorders." Her research group analyzed these patients' sexual functioning and behaviors, thoughts, fantasies, and feelings, as well as their histories, to try to understand the cause, or causes, of low sexual desire. They concluded that patients with low sexual desire actually "turn themselves off."

This is an extremely important discovery because it means that many women with low sexual desire CAN do something to improve it.

In contrast to those with low sexual desire, women (and it is true for men as well) with a normal sexual drive naturally focus on their partners' positives, selectively seeing their good points, as well as overlooking their partners' negative features. Women who are in love also "prime the pump" by thinking about spending time with their partner and imagining (daydreaming, fantasizing) about time spent together, sharing affection, and physical pleasure. There is an ongoing high expectation for pleasure with their partners. This is absent in women with low sexual desire.

Partners who are looking forward to lovemaking invest time and energy into creating a romantic, beautiful, private environment conducive to sexual intimacy. When we "fall in love" we automatically put our best foot forward. We pay attention to how we look and how we behave. We try to smell attractive. We choose what we wear, what we drive, how considerate

> **Partners who are looking forward to lovemaking invest time and energy into creating a romantic, beautiful, private environment conducive to sexual intimacy.**

and polite we can be. Also, when we fall in love we tend to idealize our partner and make excuses for their weaknesses. We overlook minor offenses or inconsistencies. We focus on kissing, hand-holding, time together, dating, romantic dinners or lunches, and little gifts. We also focus on our erotic sensations when kissing and fondling and tend to anticipate pleasure, literally tuning out unpleasant distractions (like an uncomfortable position or the noises made by children). We stay very focused on the good feelings. This is the environment in which sexual desire thrives. Without it, desire wanes.

Women (and men) with low sexual desire not only neglect the ingredients for romance but they also do just the opposite. They unconsciously, or consciously in some cases, put up barriers and step on the brakes. They focus on the negative qualities in their partner, harbor resentments, maintain unforgiving attitudes,

---

Tuning in to Sexual Desire

Periodically, take time to think about the following questions. You might find it more valuable to write your thoughts in a private journal so that you can review them from time to time:

What makes you feel alive? Being alive is to be filled with alertness, activity, or briskness, movement, vigor, zest. What invigorates you? What fills you with awareness? What activates you?

What makes you feel sensuous? *Sensuous* means "relating to the five senses." It implies delight in beauty of color, sound, texture, or artistic form. What colors, sounds, textures, smells, and tastes delight you?

What stimulates you? To stimulate is to excite to activity or growth or to excite to greater activity; to animate, to arouse. (Sounds great, doesn't it?) What stirs you? What excites you? What awakens you?

What makes you feel sexual (as opposed to sensuous)? What arouses you physically? What causes you to feel stirrings that draw you toward touching, sharing, holding, giving, and receiving?

---

pay too much attention to unpleasant environmental input, and blind themselves to their partner's positive, attractive qualities. (See Figure 4.6.) They also tend to put their worst foot forward in their own personal hygiene, appearance, and behavior. The result is they create an atmosphere and environment that hinder romance or sexual expression. In short, they reap what they sow!

Why Does Desire Diminish?

One reason people "turn themselves off" is for protection from perceived danger. This can be for a variety of real or imagined reasons. If nearly every time you have sex you come away feeling disappointed, criticized, bored, or experiencing pain, it is unlikely you will want to repeat the experience in the near future.

We asked the women in our study what negatively impacted their sexual desire. The results are shown in Figure 4.7. In addition to these statistics, many women wrote additional

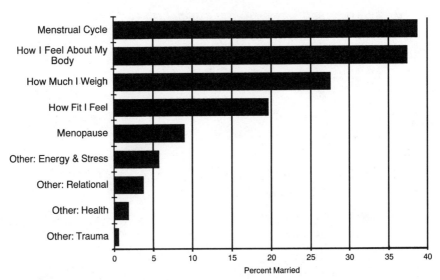

WHAT AFFECTS MARRIED WOMEN'S SEXUAL DESIRE
Figure 4.7

responses to this question, showing how important the issue was for them.

1. Fatigue and overextension

This cause is as common as the occasional cold among all women! It is so common that we will touch on it several times and in different contexts in this book. We cannot overemphasize the damage we do to our sexuality when we demand the impossible from absolutely exhausted bodies. If you are overly fatigued nearly every day for over two weeks you may be depressed.

Many women wrote about being overextended. The following comments were typical:

> *"Presently, sex is very low on my list of priorities. I know it is important to my husband, and it pleases him. This is often my primary motivation. With two small children, I don't feel like touching or being touched sexually at bedtime—mostly I'm exhausted. I wish it were more important to me—but I can't figure how to do things differently. How do I balance my partner's greater desire with my own exhaustion/lack of desire without feeling guilty or 'used'?"*

Another summed it up this way:

> *"I used to think about sex all the time—but a lot has changed! I've been married six years and have two children under three. I stay at home with my children and work part-time out of my home. I haven't lost all the weight from my last baby, and I'm tired all the time. I have to pray every day that God will help me be responsive to my husband. I find it difficult to respond to him when I hardly ever think about sex!"*

Fatigue, alone or in combination with other energy-sapping disorders, can cause low sexual desire. In order to combat fatigue, make some drastic lifestyle changes, and learn to sleep more. Sleep is the body's natural rejuvenator. Unfortunately, the majority of us are sleep-deprived and pay for this in reduced energy and desire. One comment was most telling: "I would rather sleep than have sex!"

You cannot keep pushing your body to the edge and expect it to be able to perform sexually. Exhaustion affects hormone levels, the brain's response to the hormone signals, and physical chemistry, causing headaches, muscle pain, and increased vulnerability to colds and other viruses. It also tends to make you irritable or volatile.

2. Depression

Apart from its connection to fatigue, depression can stand alone as a cause of low sexual desire. Almost all depressed individuals lose their desire for sex. Lack of interest in sex is one of the symptoms that doctors and therapists look for when diagnosing depression. One woman wrote:

> *"I love sex. Or I used to. Now I suffer from depression, and I no longer care for sex. I don't desire it, look forward to it, or delight in it. I am sad that I no longer have joy for sex or enjoy a romantic time with my husband."*

To this woman we would like to say that if you get treatment for your depression it is very likely that your sexual desire will return. So, be encouraged! Treatment of depression has improved dramatically over the past few years.

> **Apart from its connection to fatigue, depression can stand alone as a cause of low sexual desire.**

Not only can depression kill your sexual drive but it can also blunt your ability to become aroused. You may have some desire, but your body just won't respond to the signals you send it. Every erotic switch seems to have been inactivated. As another woman wrote:

> *"At this time in my life, and probably for a long time now, sex has played a very small part in my life. I wish I could feel more. I have dealt with a lot of problems—loss of my father and depression—and sex just seems to not be a part of me."*

A more complete discussion of depression also follows later in this book.

3. Self-fulfilling prophecies

Not only is it possible to learn how to allow yourself to be aroused but you can also learn how to turn yourself off. The underlying problem is in your attitude and thought process. Clinging to erroneous beliefs such as "I'm just not very sexual" becomes self-fulfilling. Or, due to early negative messages about sex, being made to feel ashamed about sexual exploration, or promiscuity, one can come to label sex and sexuality as dirty or bad. The feelings of arousal then create high levels of guilt, which inhibit sexual functioning.

4. Marital conflict

Sex happens in the context of a relationship. If your relationship is strained and you believe your needs are ignored, you will not be receptive to lovemaking. As one woman wrote:

> *"Sex has little importance for me. I don't have high needs, but our sex life has seldom been about my needs—always about his needs."*

There are many opportunities for resentment to grow in close relationships. As someone has said, "Marriage makes more enemies than almost any other relationship." Small problems that are not resolved can accumulate and grow into huge problems.

Some of the common issues that tend to eat away at healthy marriages are:

- Power struggles
- Communication breakdowns
- Unresolved past hurts
- Dual-career demands
- Disagreements over children or child rearing
- Jealousy over outside friendships

- Handling of finances
- Use of leisure time
- Selfishness
- Needing time alone
- Extended-family demands

One woman wrote about the accumulation of resentment:

> *"My sexual feelings fluctuate according to my continuous up and down feelings toward my husband. After eighteen years I've mellowed, and a lot of things that used to bother me don't as much anymore. However, I almost prefer romantic fantasies to the 'real' thing."*

Without improved communication, forgiveness, and problem solving and resolution, the accumulation of resentment can sink your sexual relationship as well as your marriage.

5. Past painful experiences

Molestation as a child, rape, or betrayal in previous love relationships can create the belief that sexual relationships and sexual feelings are not safe—they can be downright dangerous. As one woman put it:

> *"Sometimes my husband and I discuss my father's inappropriate sexual actions with me and wonder if that affects my desire for intercourse now. Once in a while my husband will do something my father did, and that instantly turns me off."*

Several women wrote comments similar to this:

> *"I am afraid of sex, so it is not important to me. I was abused at age six, and I can't get the hang of enjoying sex.*

How do you overcome past abuse so you can enjoy sex with your husband?"

Because sexual trauma of some sort is an extremely common cause of diminished sexual desire, and in many cases can kill it altogether, we will also devote a full chapter to this topic.

6. Other sexual problems

One sexual difficulty can impact other aspects of sexual functioning. For instance, if you are having difficulty achieving orgasm or if intercourse is painful, this will lower your interest in sex. Other sexual problems must be addressed prior to working on low desire. One woman in our study gives clear testimony of this:

> *"Due to pain with intercourse, my husband and I could only have satisfying sex without intercourse for a long period of time. Over the past twelve years, before I was finally diagnosed and obtained some relief, we experienced a lot of confusion, frustration, and even anger. But we did not give up and finally conquered the problem. I cherish my loving, thoughtful, and selfless husband!"*

7. Physical changes and body image

Two-thirds of the women in our study said they are affected sexually by one or more aspects related to their body image (how fit I feel, 20%; how much I weigh, 28%; how I feel about my body, 37%). (See Figure 4.7.) Thirty-nine percent also said their menstrual cycle had a major impact. Stress level and accompanying lack of energy were mentioned by 6%.

Natural changes to the body are inevitable. We all age and gravity reminds us of this. Busy yet sedentary lifestyles, physical changes that accompany bearing children, illnesses and the other effects of aging all impact our appearances. We feel disappointed in our body and this negative body image depletes our sexual desire. We don't want anyone, least of all our partners, to see our downwardly mobile bodies.

Most women suffer from unrealistic expectations about how their bodies must look and must continue to look. An insensitive partner doesn't help a woman to accept her body for what it is. They would like things to be different also. One woman wrote this to us:

"Sex is not as important to me as being loved and uncondition- ally accepted by my husband. I believe that if he were less criti- cal and more affirming of me, I would feel better about myself and have more sexual desire for him. I am slightly overweight, and it is a huge issue for him. I have tried all sorts of diets. He makes me feel ugly and unwanted. This kills my desire, but he still wants me to satisfy him in bed every other day. I do it out of duty to satisfy his libido. I am so frustrated I nearly had an affair to prove I am desirable. If it were not for my commitment to Christ, I would have."

An older woman shared this concern:

"I know that most women are not comfortable with their own bodies. I have young friends who have sex in the dark and are afraid to touch their own bodies."

Physical decline is inevitable, so every woman has to do some ongoing readjustment of her body image as time goes by. A high level of self-acceptance can work wonders for your sexual desire.

A mastectomy, colostomy, amputation, or paralyzing spinal cord injury can alter your appearance significantly. While pros- thetic substitutes may superficially restore your appearance, it would be callous of us to suggest that it is easy to come to terms with any such disfiguration. Frankly, it is a problem that must be faced with courage and determination. Do not let such trauma destroy your respect for yourself. It can also be a problem for your partner. His adjustment, as well as your own, requires some seri- ous mental and emotional effort.

8. Fear of intimacy

Men are labeled as those who can't handle intimacy. If the truth be told, a lot of women also have trouble with it. For some this can become an obstacle to sexual desire.

Most of us can recognize our need for intimacy because God created us with innate longing. But a lot can happen to spoil our ability to enjoy intimacy. People hurt us. Those who supposedly love us the most are often the ones who hurt us the most. We lose our ability to trust others with our deepest secrets and feelings. Intimacy can be a real problem for many, and this can inhibit sexual desire. More so than men, women can only give themselves sexually to someone they feel they can trust.

The marital relationship or friendship between partners is an aspect of intimacy that is often overlooked. Many couples do not have what we would consider to be very intimate marriages, yet they report that the sex is satisfactory. Somehow they are able to overcome their emotional distance for the benefit of a sexual outlet. But there is a limit to how distant you can be before sexual desire is affected. Some of the women in our study commented that the following inhibited their desire for sex:

- Bitterness toward husband
- Words husband says or does not say
- How the husband treats her
- A very strained marital relationship

It stands to reason that if the partners cannot maintain a basic friendship, sexual desire cannot thrive.

9. Medical conditions and physical problems

Much of what we have discussed thus far about sexual desire presupposes that normal health prevails. Medical conditions, or their treatments, that affect sex hormones or increase prolactin (the hormone causing milk production in mothers) can decrease desire. As one woman wrote:

> *"I have been either pregnant or breast-feeding for six years straight! I used to like sex, but now we have it because I know we need to have it as a couple. I know my drive will eventually come back when the kids are older, but my husband and I need to be assured that we will see the light at the end of the tunnel."*

Another woman wrote about her hormone difficulty due to birth control:

> *"My biggest frustration is that my sex drive is markedly lower when I am on birth control pills. All other forms of birth control are unsatisfactory—as soon as I get off the pill I get pregnant. It is frustrating to me to have all this time go by without a good sex life."*

Another common medical reason for low sexual desire is any condition that produces fatigue. A woman wrote:

> *"I have been sick with chronic fatigue for nine months. This has really impacted our sex life. When I feel so tired most of the time, I have little sexual desire. I am starting to feel somewhat better so I hope our sex will improve."*

The physical effects of injury or childbirth also impact desire:

> *"I wish I had known how painful it would be to have sex after childbirth. Finally the pain from being torn badly is going away and sex is starting to become fun again."*

And seemingly small medical problems can aggravate desire in many ways:

"I get bladder infections from intercourse, and that has always put a damper on my enthusiasm."

A hysterectomy, diabetes, thyroid problems, chronic pain, and many commonly prescribed medications were also specifically mentioned by the women in our study as negatively affecting their sexual desire.

Obviously, the solution to each of these problems is to get competent treatment for the underlying medical disorder.

How Can I Increase My Sexual Desire?

To what extent can a woman help herself to raise the level of her sexual desire? First, let us say that problems of low sexual desire *can* be changed. Second, while change is possible, it takes commitment and a lot of time and effort.

There are exceptions, of course. Some couples choose a platonic type of relationship without any sex. We respect this. Sex, after all, is only icing on the cake. It is not the cake! Or, perhaps you are not married and don't intend to marry. A sexual relationship therefore, is not on your life's agenda. Or your marital relationship may be such that you

> **Problems of low sexual desire *can* be changed . . . but it takes commitment and a lot of time and effort.**

and your partner no longer have sexual intercourse. Your priority, then, becomes building the strongest friendship you can and finding other ways to express your sexuality together. In fact, this should be a high priority for all of us.

But where low sexual desire is a problem, there is help. To improve your sexual desire means you will have to rearrange your priorities and, therefore, your life schedule. Your partner may have to also. You will probably have to let go of some other things in your life in order to make time for this to work.

What are some of the changes needed to create time? They may include: working out one day less a week, working less overtime, not bringing work home some nights, letting the dinner dishes sit overnight, sending the kids to Grandma's for a few hours this Sunday (or better still, for the weekend), hiring someone else to clean the house this week, taking more naps to restore energy, arranging for someone else to drive the kids to soccer practice, gymnastics, swimming, and parties, and finally—and for many the most important—turning off the television. Hard assignment? You bet! But we warned you!

Low sexual desire can be a difficult and stubborn obstacle to overcome, so be patient. You may need professional help at some point. "Phobic sexual avoidance" (we'll talk about it later in this chapter) almost always requires the assistance of a trained professional. Try the following suggestion: If after working on your problem for two months you do not see any improvement, seek out a therapist, preferably Christian, but especially one who is trained and experienced in dealing with sexual problems.

Pray over your problem. Both of you pray. All sexual problems are the couple's problem. Ask God to help you to rekindle your desire. Ask Him to give you both the desire and the energy to do what pleases Him.

Accompanying issues must be resolved first. If either you or your partner is depressed, solve this problem first. Depression takes precedence, and it can be treated. If severe marital conflicts are part of your relationship, solve that problem first. Dr. Kaplan sums up the view of many therapists when she says: "Couples whose relationship is in serious trouble are poor candidates for sex therapy. These patients should be offered marital therapy and then re-evaluated for the treatment of their sexual dysfunction after their relationship has improved to a point where helping them make love together starts to make sense."[8]

De-clutter your schedule. Where are the time-eaters and time-wasters for you? How much time do you spend watching television? Talking on the telephone? Do you spend every moment up until midnight making dinner, doing dishes, cleaning, and preparing for the next day, then stumble bleary-eyed into the bedroom "just too tired for sex"? Do you allow your small children to stay up too late so you have no time to yourself, and no time alone as a couple? Do you say yes to every worthy cause and work on every committee of your child's school or athletic teams? Do you permit your children to play multiple sports all year so you and your spouse spend any free time driving to or from attending practices or games, coaching, or working in the snack booth?

Get real about lowering your fatigue. You will never catch up on your rest if you do not make getting rested a high priority. You will not be able to be in touch with your sexual desire if you are exhausted. How much sleep do you get each night? Eight or nine hours are what is needed! (Read Dr. Hart's book *Adrenaline and Stress.*)[9]

Focus on your partner's attractive qualities, and actively choose to ignore negative characteristics. Remember how you used to act and feel when you were first in love? What did you do then? Make it a point to leave notes for each other, send cards to each other, go out to dinner, walk on the beach or in the park hand in hand. Celebrate special days in special ways. Dress up for each other. Look at some old pictures of the two of you together. Revisit some of the places where you spent time in the early days of your relationship.

Use your imagination. Think about your partner (positively) when you aren't together. Visualize a good physical experience you had in the past. Relive it. Fantasy about your spouse is always healthy. Do something surprising: Wear a new outfit that makes you feel sexy; have a picnic on the living room floor instead of the kitchen table; forget cleaning Saturday morning and instead drive somewhere beautiful together; drape yourself naked over the television with a rose in your teeth; buy satin sheets.

Laugh and play. Don't make working on your relationship

and desire problem too serious. Keep a sense of humor. Try to find things to laugh about—together.

Educate yourself on the effects of any medications you take, as well as alcohol or other drugs. Many common medications affect sexual desire. These include antiandrogen drugs, chemotherapeutic agents, antidepressants (particularly SSRIs and MAOIs), stimulants like Dexadrine, neuroleptics like Haldol and Stellazine, antihypertensives and cardiac drugs, Pondomin, anticholesterol drugs, steroids, narcotics like heroin and morphine, alcohol, benzodiazepines, and barbiturates. Ask your doctor about the sexual side effects of the medications prescribed for you.

Address health issues in your life. Any medical condition that causes chronic pain, fatigue, or malaise will affect sexual desire: arthritis, cancer, anemia, chronic infections, traumatic injuries, extreme obesity, and so forth. Thyroid problems can affect desire, as can pulmonary diseases, neurological diseases such as MS and Parkinson's, and various gynecological (including painful intercourse) and urological conditions. It doesn't make sense to try to work on your desire when the underlying cause of low desire is being ignored.

Prime the pump. Spend time and energy putting yourself in the mood. Think about spending pleasurable time with your partner. Imagine sharing affection, enjoyable sexual touching, and how good it feels to be aroused.

Try to gain God's perspective on sex. He created sex, and not to make you miserable either! Sometimes we lose (or never had) God's meaning for sex. We need to meditate, pray, and study what the Bible says about sexuality and allow the Holy Spirit to heal and transform us. God wants to give us His gift of sexual giving and receiving.

When Low Sexual Desire Is a Serious Problem

Physical hunger is a good analogy for sexual hunger. In animals (and humans) the brain's "appetite centers" can be damaged, causing the animal to stop eating and starve to death, even when food is present. Or these same centers can be overactivated and the animal will gorge itself and become grotesquely overweight and unhealthy. Sexual motivation also can be affected in either direction: suppression or hyperactivity.

Dr. Kaplan described our sexual desire as a balance between the accelerator, which fuels our desire to pursue sexual intercourse, and the brakes, which keep our desires controlled so "we do not crash headlong into disaster. However, if the normal control mechanism that adjusts and modulates our sexual motivation goes awry, the person will experience an abnormal or dysfunctional increase or decrease of sexual desire."[10] These two extremes are called sexual aversion and sexual compulsivity.

Sexual Aversion

Sexual aversion is an intense reaction that involves being repelled by any sort of sexual contact with all partners or, instead, involves panic when a person tries to engage in a specific type of sexual activity or sex with her steady partner. Sexual aversion is less common than low sexual desire. In one study of over two thousand patients, 80% were diagnosed with low sexual desire and 19% with sexual aversion disorder. More women than men experience sexual aversion.

Sexual aversion is a phobic avoidance of sex and is the most severe form of sexual desire disorder. Dr. Kaplan writes: "In these sexual anxiety states, sexual contact with the partner is associated with a feeling of imminent peril, and the accompanying emergency emotions override all sexual feelings."[11]

What's the difference between low sexual desire and an aversion disorder? A woman with low sexual desire has little or no appetite for sex, but is not repelled by physical contact with her partner. A woman with a sexual aversion disorder would be intensely frightened of, or even repelled by, sexual activity. She phobically avoids it.

Sexual aversion may be caused by childhood sexual abuse or rape at any age. It can also be caused by painful labor and delivery or lengthy and invasive infertility treatment. It is also more common in those with anxiety disorders or generalized phobias (such as a fear of heights, a fear of enclosed places, or a fear of flying).

Sexual aversion can range from relatively mild to severe. A woman with a mild phobia would, with work, be able to calm herself and push past her anxiety. She might even enjoy sex at times. A woman with a severe aversion would experience intense disgust and revulsion toward her partner at all times. She might not be able to tolerate even the slightest physical contact with her partner. He might not even be allowed to hold her hand.

How Can I Recover from Sexual Aversion?

It appears to us from the comments we have received that some women in our sample are experiencing sexual aversion. As with all phobias, professional help is needed.

To work on sexual aversion, it is necessary to break the learned association between fear and sex. This requires sex education and gradual planned exposures to the sexual situation that frightens you. If you believe you are sexually avoidant, we recommend you work with a therapist or doctor who is trained and experienced in treating these problems. You will need help in designing a treatment plan, which must be carried out under calm, safe conditions.

It may be necessary to use antianxiety or antipanic medications during the relearning process. Without it the anxiety is just too high for effective treatment. But take heart. If you are in need of medication, you will not have to take it for the rest of your life in order to have sex!

When Hyperactive Sexual Desire Is a Problem

Although hyperactive sexual desire in a woman sounds like a man's fantasy come true, hyperactive sexual desire, especially in women, is rare. Dr. Kaplan reports that out of over five thousand patients, "only eighteen were distressed by their excessive sexual needs, and only two of these were women." Out of the two thousand or more patients diagnosed with sexual desire disorders, 1% were diagnosed with hyperactive sexual desire. We received only a few comments (two or three) that indicated a slight tendency toward sexual hyperactivity.

Sexual hyperactivity is also called sexual addiction or compulsive sexuality. It is far more common in men. Typically, the person is preoccupied with sexual thoughts or feelings, and this interferes with their effectiveness at work or creates problems in their relationships. They have sex frequently, often having several orgasms each day.

A hypersexual person feels driven, almost out of control. Their self-control is so inadequate that they will engage in sex even when they risk losing their job, spouse, or life due to AIDS or other sexually transmitted diseases (STDs). If a hyperactively sexual person tries to stop, they often become tense, anxious, and depressed (withdrawal symptoms), and this pushes them to resume their compulsive sexuality.

Many women have been helped to stop sexually compulsive behavior. Groups such as Sexaholics Anonymous or Love and Sex Addicts Anonymous have been helpful for some. Several churches have begun Christ-centered recovery groups for those struggling with sexually compulsive behavior. These are mainly for men, but a little prod to the pastor may help establish a women's group as well. Many therapists specialize in working to help women (and men) to overcome sexual compulsivity.

Conclusion

As you can see, sexual desire is a necessary prerequisite to a fulfilling sexual relationship. Throughout our life cycle, sexual desire will be impacted by many factors. Most of us will struggle at one time or another with sexual desire. It is well worth investing your prayers, time, energy, and money to resolve difficulties with desire.

Points to Remember

1. Many women are puzzled and challenged by fluctuations of their sexual desire.

2. Low sexual desire is one of the main areas of difficulty identified by the women in our study. Many wished they could increase their desire for sex.

3. The stronger a woman's sexual desire, the more often she thinks about sex. This was a very strong finding of our study.

4. Sexual desire is influenced by many factors, including hormonal fluctuations, fatigue, depression, medical conditions, past traumatic experiences, and marital conflict.

5. Sexual desire ranges across a spectrum that includes normal-low and normal-high sexual desire.

6. Sexual desire can be increased by: prayer, rest, focusing on your partner's attractive qualities, addressing health issues and medication, and playfulness.

Chapter Five

The Quest for Orgasm

"By night on my bed I sought the one I love."
—*Song of Solomon 3:1 NKJV*

Twenty-five percent of the women in our study specifically mentioned or asked about orgasm in their comments and questions. It seems incredible that with so much literature being published about sexuality, there is still misinformation and confusion surrounding this topic. But there is! Hopefully, we can help dispel some of this confusion.

> *"Orgasm. . . . What does one feel like? How do you get them? Can you increase their intensity?"*

> *"What percentage of women have orgasms with intercourse only? How do they do that? I never have! It sounds great in novels. . . ."*

The ideal sexual experience, at least as portrayed in popular magazines and romantic novels, is mutual and multiple orgasms achieved solely by vaginal thrusting and without any other assistance whatsoever. Is this goal realistic? Absolutely not. Couples have to find their own unique way of expressing their sexuality, and it may be nowhere near this "ideal."

This does point out, however, just how destructive myths are in the area of orgasm. Myths create unreasonable and sometimes unattainable expectations, and they need to be challenged at every opportunity, which is one goal of our study. Just listen to the frustration surrounding the topic of orgasm, often fed by misinformation and myth:

"Orgasms? Why are they so hard to achieve? What am I doing wrong?"

"Do other women experience pain and pleasure during orgasm? So much so that I can't bear it. We are so ignorant about what is normal!"

"How do women have orgasms without manual stimulation? Are they telling the truth? And why does it take so much foreplay for women to be sexually aroused for intercourse?"

A damaging myth is that orgasm is necessary to a satisfying sexual experience. Listen to the following story:

"Sex is a fundamental part of our marriage. But let me make one very important point: It is not the actual orgasm that is important to me but the lovemaking. It is our emotional and physical closeness during intercourse that really satisfies me. I love giving myself to my husband and satisfying his needs. This is more important to me than orgasm."

This communicates several important points. First, for a woman at least, orgasm is not always the goal of lovemaking. Rather, orgasm is to be seen as a delightful experience that may happen, but not necessarily every time.

A damaging myth is that orgasm is necessary to a satisfying sexual experience.

Second, for a woman and hopefully for well-adjusted men also, the emotional experience of intercourse is more important than the physical. In preparing couples for marriage, we often fail to help them understand this. We overemphasize the physical and neglect to emphasize the emotional needs that are satisfied through sex. As a consequence many couples quickly become dissatisfied with their sexual experience. They are looking for satisfaction in the wrong place! We will have more to say about this later.

What Is Orgasm?

"I really don't know what orgasm is for a woman. I've experienced joy, exhilaration, and great happiness, but if orgasm for a woman is supposed to replicate a man's release—then I've never experienced it. After forty-plus years, I'm still uneducated in this area."

"How can a woman know when she has had an orgasm? I have no idea what to expect."

One of the reasons women are confused about orgasm is that they don't understand what is happening in their bodies. We need to pause here to describe the physiological orgasmic response. If you are going to try to enhance your sexual experience, you need to understand how it works.

An orgasm is a reflex—as natural as sneezing. Physically, it is a series of vigorous, rhythmic muscle contractions that come from the pelvic and clitoral muscles. But an orgasm is not an isolated event. It is a part of a series of changes that occur in the body when you are sexually stimulated. Without stimulation and these changes in your body, you cannot reach orgasm.

When a woman becomes sexually aroused, her body goes through several physical and emotional responses: increased heartbeat, perspiration, lubrication (the moistening of the vaginal walls through a process similar to sweating), the body flushing, and nipples becoming erect. There are also many internal responses that she may not notice: The uterus lifts, the inner two-thirds of the vagina expands about one inch in length and doubles in width, the outer one-third of the vagina expands as it becomes more congested with blood, and the vaginal opening decreases about one-third in size. The clitoris and the many tissues attached and surrounding it internally fill with blood and increase dramatically in size.

The entire clitoral system, the nerves, veins, arteries, and spongy tissue (the glans, shaft, and hood of the clitoris, the crura, the inner lips, the hymen, several bodies of erectile tissue, the clitoral bulbs, the urethral sponge, and the perineal sponge) muscles, nerve endings, and networks of blood vessels become swollen in the same way that a penis does. It is the equivalent of the male's erection. When fully aroused, the internal part of the clitoris is roughly thirty times as large as the external clitoris glans and shaft.

Barbara Seaman, in emphasizing how the female's "erection" differs from the male's, writes:

> *"Our sexual structures expand as much or more during arousal as men's; the only difference is that male erection (engorgement) takes place outside the body, and is therefore more visible, while ours takes place underneath the surface—under the vaginal lips. The total size of our engorgement is no smaller than the size of an erect penis."*[1]

In both women and men, the arousal response depends on two processes: blood filling body tissues (vasodilation) and increasing muscle tension (myotonia).

All of these physical responses, the building of muscular tension and the swelling of body tissues, are necessary in order to reach orgasm. When the sexual response reaches its climax (orgasm), the muscles contract and then relax, and the blood is pushed out of the tissues and returns to normal circulation.

How Can You Tell If You Are Having an Orgasm?

Each of us is physiologically and psychologically different, so the experience of orgasm is unique for each of us. Also, orgasm differs from experience to experience in the same woman due to a variety of factors: dynamics in the relationship, what is going on in the physical environment, her personal beliefs about sex and the meaning it holds to her, her menstrual cycle, and her physical health. An orgasm can be extremely intense so that you are totally absorbed in it, or it can just be a pleasant, local sensation.

Orgasms have been described as: "warmth throughout my body," "tingly," "a fantastic rush," "a pervasive sensation, wide waves of feeling through my whole body," and "high, joyous."

Many women have difficulty knowing whether or not they have had an orgasm. This is not all that surprising since in popular literature orgasms are supposed to cause the earth to move, make you hear singing, and cause any number of other unrealistic expectations.

What are the signs of orgasm? They are *not* bells and whistles. Though some women experience "fireworks," not all do.

You can look first for physical signs that lead up to orgasm: a sexual flush, nipples that are erect, contractions of the pelvic region. Even these signs may not be clear because orgasm is a more subjective experience for women than it is for men. Pay attention to how you feel. Are you warm and relaxed? Do you feel satisfied and "nice" all over? Do you sense that you don't need to go on any further, as if the experience is over? Or, do you stop seeking stimulation because your partner has had his orgasm or because you feel exhausted? A pleasant feeling of relaxation and satisfaction is the best sign that orgasm has occurred.

Women also differ in their personal preferences and/or pattern in orgasm. Some women are multiorgasmic. Other women prefer a single orgasm and find more unpleasant. Some women describe having several mild orgasms, others one long one. And still others describe patterns of "mixed" orgasms.

All this means is that there is no pressure on you as to what type of orgasm you should be having. There is no one, right type. Some researchers have described women's unique patterns of orgasm as "orgasmic fingerprints"—no two are the same.

Who Has Problems with Orgasm?

Orgasmic problems are common. One medical textbook estimates that roughly 10% of women report a lifelong total lack of orgasm. This agrees with our study where a little under 10% of the women reported they never reach orgasm.

In another study, at least 50% of women report having problems reaching orgasm off and on over a certain time period or in certain situations.[2] Fifty-eight percent of women aged eighteen to seventy-nine reported orgasmic "difficulties." That is a high percentage of women. If you are having difficulty reaching orgasm, you are not alone!

What about Christian women? Twenty-six percent of the women in our study reported that reaching orgasm was a difficulty. Of these, half feel it is a moderate problem, and almost a quarter believe their problem is severe.

We asked the women in our study what percentage of the time they were able to reach orgasm. As you can see from Figure 5.1, about one-third of the women were able to reach orgasm 75% of the time. One quarter reported that they could achieve orgasm all the time. Nine percent say they are never able to reach orgasm.

We also discovered that there is a significant association between sexual satisfaction and frequency of orgasm. As shown in Figure 5.2, the pattern is very clear. Those who reach orgasm 50% or more of the time are more sexually satisfied than those who reach orgasm 25% of the time or less. While orgasm alone is not a direct indicator of sexual satisfaction (as you can see, one in five women who always reach orgasm still report feeling sexually unsatisfied), the

> **While orgasm alone is not a direct indicator of sexual satisfaction, the relationship between orgasm and sexual satisfaction is nevertheless very strong.**

relationship between orgasm and sexual satisfaction is nevertheless very strong.

HOW OFTEN WOMEN REACH ORGASM
Figure 5.1

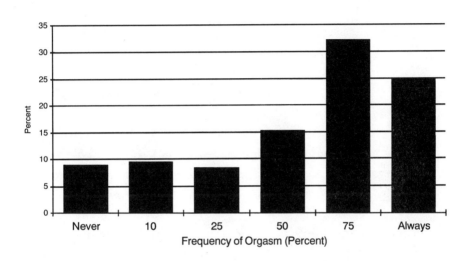

SEXUAL SATISFACTION AND FREQUENCY OF ORGASM AMONG MARRIED WOMEN
Figure 5.2

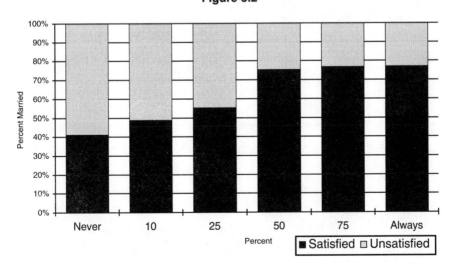

We do not want to overaccentuate the importance of orgasm. But we do want to encourage women who desire it, yet struggle to achieve it, to persist. Orgasm is a very pleasurable experience that provides many benefits, not the least of which is a healthy release of sexual tension. It is a part of the God-given gift of sexuality and worth pursuing.

How to Achieve Orgasm

"Why is it so hard to reach orgasm? What am I doing wrong? What do I need to do?"

"What ways—mentally or physically—can help me to be able to reach orgasm? It would please me and my spouse. On our honeymoon we both reached our peaks. Now I can't. I don't understand."

We received many questions like these. Many factors need to be considered when looking at sexual complaints, including problems reaching orgasm. These factors include: the way you make love (i.e., sexual technique), relationship problems, medications you are taking (some actually inhibit orgasm), unpleasant sexual experiences earlier in your life (psychological factors are very strong in orgasm), sexual trauma such as abuse or rape, and early family history and sex education (including negative messages regarding sex and whether or not your parents were trustworthy or abandoning). We will examine each of these in turn.

1. Technique

One of the first areas to look at when there is a problem with orgasm is how much time you devote to having sex. Men are capable of becoming aroused and climaxing within minutes. Most women are physiologically not capable of such a rapid response! So unless you and your partner devote enough time to lovemaking you cannot become orgasmic.

Often a woman may worry, or her husband may complain, that she is "taking too long." Invariably the woman will blame herself. After all, she sees how fast her husband responds and she compares herself to him. But it may not be her problem at all. Her partner's technique may be wrong or he may not be creating the right atmosphere for lovemaking. It is possible that the difficulty may arise from within the woman herself. She may not be able to abandon herself to the experience because she fears the loss of control necessary for orgasm. She may have a hard time believing that it is "acceptable" for her to enjoy any sexual pleasure. Perhaps old tapes about how "sinful" sex is are playing in her head. When she becomes frustrated, orgasm recedes further over the horizon. Both partners need to accept that it takes time to really enjoy the sexual act and to receive the stimulation necessary for orgasm.

Most women *do* require a long period of time to become excited and reach orgasm. How much time? Roughly ten times that required for most men. And it may take even longer for some. This time difference between men and women can make achieving a simultaneous orgasm a real challenge.

This difference in partners' timing was confirmed by the data in our study. We compared how long women said they needed with how frequently they reached orgasm. Figure 5.3 shows the results.

There is a definite association between how long you take to make love and how frequently you reach orgasm. (This finding is comparable to the *Sex in America* study, for both their entire sample as well as for the Protestant sample.) Reflect on the data. Those who reach orgasm 10% of the time only spend five minutes making love. Those who reach orgasm 50% of the time take thirty minutes. Good sex takes time, no doubt about it. And time is a precious commodity for most couples these days!

To understand the time factor in the female orgasm, look at Figure 5.4. Here we illustrate three different "response styles" of orgasm. Notice also that there are five distinct phases: the desire phase (interest or openness to lovemaking), the excitement phase

DURATION OF LOVEMAKING AND FREQUENCY OF ORGASM AMONG MARRIED WOMEN
Figure 5.3

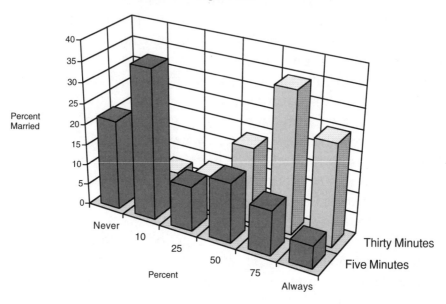

FEMALE SEXUAL RESPONSE CYCLES
Figure 5.4

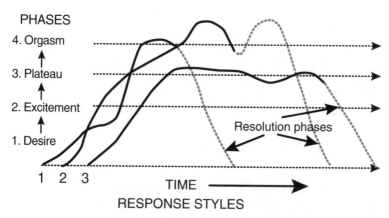

RESPONSE STYLES

1. Female 1 (Resembles male's response)
2. Female 2 (Rapid orgasm, no plateau)
3. Female 3 (Extended plateau, no orgasm)

(buildup of arousal), the plateau phase (the high level of excitement just before orgasm), the orgasm phase (the release of sexual tension), and resolution (a gradual return to the normal physiological state). Men typically drop away rapidly from the plateau phase, but women can remain there for much longer, hence the ability to have multiple orgasms. Female 1 most closely resembles the male response. Unlike the male, however, the female can have more than one orgasm without falling below the plateau level. Female 2 shows a rapid ascent to orgasm—without much of a plateau—and quick resolution. Female 3 has an extended period at the plateau stage without orgasm.

Note that there are different response styles. You might find yourself identifying with one of these styles at different times or stages in your life. Notice also how important time is in achieving a satisfying response.

Orgasm: The Seven Habits of a Satisfied Woman

1. Think about sex more frequently. Think in advance about the coming sexual encounter. Anticipate desire and arousal (prime the pump).

2. Don't hurry lovemaking. Allow ample time to reach arousal levels required for orgasm.

3. Get rested. Combat fatigue. Allow enough time and energy to be truly present in the sexual experience.

4. Don't use alcohol. Small amounts of alcohol initially lower inhibitions which can increase desire and enjoyment of foreplay. But moderate amounts of alcohol may cause fewer or no orgasms, less satisfying orgasms, less lubrication, and the need for longer foreplay. Large amounts of alcohol cause women to be nonorgasmic.

5. Stay focused. Tune in to the areas of your body that are experiencing pleasurable feelings. Go after the good feelings. Be aware of your mind wandering ("Did I defrost the roast?" "Did I fax that important memo?") and bring it back to the here and now.

6. Learn about your own body. Examine its structures and explore their reactions and functions. What feels good?

7. Examine your beliefs about your body, sensuality, your sexual parts, and sex itself. What meanings do each of these hold for you? Is it time to ask God to help you process and re-create your sexual belief system?

How much time of sexual stimulation is needed for a woman to become aroused and reach orgasm? We asked this question of the women in our study. Figure 5.5 shows the results. Just over 62% (the largest group) said they needed fifteen minutes of *stimulation*. It is important to notice that this is not total duration of lovemaking (which of course would be even longer) but duration of sexual stimulation. Twenty percent needed only five minutes, but 15% needed thirty minutes. A very small percentage, about 2%, said they needed more than forty-five minutes.

STIMULATION TO REACH ORGASM FOR MARRIED WOMEN
Figure 5.5

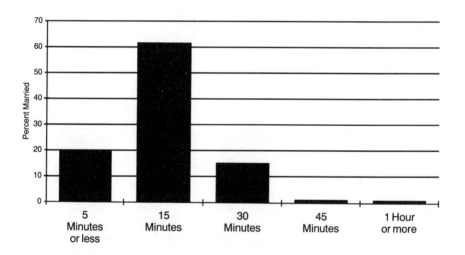

Clearly, therefore, time is a significant factor in achieving orgasm. The reason it takes time is that important biological changes must occur. If a woman is thinking, *Let's just hurry up and get it over with,* or is anxious that she is "taking too long" these pressures will keep her from enjoying what *is* happening and short-circuit the arousal process. A woman cannot reach orgasm without adequate time being given to the excitement phase, and this explains why many are not able to achieve an orgasm.

2. Overcoming relationship problems

Orgasm problems that are intermittent (at intervals over your life) or in specific situations are often connected to relationship problems. Why else would you be orgasmic at one time and not the next? Varying environmental or life conditions can also be the cause.

Relationships that are filled with conflict, bitterness, and hostility tend to stifle orgasm. There is no way you are going to be able to achieve an adequate level of arousal when you don't feel safe, secure, and loved. The solution? Heal the breach that is causing the conflict. Seek marital counseling if necessary.

Also, women who have been sexually traumatized earlier in life often find it difficult to be orgasmic. Because sexual trauma is so important as a cause for orgasmic problems, we will devote a separate chapter to trauma (chapter 10).

When you are under too much pressure to perform for your partner or if your partner seems unconcerned about your problem, you may become angry and resentful. This can also inhibit orgasm.

In all intermittent orgasmic problems it is essential that you open up a frank and honest discussion with your partner. You probably both need some educating. Blaming one another won't solve anything, so you should own it as your joint problem. You are *not* responsible for each other's orgasms, although you can each do a lot to help the other. Your main responsibilities are to give and receive pleasure and to focus on your own body's responses. Sex is most satisfying when a couple love each other and want each other to receive pleasure, while each person *also* focuses on feeling his or her own pleasure. This means resisting all distractions. Don't turn yourself off—turn yourself on!

3. Attending to medical problems and medications

It is alarming how often we encounter couples in counseling who are not aware of how medical conditions, and treatment, can inhibit sexual arousal and orgasm. Diabetes, alcoholism, hormone deficiencies, and some neurological disorders can cause orgasm difficulties.

Many medications inhibit orgasm. You may be able to become aroused but are unable to climax. The list of drugs that *may* cause sexual side effects include (and don't let your imagination influence you too much here): antiandrogens, antiarrhythmics, anticancer agents, anticholinergics, antihistamines, antihypertensives, diuretics, hormones, antianxiety drugs, anticonvulsants, antidepressants, antipsychotics, sedatives, hypnotics, stimulants, Demerol, methadone, alcohol, amphetamines, cocaine, heroin, marijuana, and nicotine. Note the nicotine. Women who smoke a lot can expect some problems. Note also that almost any drug that starts with the prefix *anti* is going to be *antiorgasmic!*

Since many are concerned about taking medications, we strongly suggest that any time a medication is prescribed for you, you ask your physician to tell you what the sexual side effects of the drug might be.

One other important point about medication. New drugs are being discovered all the time. While they are very effective in treating the primary problem for which they are designed, their sexual side effects may not yet be well established. Keep a careful note of all changes so you can show them to your doctor.

4. Overcoming early family experiences and faulty sex education

We receive much of our training in sexuality in our childhood. Some of it is deliberate and good. Some of it, however, is accidental and destructive. In fact, more harm can often be done by silence than by what is spoken even if the information is faulty. Homes in which sex is never talked about can be the most damaging. Inevitably, children will develop beliefs about attractiveness and its importance, about their bodies and body parts, and whether sex is dirty, good, or unmentionable.

Because sex education is such an important topic, we have devoted a separate chapter to it.

5. Getting help for total lack of orgasm

A substantial number of women have not been able to have an orgasm. An inability to reach orgasm in any situation and over your entire life rarely has a physical basis. Overall lack of orgasm can be caused by: emotions, attitudes, lack of knowledge, and lack of experience. Treatment involves identifying the thought patterns and feelings that keep a woman from being able to "let go." Women also learn more about how their body functions and their sexual response cycle. They privately explore their own bodies and learn what is sexually pleasurable to them. All of this information is brought into the sexual relationship with their husband as treatment progresses.

In most cases (75–90% of cases where there is adequate desire and arousal but no orgasm), by working with a sex therapist or joining a woman's treatment group, you will achieve orgasm. There are also excellent self-help books available if you would prefer to work on reaching orgasm on your own.

Orgasm During Intercourse

One of the most frequently asked questions surrounding the topic of orgasm had to do with having an orgasm during intercourse—preferably simultaneously with the woman's partner. Here are some sample questions:

> *"Is there something wrong with me that I can't have an orgasm during intercourse, only when I stimulate myself?"*

> *"How often do women really have an orgasm during intercourse? It makes me feel a little inadequate to think I might be the only one who needs direct stimulation to the clitoris in order to have an orgasm."*

"I know that the majority of women need to have their clitoris stimulated in order to achieve orgasm. Somehow I see this form of orgasm as inferior to the kind of orgasm my husband has. Please address this."

We asked the women in our study whether or not they could reach orgasm with intercourse alone. We were not surprised by the answer: 59% said no, they could not. How does this compare with other studies? It is in close agreement with what most sex researchers and

> **Two-thirds of women cannot reach orgasm through intercourse alone.**

therapists have found. Some claim that it is as high as 67%. We can safely conclude that about two-thirds of women cannot reach orgasm through intercourse alone.

This fact alone should be freeing to many women who have labored under the belief that if they were normal they should reach orgasm through intercourse alone. There is no basis in physiology to support this idea. While some women are able to develop their ability to have an orgasm with only vaginal thrusting, many need direct stimulation of the clitoris to achieve this. This stimulation must be achieved by finding an appropriate position, or by stimulating the clitoris yourself, or by having your husband stimulate your clitoris before, during, or after intercourse.

Also, if you can't reach orgasm with intercourse alone, our research says that both increased frequency and increased duration can help. In other words, take more time and have sex more often. This can improve your orgasmic response during intercourse.

A lot of the faulty belief that orgasm should be achieved through intercourse alone and without any other help can be traced back to Freud and his theory about vaginal versus clitoral orgasms. In reality, there is no such difference. An orgasm is an orgasm. It is triggered primarily by clitoral stimulation, but it is expressed by contractions of the pelvic muscles and the outer one-third of the vagina. The thrusting of the penis either stimulates the clitoris directly when, in certain positions, it has contact, or indirectly by pulling the clitoral hood across the clitoris.

We also asked women how they reached orgasm if not from intercourse. Fifty-one percent said by manual stimulation (their hand or their partner's hand). Twenty-five percent said it was by oral stimulation. Many women wrote that they needed a specific position (woman on top) or a vibrator to reach orgasm. Others also mentioned stimulation by the penis directly (external stimulation without penetration).

It is usually helpful for men and women to understand that the vagina has about the same sensitivity as a man's testicles. Imagine a man trying to reach orgasm by stimulating the testicles alone. It's not impossible, but it is extremely difficult. That is the equivalent for many women of trying to reach orgasm by intercourse alone. What we are stating is that you are normal if you can't reach orgasm with intercourse alone—most women can't!

For many Christians who reject all forms of masturbation, this can be a real problem. They wish not to touch themselves for fear that it is wrong. But stimulating yourself before, during, or after intercourse as part of lovemaking with your partner is not masturbation. Masturbation, by definition, is "autoerotic," meaning that you do it by yourself, for yourself. We want to clarify the confusion that prevents many otherwise healthy women from achieving a complete orgasmic experience. They put the wrong label on their self-stimulation, the label of masturbation, and this label is charged with feelings of guilt.

Frequently, one of the obstacles to orgasm is that a woman doesn't know how she needs to be stimulated. In this case, we would encourage her to experiment and find out what is most pleasurable for her. Or, if she does know how to stimulate herself to orgasm, she has a difficult time communicating this to her husband. The only way he can learn is through more complete communication—she must describe it to him, demonstrate with him, and encourage him to practice with her. It is also perfectly acceptable for her to stimulate herself during love-play and intercourse.

Orgasm and Masturbation

"Is it normal for women not to reach orgasm as easily by inter-course as by masturbation?"

Yes, it is quite normal for some women to feel that it is easier to have an orgasm through masturbation than by intercourse. As we have already indicated, most women must receive direct stimulation to the clitoris, even during intercourse, to reach orgasm. The advantage of self-stimulation is that you have immediate feedback. You control the stimulation. You can apply more pressure, less pressure, change the direction, get more lubrication, and so forth. You know immediately what gives the best results. Stimulation through intercourse alone usually means you don't have as much control over the amount, type, or speed of stimulation, and there-fore you may not get exactly what you need in order to reach the level of arousal required to climax. In that sense, for many women it is easier to reach orgasm through self-stimulation.

But as the following quotes from the Hite Report indicate, easier is not always perceived as better.

"My most satisfying orgasms, both physically and psychologically, are those during intercourse. My most intense ones are those from masturbation."

"Clitoral orgasms are stronger; orgasms from intercourse alone are weak and unsatisfying, and extremely frustrating sometimes!"

"Intercourse orgasms are stronger and better and satisfy my whole body rather than just the genital area the way direct stimulation does."[3]

Orgasm is a very individual, very personal experience. Some women experience intercourse orgasm as the most satisfying; others prefer orgasm through self-stimulation or masturbation. So much depends on a myriad of factors that it is impossible to say whether one way is superior to another.

Multiple Orgasms

"How common or attainable are multiple orgasms?"

One of the most striking sexual differences between men and women is that men enter a refractory phase after they have ejaculated so that they are unable immediately to become physically aroused again. They have to wait. For some it may be just a few minutes (younger men), for others a few days even. Women, however, are able to reach a second or third orgasm immediately after the first. These are referred to as multiple orgasms.

How is this possible? Once again it is due to anatomy. Because the blood congestion during arousal encompasses such a large area, as opposed to the male's penis only, resolution or the lowering of arousal is a much slower process in women. With continued stimulation, therefore, a woman can quickly build again to the point of climax. Not all women enjoy it, but they are capable of it.

One unsatisfactory side effect of this ability is that you can easily feel a pressure to perform. The pressure can be inside you ("Everybody is talking about multiple orgasms, so I better get with it"), or your partner can pressure you ("I'm not a good lover unless I give you a lot of orgasms"). Either way, the real point of lovemaking is lost. Sex is for expressing love, feeling good, having fun, becoming one with your partner. It is not a competition or a way to prove to yourself, to your partner, or to your girlfriends that you are a total woman.

Multiple orgasms are definitely attainable by many women, but do not feel pressured in any way. Find the pattern you feel most comfortable with and enjoy it. The important question is: What satisfies you?

Simultaneous Orgasms

"Is it reasonable to want to have simultaneous orgasms?"

That depends. It is reasonable to expect that you might reach orgasms simultaneously with your partner some of the time. But we don't think it is a constructive goal to want to climax simultaneously most of the time. Certainly, it's unreasonable to expect it all of the time.

To achieve a simultaneous orgasm requires a great deal of coordinating and concentration on your partner's response. You and your partner have to learn how to hold back your orgasm without switching it off, or to speed up your arousal. None of this encourages letting go—a necessary ingredient for reaching your own orgasm.

Most couples have "consecutive" orgasms. Some women prefer to reach orgasm before their partner. Once they reach orgasm they feel close to their partner and can focus on bringing their partner greater pleasure. Some prefer to reach orgasm after their partner so they can focus totally on their own sexual arousal and orgasm. Find the pattern that works best for you and your partner.

In another study of sexual behavior, respondents were asked whether simultaneous orgasm was a must for gratifying sex. Fourteen percent of women said yes. Seventy-six percent said no.[4] We stand with the *no*s. It's a nice experience, even a grand experience when it happens; but it is not the only grand experience. To put that expectation on your sexual relationship isn't helpful.

Orgasm and Menopause

Many of the women in our study expressed concerns about menopause. We have all heard stories of women who lost their sex drive or women who could no longer reach orgasm after they passed menopause. Usually it is not the physiological effects of aging that decrease our sexual responsiveness but our fears and false beliefs about becoming older.

In a recent survey of thirteen hundred postmenopausal women (ages forty-five to sixty-five), 90% of the women were sexually active and believed sex to be a positive part of their lives. Seventy-five percent reported that menopause hadn't reduced their ability to enjoy sex one bit. According to the Masters and Johnson studies, as a woman ages lubrication may take longer and be less plentiful, and arousal and orgasm may be less intense. Actually, this slowing of response may serve to increase rather than decrease pleasure since it means you have to spend more time caressing and stimulating each other to reach high levels of arousal.

The decrease in estrogen during menopause can cause the vaginal walls to lose their elasticity, become thin, and become more susceptible to damage. Women in this era of their lives need to take steps to maintain their vaginal health by having consistent sexual activity. If discomfort is a problem, use a lubricant, vaginal estrogen cream, dietary estrogen, or hormone replacement therapy.

The best preventative for sexual problems caused by aging is an active sex life. Masters and Johnson found that women who had intercourse once or twice a week had little difficulty with lubrication and little or no discomfort during sex. Those women who did not have consistent sexual activity were the ones with the greater problems.

There are many older women who, throughout their marriages, rarely or never enjoyed sex. These women are relieved that they can finally have a reason (menopause, hysterectomy, or aging) to avoid sex altogether. One of the women in our study wrote this to us:

> *"I want to know if it is normal procedure that after the reproductive years the sexual struggle stays on? To me it seems impossible that the average woman of fifty, sixty, or seventy*

should enjoy the mess, the pain (dryness), and the inconvenience of her partner's activities in which she is involved by definition."

Another wrote:

"A lifetime of sexual intercourse on a regular and more or less compulsive basis is a heavy burden for a partner to bear."

We accept that there are those for whom sex has no appeal and who are glad when the obligation to have sex is over. But aging alone is *not* a reason to stop being sexual. God created our bodies with the ability to give and receive love, affection, and sexual fulfillment *throughout our life*. Sexual fulfillment does not require sexual intercourse. There are many additional ways to give and receive sexual pleasure.

Many older women wrote to us affirming the positive aspects of sex and love in their lives. One said her ideal sexual experience would be cuddling in front of a fireplace with candles and wine. Here are what other women had to tell us:

"We'd give each other a massage with music playing in the background. We'd take lots of time with lots of foreplay and drive each other wild."

Another woman, in her eighties, wrote that after thirty years of being celibate she had recently experienced a relationship with a man (her husband) who was "the perfect lover at this time of my life." She went on to say:

"When I was young (eighteen to forty-five) sex was hot and forceful—different from the passion now, which is at a slower but no less satisfying pace."

It's good to hear it!

Points to Remember

1. Many myths surround the topic of orgasm. The most damaging is that orgasm is absolutely essential for women if they desire a complete sexual experience. Furthermore, this orgasm must be purely vaginal and multiple!

2. For many women, the emotional experience of intercourse is more important than the physical. The ultimate goal of intercourse does not have to be achieving an orgasm. Many women are content to have physical and emotional closeness.

3. Women need longer periods of lovemaking than men in order to achieve orgasm. Our study found that women cannot reach orgasm without adequate time being devoted to arousal.

4. Factors that interfere with orgasm include relationship conflicts, previous sexual trauma, medical problems, and lack of education in how to achieve an orgasm.

Chapter Six

The Energy Crisis

"I sleep, but my heart is awake; it is the voice of my beloved! He knocks, saying, 'Open for me . . . my love . . .'"

—*Song of Solomon 5:2 NKJV*

We read it again and again as we pored over the comments of the women in our study. It sounded like a refrain from the "Song that Never Ends." Only this song is serious. Many marriages fall apart because couples can't figure out a way to resolve a major dilemma: They want to enjoy a rich and fulfilling sex life but do not have the energy to achieve it. The spirit is willing, but the flesh is weak! We call it "The Energy Crisis."

Cliff and Joyce Penner, in their classic *The Gift of Sex*, report that they regularly survey couples at seminars, asking, "What area of concern would you like to work on?"[1] Roughly 75% of couples say that it is difficult for them to find the time to be together. While it is true that most couples these days are in a time crunch, our study seems to show that the problem now goes beyond the matter of time. Even when couples can find the time to be together, they cannot find the energy to engage in satisfying sex.

This chapter is not based so much on statistics as it is on the narrative responses of the women in our study. From their highly personal and emotionally charged comments on this topic we discerned several themes. Some women complained of their own busyness that left them too exhausted to think about sex. Others complained of their husband's busyness. They were available, but he wasn't. And quite a few blamed their combined frenzied rush through life. They were ships passing in the night. "Hi" and "Bye" were the sum total of their relationship. Read what some had to say:

> *"I just don't have the energy to be bothered with sex. This may only be temporary, but right now I don't even care if it is or it isn't."*

> *"I've told him many times it is difficult for me to make love to a stranger. He's involved in everything—church boards, soccer programs, stuff at his work. And then he has his buddies to do things with. We just never spend time together getting to know each other. He's promised to resign from some of his activities this spring, so we'll see!"*

> *"I think our sexual relationship would be better if we could eliminate the stressfulness of our busyness. I don't think we were created to be busy and sexual at the same time. One has to make room for the other, or else both lose out."*

Quite a common theme was expressed in the following comment:

> *"We both don't have the energy to be troubled about sex. We both work at full-time jobs and come home exhausted every evening. On weekends church and our kids consume all our free time. Sunday evenings we can hardly make it to bed and often fall asleep exhausted in front of the television set. Will we ever escape this frenzied cycle?"*

Children, Children, Children

Perhaps the most important complaint we received about low energy and its effect on sexual desire came from mothers with children still at home. How does this affect energy for sex? Figure 6.1 shows the answer. Fifty-five percent of women with

> **The most important complaint we received about low energy and its effect on sexual desire came from mothers with children still at home.**

children at home report that they have difficulty finding the energy for sex. Only 33% of women without children complain of difficulty finding energy for sex.

DIFFICULTY OF FINDING SEXUAL ENERGY WITH CHILDREN AT HOME
Figure 6.1

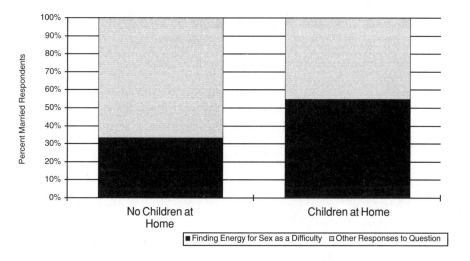

This was corroborated by many personal comments:

> *"Since having children (ages three, four, and six) I find it hard to summon the desire and energy for sex. I sometimes wonder if this is normal. After kids all day the last thing I want is more physical contact (sex) at night. When we first married, I wanted sex more than my husband—now it is reversed, and*

he's frustrated and feels the withdrawal of my love and support. Help! Will this change?"

"As a mother of three small children, sex is low on my priorities. I'm usually too tired. Unfortunately it is high on my husband's list and occasionally causes disagreements. Thank You, Lord, he has proven himself to be loyal even though I know his needs for sex are not always met. Maybe when the kids are grown!"

"I have been pregnant or breast-feeding for four years straight. I used to like sex, but now I know we need to have it. My drive will eventually come back when the kids are older, but right now we can't see the light at the end of the tunnel."

Yes, energy for sex does get a lot better when the kids are grown. In many respects, this is a temporary, though protracted, stage in a married couple's life.

Effect of Aging on Sexual Energy

Does the energy crisis get some relief as one gets older? We looked at the effect of age carefully. We found that for married women with children, difficulty finding energy for sex peaks between the ages of thirty and forty-nine, then improves progressively as you get older. The most difficult period was between the ages of forty and forty-four, with 44% of women reporting difficulty finding energy. By ages fifty-five through fifty-nine, only 23% reported difficulty in finding energy for sex. (See Figure 6.2.)

It does pass, but there is a need to find ways to get around this problem in the interim. We will have more to say about how to escape from this low energy trap as we proceed in this chapter. But here let us make two important points:

1. You must discipline yourselves as a couple to take breaks from your kids regularly. Take mini vacations, like a night

out alone once each week, or a weekend away while friends or family watch the kids for you.

2. Husbands need to be more understanding about the tremendous stress of being a mother. If a woman must also work outside the home, all of her responsibilities and demands can become a nightmare. Hopefully, as husbands understand their wives' struggles, this understanding will result in more help around the house! Husbands, take a day's vacation from work periodically if you can and give your wife a day off. It can work miracles.

THE EFFECT OF AGING ON SEXUAL ENERGY
Figure 6.2

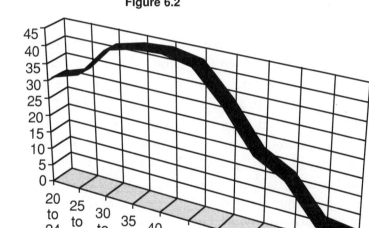

The Too-Busy Wife

In addition to the role of children in depleting women's energy, it is just possible that the family's lives are too busy.

"I am a very busy and active person with a high-pressure career, so I feel tired, fatigued, and pressured from work. It has caused less sexual interest as my mind is always busy with other things."

"My answers to this questionnaire would have been much different a year ago when I was working very hard and under a lot of pressure and stress. Reducing my workload and stress, and getting Norplant have significantly improved my sexual energy and response to my husband."

"I'd like to know what other women tell their husbands when they don't have the energy to give a lot to them. My husband says I should just lie there. Would it be more healthy to say 'not tonight' sometimes?"

Work, these days, consumes the lives of women as well as men. And if they're not working, they are networking. They power-exercise, power-lunch, and power-parent. The pace of life has accelerated for the average woman today. Their average working day has increased as business and industry have demanded more and more commitment.[2] But women have to cope with a double load of work. They have to cope with their traditional duties in the home *and* earn a paycheck. Couples usually can't survive anymore on one income. It is not surprising, therefore, that most women today operate in overdrive.

The result? She's too exhausted to be interested in sex. And if a husband is bored with his job, doesn't feel satisfied or challenged, and lives for the moment when the clock sounds quitting time so he can head for home and some excitement, she has a huge problem on her hands. If a husband isn't gratified by a challenging career or other outside interests, there may be only one thing that excites him—sex. He's ready. He's charged and energized. After all, his day hasn't been too demanding. So why can't he have sex?

Many husbands have great difficulty understanding women's fatigue. A mother rises early, gets in a load of laundry before dressing and feeding the kids, cleans up a bit, makes lunches, and sees that the kids get to school. Then she heads for her job and rushes during lunch to get what she needs for dinner. After an exhausting day she hurries home to fetch the kids, prepare dinner, see to homework, clean up, get in another load of laundry, arbitrate conflicts, make those PTA calls, call her mother because she hasn't heard from her for days, see to baths, pray with the kids, then finally get them to bed. Then her hair desperately cries out to be washed, and her nails need doing. All the while her husband innocently stands there waiting for his turn and can't understand why she's exhausted! And she doesn't even have the energy to explain.

Working mothers today are overextended. They are on overload and bone weary. Not all husbands are in a position to help. They are in a bind, too. As one factory worker once told one of us: "Either I can spend time with my family, or support them financially—not both." Many fathers have to work long overtime hours, even carry more than one job just to make ends meet and give their families a decent living. Families must make a real effort to spend time together as a family.

The Too-Busy Husband

The too-busy husband differs from the too-busy wife in one important respect: While her busyness usually involves the family, his seldom does. Even when a working wife is overextended, she generally manages to devote a great deal of attention to her husband and children. And while sex may have to take second place for a while, at least the family doesn't suffer from her neglect. The too-busy husband tends to neglect his family. And that's the tragedy.

These women's comments illustrate the effect of a husband's busyness on the sexual relationship:

"I love my husband deeply. Sex would be fine if he would slow down and give me more of his time. I submit to him because I

*love him and I enjoy his closeness. But as far as orgasms are con-
cerned for me, well, he can't seem to give me enough time for it
to happen."*

*"Sex is frustrating and confusing to me. I desire more intimate
times together—but my husband, a professional man, is too tired
most of the time and stressed out from his day."*

Some husbands can't avoid being too busy. Their survival and
the survival of their families depend on it. This came home
forcibly to Dr. Hart a short while ago. He was returning from a
speaking engagement and arrived at the airport late in the
evening. He caught a limo for the forty-five-minute drive home
and was the only person in it. So he and the driver started talking.
The conversation turned to a comparison of their lives. Dr. Hart
sensed a real sadness in the man's voice when he told him how
much he missed being with his family in the evenings and weekends like "normal dads."

But not all husbands are overly busy because they can't avoid
it. Even Dr. Hart's newfound driver friend admitted that he
could ease up a little over the summer when his boys are out of
school and his wife needs some extra help. Busyness is a choice,
more often than not. Another story might make this point more
clearly.

Peter is a senior-level executive in a large business making an
enormous salary. He was only thirty years old when catastrophe
struck. He woke up one morning and found himself in a profound
and debilitating depression. At first he tried to overcome it with
sheer willpower. A devout Christian, he tried to pray it away. But
quickly he realized he couldn't fix it as easily as he fixed business
problems. At his wife's insistence he went to see Dr. Hart for help.

Sure enough, Peter was in a serious depression. But he was also
suffering from high blood pressure, an extremely high cholesterol
level, frequent headaches, and several other stress symptoms. He
was in a bad way. His crazy, driven, and frantic work life had not

only precipitated a major depression but it was also killing him. Peter was a strong candidate for early heart disease!

Restoring Your Energy

So what can a busy, exhausted woman do to restore the energy needed for sex?

1. Reorder your priorities. Sit down with pen and paper and write out your priorities. We often write lists with God on top, then spouse, and then family. But in reality, our lives aren't lived out in this order. It might be more helpful to begin with two lists: "actual priorities" and "priorities I'd like." Then you can try to reconcile the two lists, making the necessary changes in your daily life.

2. De-clutter your schedule. Look at your daily life in light of your priorities. Decide to give time to what really matters the most to you and your family. It might mean having to say no to some extra activities. Family life these days is so hectic with so many opportunities and demands on everyone. It takes a conscious effort to evaluate priorities for all family members, then set boundaries so your daily life is lived out according to your priorities.

3. Make sleep a high priority. Most health experts agree that a large percentage of Americans don't get enough sleep. Most humans need eight to nine hours of sleep per night. Sleep deprivation causes traffic accidents, mistakes on the job, marital conflict, depression, and a host of other problems. It can also affect your sexual desire and functioning. Get to bed earlier, and take naps if possible.

4. Get treatment for physical conditions. Many physical conditions such as anemia, thyroid problems, hormonal imbalance, and depression can cause fatigue and exhaustion. If you get enough sleep and you are living according to your priorities but you still feel exhausted, get a complete medical checkup.

5. Exercise. Exercise of any type (walking, in-line skating, biking, aerobic dance, and so forth) increases the release of chemicals in the brain that give a sense of well-being and increases your stamina and energy. One twenty-minute walk a day is enough to make a difference in your energy level.

6. Resolve emotional issues. Fatigue is a normal and frequent experience as a result of the grief process, job stress, marital conflict, problems with children, or other relationship and life stresses. Do what you can following points 1 through 5, then give yourself more grace for this season. Pushing harder or getting angry and frustrated at yourself will only make it worse. Get additional emotional support if you are feeling overwhelmed. Meet with your pastor or a counselor to help guide you through this difficult time.

His marriage was a mess, even though he loved his wife dearly. His recently arrived baby never knew what it was to be held by her father. After a very satisfying start to their sexual life when they got married, Peter slowly lost interest. He never had any energy to make love. His wife began to think she was the problem so she withdrew emotionally. They were headed for disaster.

He started treatment for the depression and only after many months of trial and error on several antidepressants did he finally see relief. But Peter's reaction was, "Well, it's back to business as usual!" Dr. Hart protested, and with the help of Peter's wife, they convinced him he needed to continue in therapy and work on his value system. He was obsessed with the need to succeed and make a lot of money. But this obsession was killing his sex life and his wife's love for him. Eventually it would have impacted their young baby. Peter listened and decided his life had to change.

He began by reevaluating just how rich he wanted to become. He renegotiated his salary contract to "buy back" some of his personal time, changed his working habits to be home on weekends, and took up gardening as a hobby so that he would have an added incentive to stay home more.

> **Love revives when it is nurtured. It thrives on intimacy, but intimacy takes time and energy.**

Did it make a difference to their sex life? Absolutely. Love revives when it is nurtured. It thrives on intimacy, but intimacy takes time and energy. And Dr. Hart is pleased to report that the changes Peter made have remained to this day, nearly six years after they were first made.

The Too-Busy Marriage

One of the most dramatic changes in our society during the past decade is called the "time squeeze." The time squeeze is a major factor causing the energy crisis in a couple's sexual expression.

The faster we move, the faster we want to move. Time is a relative thing. When we traveled by ox wagon, a delay of a few hours to let a storm pass over the wagon trail was not a big inconvenience. Now, because we travel on high-speed jets we become frustrated when the plane is delayed twenty minutes.

Juliet B. Schor, Associate Professor of Economics at Harvard University, tells of employees at a fast-food restaurant who used their creativity to develop a way to serve a drive-in customer in twelve seconds flat. The problem is that the twelve-second service, as opposed to the previous twenty-second standard, became the new standard. One day things went wrong and the delay crept up to fifteen seconds, still five seconds better than the old standard of service. But the horns started honking and the customers went crazy. They had come to expect twelve-second service. The three extra seconds of delay were unacceptable! This is the "time squeeze." And we are all feeling its pinch!

While the lack of time contributes to our sexual problems, *time isn't the only problem.* The problem is spending too many hours working without adequate time for rejuvenation of exhausted bodies.

> *"My husband and I always seem to be too rushed, too tired, and too busy for sexual encounters. But when we do make the time we love it."*

> *"I have found that having children has greatly affected our sexual relationship. I don't feel great about the after-baby looks, although my husband has never made me feel as though it bothers him. It's just that the children need a lot of attention, and my husband doesn't understand. I find myself very tired at the end of the day —also at the beginning and middle of the day!"*

One of the surprises couples are not prepared for is the dramatic change that happens to both the wife's energy level and her

> **One of the surprises couples are not prepared for is the dramatic change that happens to both the wife's energy level and her love priorities when the first baby arrives.**

love priorities when the first baby arrives. Subsequent children only add to this. The wife becomes focused on the child or children, and the husband becomes more focused on work or external priorities.

Because you cannot adequately prepare for these changes, new fathers often feel angry and hurt and new mothers feel overwhelmed. Sexual needs take second place. Baby must be fed and cared for, and for the wife sleep is at a premium. Time and energy for sexual experimentation and enjoyment are not available.

This inevitable transition (really a developmental stage in the marriage) requires endurance. A father can turn his energy towards becoming bonded to the baby and supporting his wife in her new role. Instead of burying himself in work, he can participate in the childcare tasks. The emotional confusion he feels can also be reduced by the wife including him and by the couple talking together about their frustrations. Understanding and accepting each other and their new roles is essential to adjusting to this new season of life.

A Married Couple's Guide to Dating

Perhaps the most important solution we can offer a busy married couple, young or not so young, is to institute dating. Dating worked while you were courting, why shouldn't it work now?

Do married couples have to think about dating? You bet they do, because one or both of the partners is involved in a job, a career, child rearing, sports, hobbies, and other activities. The marriage relationship must take priority over all other matters—including a baby—and the only way to do this is to schedule times together. Start dating again, and keep it going!

As we have seen, the scarcest commodity in all our lives is *time*. As we move into the next millennium it is going to become even scarcer. There just isn't enough of it to go around two busy lives. Work, chores, social activities, church, families, and kids can only be nurtured by devoting time to them. Time

> **Dating in your marriage is even more important when your relationship suffers from an energy crisis.**

together is to a family what water is to a plant. It will die without it. The challenge facing all of us, as we think about improving our personal relationships, is how to find more time. Since time is fixed, the only way to free up some of it is by stealing time from the other activities that are hogging too much of it. And we really mean *stealing* it. That's the attitude of determination it takes.

Dating in your marriage is even more important when your relationship suffers from an energy crisis. Here are some suggestions:

1. Plan ahead. We mean really ahead—not just days ahead, but weeks and even months ahead. Sit down together and talk about activities you would like to do: a concert, a picnic, a sports event, a play, a quiet evening by the fireplace. This requires making reservations, getting tickets, and arranging childcare. Dr. Hart recently counseled with a pastor and his wife. She complained that they could never find time for love-making. Who was at fault? She blamed him; he blamed her. She was never ready when he was (one o'clock in the morning), and he was never available when she wanted some romance (some Saturday evenings when their kids would stay over with grandparents). After some encouraging, the husband said he could certainly have someone else lead prayer meetings on those Saturday nights when the kids were away. It felt corny to him to call it a date night, but he complied. It only took two such Saturday nights and he was hooked!

2. Find time to talk as part of your date. Jumping into bed is not the first, or necessary, thing to do on a date. If movies are on the dating agenda, plan on a dinner or after-movie coffee time to talk.

3. Have fun! Don't talk about problems you are having in the relationship or with the kids. Set aside other times for problem solving. Don't contaminate your dating time. Dates are just for the two of you.

4. If possible, never cancel the date. Don't allow patient emergencies, parishioner catastrophes, the stock market crashing, your car breaking down (take a taxi), or your tiredness to interfere with your plans. If something really important comes up, work around it. Have people wait. Find someone to replace you. Resign from the committee if it's the only time it can meet. Nothing should be allowed to get in the way.

Chronic Fatigue

"I have been sick with chronic fatigue for nine months now. This has devastated our sex life. When I feel so tired most of the time I have little sexual desire. I am starting to feel somewhat better so I hope our sex will improve."

Overwork, sleep deprivation, poor nutrition, lack of exercise, and emotional stress can all cause fatigue. We all experience short periods of fatigue. We sleep a little more, and it usually goes away. Serious fatigue falls into two categories: *prolonged* and *chronic.* Prolonged fatigue is defined as self-reported fatigue lasting one month or longer. Chronic fatigue is defined as self-reported persistent or relapsing fatigue lasting six months or longer.

How common is chronic fatigue? The International Chronic Fatigue Syndrome Group (you can find them on the Internet) estimates that in the United States, 24% of the general adult population has had fatigue lasting two weeks or longer. About 60% of these persons report that their fatigue has no medical cause.[3]

Many physical conditions can cause fatigue, including diabetes, anemia, hypothyroidism, cancer, immune problems, and a heart problem called mitral valve prolapse (MVP), which is quite common in women and is often associated with panic anxiety. Many emotional conditions, such as severe anxiety or depression, can also cause fatigue, as can drug and alcohol abuse, excessive use of caffeine, and nutritional deficiencies.

A woman we'll call Barbara had a bout with the flu and never seemed to be able to recover from it. Her glands were swollen, she had trouble thinking clearly, and she dragged her body and mind through each day, feeling like a zombie. She became oversensitive to everything in her environment—noise, cold, and social pressure. She didn't want to go out or talk to anyone. After going the rounds with many doctors, blood tests, and probing, the diagnosis returned: chronic fatigue syndrome (CFS).

CFS is controversial. Some doctors believe it is a genuine illness, and others contend that it is not. Differentiating between other medical conditions and CFS is difficult.

What are the symptoms of CFS? In addition to fatigue that is not being caused by ongoing stress or any other medical condition, the Centers for Disease Control published the following symptoms in 1994:

1. Short-term memory or concentration problems

2. Sore throat

3. Tender lymph nodes

4. Muscle pain

5. Joint pain without swelling

6. Headaches

7. Unrefreshing sleep

8. Debility after exercise that lasts for more than twenty-four hours

Any four of these symptoms must be present in addition to fatigue for a diagnosis of CFS.

A close cousin of CFS is depression. How does depression differ from CFS? In depression, sore throat and swollen lymph nodes are not present. Depressed patients do better after exercise. For at least twenty-four hours after exercise CFS sufferers do worse.

If you are fatigued much of the time *for no apparent reason,* you should consult a physician. Because so many CFS sufferers are not able to find relief with our limited current knowledge about what causes the disease, we recommend that you also become involved in a support group. Check your local telephone directory, or use the Internet.[4]

The "DINS" Marriage

"I work a lot of night shifts and am often eager to get to sleep when I get home. My husband works too hard and is tired as well at bedtime. Holidays are the only great time for sex. I have a thing about getting my sleep!"

Someone has labeled the average young marriages of today as "DINS", which stands for "Dual Income, No Sex." This sums up many modern, and dare we even say it, "yuppie" marriages. But DINS afflicts many older marriages as well. And it can be resistant to cure unless a dramatic change in values takes place.

DINS couples are often forced to focus on work out of necessity. Some wives would gladly stay home and take care of the kids if they could. But it is increasingly difficult for families to survive on one income. With two careers there is little intimacy because there is no time to build it. It is not surprising, therefore, that sexual difficulties are common.

But let us strike a balance. *If* it is mutually acceptable, a marriage *can* survive without sex—for a while at least. So let us take the pressure off those couples who feel guilty or abnormal about their low sexual interests right now. Most marriages go through temporary periods when sexual interest is low, usually because there is some major distraction. For instance, in times of serious illness—a battle with cancer or children becoming seriously ill, there may be no interest in sex.

There are many distractions that come along from time to time that impact sexual interest, and they are all perfectly normal. But when a DINS couple allow their lifestyle to become entrenched, never taking a break, the low sexual bonding between the couple can result in long-term problems.

Work stress and fatigue can lead to sexual problems, such as lack of desire or arousal in women and inability to maintain an erection in men. Every time the couple tries to have sex, these problems arise, so they avoid sex more and more. A vicious cycle begins: diving into work, which decreases sexual performance, which in turn creates anxiety over sex.

The value system of a DINS couple causes them to feel very guilty when they are not performing to their work expectations. So work always comes before play. When there is *only* work and no play your value system is unbalanced. You must reorder your priorities to allow for more couple playtime!

DINS couples are performance oriented in their work lives, and they can also be performance oriented in their sex lives.[5] Play becomes work. They approach sex too seriously. As you can expect, the more they pressure themselves to perform, the more likely they are to find sex a burden rather than a pleasure.

What can a DINS couple do to solve their energy crisis? A lot. Improvement takes dramatic lifestyle changes, and there are a number of things both husband and wife can do to create more balance between work and their personal lives:

1. Learn to value each day's blessings. Try living in the here and now. Stop and smell the roses; count the birds in your garden every morning before you go to work. Stay in touch with today.

2. Revitalize yourself by developing other interests outside of work. Art, music, church life, and hobbies can all help bring balance.

3. Slow down. Try not to do too many things at the same time.

4. Get in touch with your body. Listen to your senses, your feelings, and God's promptings. Pay attention to the warnings of your body: headaches, tension, sleeplessness, and ulcers.

5. Learn to say no. Set limits—you are not superwoman. Don't try to do everything. Choose where you want to put your energy.

6. Give lots of time to your relationship with your spouse. Yes, it is a matter of priorities. We all have more things crowding our calendar than we have time to do, so choose wisely where you give your time.

7. Stay in touch with God. For many of us this means slowing down to spend time with Him.

Points to Remember

1. Lack of energy for sex stood out as a significant issue for many women. Fifty-five percent of women with children at home and 33% without children at home complained about this lack of energy.

2. In either or both partners, lack of energy can be due to overextended and stressful lives, lack of sleep, misplaced priorities, and failure to plan for times of togetherness away from children.

3. The restoration of energy requires getting adequate rest and balancing work and your need for intimacy. Also important is attending to basic self-care, including exercise, a healthy diet, and effective stress management.

Chapter Seven

Hormones and Sexuality

"For, lo, the winter is past, the rain is over and gone; . . . the time of the singing . . . is come."

—Song of Solomon 2:11–12

A little-understood fact about hormones is that they are powerful drugs. We don't usually think of them this way because we've been conditioned to think of drugs either as foreign and dangerous to the body or as medications used to treat diseases. But hormones are drugs in the sense that they can powerfully influence mood and well-being.

Many of the women who participated in our study were puzzled about the effects their hormones had on their sexual feelings. We received questions and comments about hormones and sexuality. Women posed questions like:

"How do hormones and the menstrual cycle affect my mind, mood swings, and sexual desire? At times I can't really tell what's going on inside me."

"Is there a cycle of desire related to hormones? Mine goes up and down so mysteriously that something's got to be happening and affecting it."

"I want to learn a lot more about the female hormone cycle and how it affects me. I hope you can help me."

"I want to know about the problems of PMS and how it affects sexuality. Are there ways to help the PMS issue?"

Because an understanding of the hormones and their cyclic effect on our moods and sexual responsiveness is so important, we have included a chapter on the topic.

First, we will report on the more common hormonal problems experienced by the women in this study. Then we will provide resources and lifestyle guidelines that can alleviate the sometimes debilitating side effects.

Hormones and Premenstrual Syndrome

We begin our exploration of hormones and sexuality with a look at premenstrual syndrome (PMS) because it is the most frequent health concern reported to us by our sample. Fifty-one percent of our respondents reported experiencing mild, moderate, or severe PMS. (See Figure 7.1.) Thirty-nine percent reported their sexual desire was affected by their menstrual cycle. Twenty-three percent of the women reported being in the process of completing or having completed menopause.

We posed the following question to the women in our study: "If you experience PMS, how severe are your symptoms?" Of those who have PMS, 39% reported that their symptoms were mild, 43% said moderate, and 17% said severe. Fifteen to 20% of women with PMS in the United States report that it is severe enough to disrupt optimal functioning at work and home.

Twenty-five percent of the women in this study who experienced mild PMS symptoms reported less sexual interest. This loss of interest rises to 32% for those with moderate symptoms and 26% for those with severe symptoms. The next most common effect is increased marital conflict: 19% for those with mild PMS, 31% for those with moderate, and 34% for those with severe. PMS does not negatively impact sexuality in *all* women. Sometimes there is actually an increase in sexual interest. About

17% of all the women with PMS in our study reported increased sexual interest. (See Figure 7.2.)

WOMEN'S HEALTH CONCERNS
Figure 7.1

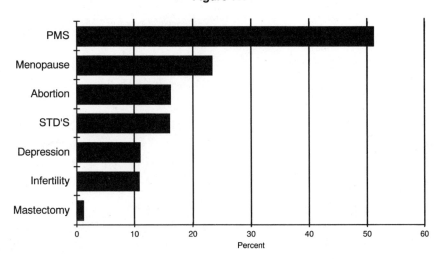

SEXUAL EFFECTS AND SEVERITY OF PMS IN MARRIED WOMEN
Figure 7.2

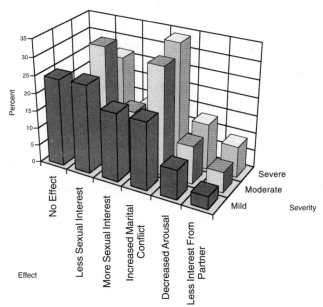

PMS can appear any time after puberty (when menstruation begins) and continue through the forties or even longer. PMS usually begins three to ten days prior to the beginning of menstrual bleeding, but PMS can begin any time after ovulation (the midpoint of the menstrual cycle). Symptoms can vary in intensity throughout a woman's life and from month to month. At least 75% of women report minor or isolated premenstrual changes. Some studies suggest 20 to 50% of women experience PMS. Three to 5% of women experience symptoms so severe they meet the criteria for Premenstrual Dysphoric Disorder (DSM IV, 1994).

Typical PMS Symptoms

Anger
Anxiety, Feeling "on edge"
Apathy
Bloating
Breast Tenderness
Clumsiness
Depression, Hopelessness
Difficulty Concentrating
Emotional Outbursts (crying, yelling)
Emotional Sensitivity
Fatigue, Lethargy
Food Cravings
Headaches
Insomnia

Up to 150 symptoms have been attributed to PMS. The most common are listed in the sidebar above of Typical PMS Symptoms.

Many mentioned that they experienced painful emotions and a gamut of other symptoms, including mood swings; headaches; tension; fatigue; lethargy; irritability; feeling less patient, less tolerant, more angry at little things; lots of tension; being in a bad mood; low self-esteem; and bouts of internal agitation. Later in this chapter we provide guidelines that will be helpful in alleviating some of the symptoms.

The Hormonal Cycle and PMS

Many women asked us to give a simple explanation of the hormonal system. So, here goes:

As shown in Figure 7.3, the brain controls the pituitary gland (the master gland) which controls the ovaries. The ovaries produce progesterone and estrogen. Progesterone and estrogen control the menstrual cycle (and pregnancy).

> **The entire hormonal cycle is an interaction between the brain, hormones, and the body.**

The entire hormonal cycle is an interaction between the brain, hormones, and the body. Therefore, the hormonal cycle can be impacted by: illness, stress, injury, emotional trauma, and eating habits. Even caffeine can significantly impact how you experience PMS.

A WOMAN'S HORMONE CYCLE
Figure 7.3

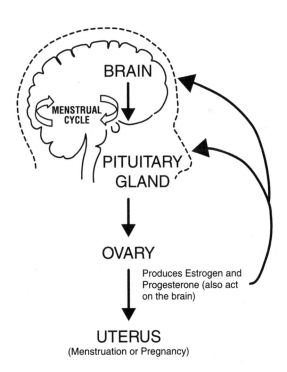

BRAIN

MENSTRUAL CYCLE

PITUITARY GLAND

OVARY

Produces Estrogen and Progesterone (also act on the brain)

UTERUS
(Menstruation or Pregnancy)

During an average menstrual cycle, a woman's body experiences a shift in the blood levels of estrogen and progesterone. After ovulation, there is a drop in estrogen and an increase in progesterone, preparing the body for menstruation. (See Figure 7.4.)

HORMONES AND THE MENSTRUAL CYCLE
Figure 7.4

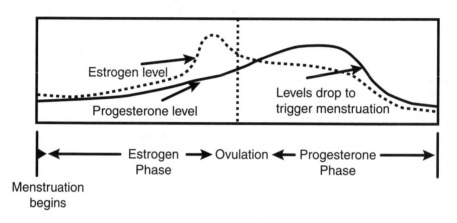

However, if the hormonal blood levels of estrogen and progesterone are not balanced (too much or too little for what the body needs), then a woman experiences PMS symptoms such as the following:

Characteristics of High Estrogen	Characteristics of High Progesterone
Optimistic	Moody
Self-confident	Gloomy
Positive	Impatient
Focused	Irritable
Reasonable	Sensitive to noise
Sense of well-being	Shaky, lacks coordination
Can overlook small irritations	Food cravings
Idealistic	Self-doubt, lacks self-confidence
Aware of sexual feelings	
(as moves to ovulation)	

Hormones and Sexual Desire

Many women in our sample were bothered by how their monthly cycle affected their sexual desire. For some desire increased, for others it decreased, and this could vary from month to month. This fluctuation in desire is also impacted by emotional and relational tensions. Here is how they described it:

> *"It seems that some days my hormones have me thinking more about sex, and other days I can't stand the thought of it. My desire is all over the place."*

> *"My sexual feelings vary so much during my monthly cycles. My husband and I practice the sympto-thermal method of birth control. This has had a big effect on our current level of satisfaction. We abstain during phase II, my fertile time and the time I feel most interest and can be easily aroused. By the time we can have intercourse, I'm usually not that interested anymore—it takes more work."*

> *"I really do want to know how hormones affect sexuality, as this has caused a great deal of frustration in my marriage. I'm totally turned off sexually during various times of my cycle, and it's like climbing a mountain to overcome that level of non-interest to be available to love sexually or to be loved."*

As you can see, the sexual symptoms of PMS are quite varied, and in some cases opposites. When asked to report on other effects of their PMS, the women in our study added the following comments:

> *"We usually have no sex during this time."*

> *"I become restless and feel emotionally in turmoil."*

"I am unable to concentrate until my period starts."

"It is harder to reach orgasm because I'm uptight."

"I crave more affection."

"I want more sex because I feel needy."

"My depression is mostly due to PMS and affects me three out of four weeks."

Although there does seem to be a biologically based monthly cycle of desire, many of the other symptoms that women listed also affect sexual functioning. It is very difficult to desire being close and making love when you're battling fatigue, anger, or "just lots of tension and being in a bad mood." So while hormones may cause sexual interest to be higher, the havoc in your life can inhibit sexual desire.

Menopause

Menopause is also a concern to women, as is evident in the following questions:

"How can I celebrate the change of life—not dread it?"

"I'm curious about what is going to happen to me when I go through menopause, and how it will change my sexuality."

"How will aging and menopause affect me physically, emotionally, and sexually? Will I have more desire or less?"

"What can I anticipate as I look ahead to menopause? How will it affect me sexually?"

Technically, menopause is the last menstrual period and marks the end of a woman's fertility. However, when people talk about "menopause" they usually mean "the change of life." This could last anywhere from two to ten years before the final menstrual cycle, and continue about a year or more after. Medically this period is called the *climacteric*. During this time many women experience difficult physical and emotional symptoms.

Menopause can be viewed as a twofold process. *Perimenopause* is the term often used for early menopause, the two to ten years prior to the last menstrual cycle. This phase can begin anywhere from age forty to forty-eight (even as early as the twenties or thirties). You can recognize this phase when your menstrual cycles become irregular, PMS symptoms intensify, or you start experiencing some of the menopause symptoms. (See sidebar under Hormones and Menopause.) In this book we will refer to the entire process, including perimenopause as menopause.

We asked the women in our study who reported having menopause symptoms to rate the severity of their symptoms. Thirty-two percent said severe, 19% said moderate, and 49% said mild. Almost half of the women only had mild symptoms.

What were the main sexual effects of menopause? Figure 7.5 shows the sexual effects corresponding to the three levels of severity. Forty-one percent of those with mild symptoms

> **One in two women with moderate to severe menopausal reactions will experience a decrease in sexual interest.**

reported no effects. In contrast, this dropped to 20% of those with moderate symptoms, and only 4% of those with severe symptoms.

The greatest sexual effect was less sexual interest. Clearly, 50% of women with moderate to severe menopausal reactions will experience a decrease in sexual interest. Only one woman reported more sexual interest, which is a stark contrast to the sexual effects of PMS.

SEXUAL EFFECTS AND SEVERITY OF MENOPAUSE
Figure 7.5

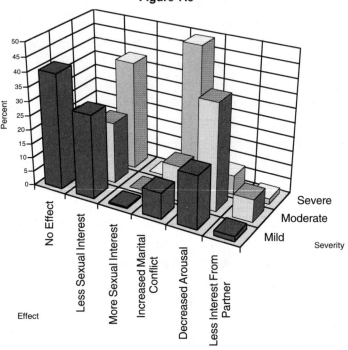

The narrative responses further illuminated the impact of menopause on the women in this study. We asked them to describe other sexual effects we did not list. These were among the responses: felt less clean; relief that intercourse was over; confusion; frustration; and mostly, just plain tired.

One woman explained transitioning into menopause this way:

> *"Aggravated PMS marked the beginning of my transition into menopause and has continued four to five years with some help from hormone therapy and diet. Some months are worse than others when symptoms are aggressiveness, sleeplessness, and forgetfulness. I find it frustrating to lose control of my body that worked well for forty-five years. The doctor is minimally responsive, and both he and my husband often seem lacking in sympathy or compassion."*

Here is how another woman eloquently described her symptoms:

"Since my last physical a year ago, I have noticed changes in my cycle, and through counseling with other women I believe I am beginning to experience some perimenopause symptoms. I feel my husband doesn't understand my mood swings, and even though he does believe they are the cause of physiological problems, he believes I cannot use this as an excuse to be out of control emotionally. I frighten myself with my emotional outbursts! I am emotionally and in a way physically sick, and my husband doesn't know how to support me in this. I turn to God for comfort, but there is still a yearning for tangible comfort. So I turn to women friends for consolation as well. My fear is that as menopause increases I will only become worse, and my husband will continue not to understand or appear not to care. My struggle is that I want to believe I should only be trusting God's comfort and strength—but at this point I feel lost and out of control. I don't find men to be very friendly toward women's special physical and emotional needs."

These comments speak for many women. Menopause can be very frustrating. Husbands don't know what's going on because they've not been educated, and if ever there is a period in a woman's life when she needs that extra hug and some reassurance, it is during these times.

Hormones and Menopause

What is happening hormonally? Menopause is caused by the degeneration of the follicles and their egg cells within the ovaries. These follicles produce less and less estrogen. Eventually, not enough estrogen or progesterone is produced to keep the menstrual cycle going and menstruation stops. This decline, however, is gradual and periodically an ova (egg) may mature and be released. This is why a woman is not considered to have gone

> **Typical Symptoms
> of Menopause**
>
> • Any of the PMS
>   symptoms
> • Depression
> • Emotional instability
> • Hot flashes and
>   night sweats
> • Insomnia
> • Irregular periods
> • Lack of energy, fatigue
> • Lowered sex drive
> • Memory lapse
>   (fuzzy brain)
> • Skin breakouts such as
>   facial acne
> • Vaginal dryness
> • Vague feelings of
>   anxiety, or even full-
>   blown anxiety attacks

through menopause until she has not had a menstrual period for one full year. It is common for menopause to occur between ages forty-eight and fifty-five. The average age of menopause in America is fifty-one, but it is normal for women to go through menopause as early as forty or as late as sixty. Apparently the age of menopause is determined by a woman's genes; it is unrelated to when she began menstruating, diet, or previous use of birth control pills or fertility drugs.

Many women wondered what to expect as they approached menopause. Although we have described the symptoms of menopause most women experience, which can be frustrating both physically and emotionally, not all the effects of menopause are negative.

Some say they have a feeling of renewed freedom and energy after this change of life. A recent report in *Time* magazine states that the rate of women who suffer from anxiety or depression drops from 11% in women under fifty-five to 5% in those fifty-five and older who are over the menopausal phase of their lives.[1] One woman described her feelings about being past menopause as, *"Happier at last!"*

Try to view menopause as a normal part of your life cycle. It is a season of challenge and change. The most frustrating part of it all might be not feeling validated by those around you and even your own doctor. We have talked to many women who have

> **Try to view menopause as a normal part of your life cycle. It is a season of challenge and change.**

been told they were too young to be going through menopause. Find a doctor who is competent to work with hormonal changes, and keep experimenting with treatment options. Be patient and persistent.

Important Questions Asked by Early Menopausal Women

"What are the differences between late PMS and early menopause?" During PMS a woman generally can chart her cycle and more or less predict the symptoms. But during early menopause the symptoms are unpredictable and seem to be pervasive. PMS symptoms could intensify, and/or some menopause symptoms may appear. Examples would be an ongoing loss of sex drive, irregular periods, depression, sleep disturbances, unpredictable irrational overreaction, outbursts of anger, or vaginal dryness due to lower estrogen levels.

"Should I still use birth control?" While the chance of becoming pregnant diminishes during perimenopause, pregnancy continues to be a possibility. Contraception must remain an important part of your health planning. Consider using a low-dose birth control pill, which has the added advantage of correcting irregular bleeding and reducing the risk of ovarian and uterine cancers.

"Is there any treatment for severe menopause reactions?" As with PMS and menopause, hormone therapy (in this case, estrogen replacement) may offer some relief and can protect against osteoporosis and cardiovascular disease. However, there are risks in estrogen supplement therapy for certain women, so consult your physician. There are also many natural alternative treatments and supplements with no known toxic side effects. This is a good time to plan for a healthy second half of your life. Exercise, good nutrition, lowered stress, and a balanced life can go a long way in helping you adjust to this transition with grace and contentment. Please refer to the Lifestyle Plan for Optimal Health, later in this chapter.

Changes to Expect During Menopause

The most common changes to expect are psychological, sexual desire, vaginal discomfort, urinary tract discomfort, orgasms, and other physical changes such as fatigue and weight gain.

1. Psychological

Your overall attitude toward the menopause process will greatly impact your experience during this change of life. In chapter 5 we talked about the brain being the most important sex organ. We also discussed how relational, psychological, and emotional factors have a very significant impact on desire. During menopause these factors are crucial. Some women may think they are experiencing a personality change, when in reality they are not. The hormonal and psychological changes during menopause often accentuate already existing tendencies or difficulties. They are now experienced more intensely or profoundly.

There are many psychological reasons why women may choose to finally say no to sexual activity. For example, if a woman has been in a painful or difficult marriage, never really enjoyed sex, or was abused when she was young, this can be the time when she finally has the excuse and feels empowered to say no.

2. Sexual desire

Respondents in our study reported some very positive changes in their sex drive:

"Sex is more important now than in early marriage."

"I enjoy sex now because it makes me feel like I'm an attractive, whole, older woman—vital."

"As I get older, the more desire I seem to have."

"As I get older, sex gets more enjoyable. I'm less inhibited and more open."

But not all the comments were that positive.

"Sometimes I wonder if my lack of interest or drive is normal, hormonal, or age-related, or if there is something wrong with me."

"It takes me longer to be in the mood than when I was in my twenties and thirties. A great deal of my drive is a decision of the will. I choose to love my husband, and I choose to enjoy love-making. His attitude can turn me on and off more than anything in the world."

"At fifty-four I've just reached menopause, and my sexual frustration tends to go up and down, presumably to match my hormones."

Can changes in sexual desire during menopause be predicted? Not really. Of those women who reported menopausal symptoms, 31% reported less sexual interest, and only one said she had more sexual interest.

Energy for life and sexual desire are closely connected. Fatigue and lack of desire often go together. Other symptoms such as pain during intercourse, vaginal dryness, frequent bladder infections, uncomfortable orgasms, hot flashes, insomnia, feeling tired, and not feeling well can also affect sexual desire. Estrogen treatment can effectively reduce many of these symptoms, thus giving an increased sense of well-being leading to more sexual interest.

3. Vaginal discomfort

Lower estrogen levels will cause a reduction of the blood flow to the vagina. The tissues of the vagina become thinner, drier, and less elastic, which can make sexual intercourse uncomfortable and even painful. Lack of interest in sex due to discomfort may also occur at this time.

Vaginal dryness can be a real problem. It can cause painful intercourse as well as uncomfortable itching. Lubricants can be used during intercourse to correct this problem, but first consult a gynecologist. In addition, hormonal therapy can help.

Women experiencing discomfort during intercourse can use a localized form of estrogen replacement cream or the new vaginal ring.

4. Urinary tract discomfort

"Having sex is more difficult for me now because I seem to always have something going on—bladder infections or vaginal irritation and infections. I'm not able to enjoy intercourse very often."

Many women experience an increase in urinary tract infections and irritation of the urethra, which causes painful urination. These can usually be treated, even prevented. Talk to a gynecologist or internist about any repeated infections.

5. Orgasms

As stated earlier, according to Masters and Johnson's studies, as a woman ages lubrication may take longer and be less plentiful. Arousal and orgasm may also be experienced as less intense. Other changes may include taking longer to reach orgasm and reaching orgasm less frequently. Sexual dysfunctions in post-menopausal women are not always due to loss of estrogen. They may also be caused by hardening of the arteries—the same condition that results in male impotence. Clogged arteries reduce the blood flow to the vagina and clitoris, interfering with normal sexual arousal.

Some women find the clitoris uncomfortably sensitive and experience painful contractions during orgasm. Although orgasms may be less intense, they are often described as gentler. Please refer to the chapter on orgasm (Chapter 6) and the section on orgasm and menopause.

Guidelines and Solutions

In this chapter we have touched very briefly on some of the major ways in which hormones can influence sexuality. In conclusion, here are some general principles that you can follow to help alleviate the difficulties associated with hormonal fluctuations.

At first glance, these may seem very simplistic. However, the basic Lifestyle Plan for Optimal Health we present has been proven to be invaluable in improving overall health, hormone balance, and, as a result, sexual functioning.

1. Get to know yourself and your body.

Accept how God has created you. All your hormonal ups and downs are a part of the complexity and wonder of being a woman. Hormonal upheavals can be very frustrating and overwhelming at times, but you don't have to feel helpless or victimized.

Begin by being proactive and getting to know your ebbs and flows. This way you can take responsibility for caring about yourself and those around you. If you don't already, start keeping a record of your menstrual cycle. This will help you and your doctor figure out

> **Accept how God has created you. All your hormonal ups and downs are a part of the complexity and wonder of being a woman.**

what is happening when. Remember, *you* are the best person to understand what is going on inside you. There are some helpful ways to balance your hormones and ease symptoms. But before you move to the treatment, it is best to have a concrete record of your symptoms.

Keep a daily journal, noting how you feel physically, emotionally, and spiritually. Also, be aware of any increase or decrease in your sex drive and note these. (It is also important to note any conflict or other external stress, which could be affecting you as well.) Every woman has a unique hormonal profile with varying symptoms occurring throughout her cycle. Get to know your unique pattern.

2. Learn all you can about hormones.

Our knowledge about hormones is rapidly changing, so keep up to date. As you read and learn more, it will reassure you. You can find current information through the Internet, books, magazines, and your gynecologist. Check out your local bookstore and library.

One of the most often asked questions in our study was: "Am I normal?" The more you know about what other women are experiencing, the less alone and confused you will feel. Some women have lived for years searching for a medical diagnosis, finally to discover they are going through menopause. Many women blame themselves for feeling depressed, tired, uninterested in sex and forgetful. It is encouraging to them to find out that these symptoms are not their fault, but a result of hormone imbalance.

We want to suggest that the best time to research and read about hormones and health is during the "positive" time of your cycle. When you are feeling down you are more likely to be pessimistic. Wait until you are feeling better, then explore solutions and implement what you've learned.

3. Get a thorough medical checkup regularly.

It is alarming just how many women don't go to a doctor until a problem is well entrenched. Prevention is always better than cure. At least once a year get a physical checkup.

See a doctor who is competent to treat hormonal imbalance. Be persistent and assertive regarding your health needs. This is especially important if your symptoms are increasing or changing.

Do your homework about prescription drugs and check out alternative treatments to make an educated decision. For example, it is crucial that you take into consideration your age and your family history of breast and uterine cancers before begining hormonal therapy.

4. PMS and Menopause Lifestyle Plan for Optimal Health.

Diet and supplements. What you eat can greatly contribute to relieving many PMS symptoms. The biggest challenge is dealing with the food cravings that usually lead women to consume foods that actually aggravate their condition. During PMS, women usually crave carbohydrates, sugar (usually combined with chocolate), or fat (combined with salt). Initially these foods seem to make you feel better, but in actuality they create a false sense of energy that only leads to greater fatigue and increased cravings. Resist all cravings for junk food!

The basics of a healthy diet include plenty of complex carbohydrates, moderate amounts of protein, minimal fats, and lots of water. Increase quality whole natural foods, complex carbohydrates such as pasta, potatoes (baked or sweet), rice (preferably brown or wild), dried beans, peas, cereal, and whole grain breads, and lots of fresh fruits and vegetables. Soy protein has many benefits as well.

These complex carbohydrates help keep blood sugar balanced while providing the body with an even source of energy. Try eating six small meals throughout the day—instead of three big ones. This will increase your metabolism and cause less weight gain. Allow yourself a few treats now and again, and make it worthwhile. Have the first bite and then the last bite. Then wait a few days before you have your two bites again.

Avoid alcohol, chocolate, dairy products, caffeine, and processed foods as much as you can. Cut back on fats, sugars, and salt.

Take a good multivitamin with minerals, if possible one that is specifically recommended for women with PMS or those going through menopause. There are additional supplements that can be taken for specific symptoms. For example, additional Vitamin E (100 to 800 international units per day) will help relieve breast tenderness.

Exercise. Exercise regularly. The best all-around option is brisk walking for at least thirty to sixty minutes a day, as many days a week as possible. This has been found to be very effective in reducing a wide range of PMS and menopause symptoms. It also reduces stress, increases energy, and gives a sense of well-being.

Don't forget your Kegels! Kegel exercises strengthen and give you voluntary control over the pubococcygeus (PC) muscle. The PC muscle encircles the urinary opening and also the outside of the vagina. To identify the PC muscle, see if you can start and stop the flow of urine while urinating. Kegel exercises involve tightening this PC muscle as you do to stop the flow of urine and then relaxing it. Begin by doing ten Kegels each day, then increase the number by ten each week working up to 50 to 100 each day.

Rest and relaxation. The general fatigue due to hormonal changes and sleep disturbances can be quite debilitating to daily life and sexual desire. Rest and relax as much as possible. Take naps if you have to. Take a hot bubble bath and go to bed early if you can. This is especially important for those needing tension taming. Some other tension tamers include a brisk walk, herb supplements and teas, deep breathing, journaling, or a venting chat with a friend. It might mean scheduling your life to avoid activities that would increase your stress level or aggravate you.

Quiet time. We all know that the Word of God and prayer strengthen us spiritually, but many of us find it difficult to touch Jesus through our "hormonal fog." During these times, simply sitting quietly meditating on His attributes, His names, or a favorite Scripture or song can be refreshing. Don't become overwhelmed trying to "do it right."

Many women struggle with emotional challenges like anger, frustration, and free-floating tension. These are very real physically based symptoms that impact your emotions and behavior. Realize you are in a spiritual battle, but God's acceptance and love for you are unconditional and forever sure. You can never "out- symptom" His love for you!

Communication—An Essential Element

"I find it helpful to talk to my husband and warn him of my hormonal state of mind and lack of sexual interest."

What a sensible suggestion. To be forewarned is to be forearmed. Many husbands report that just knowing that their wives are entering a hormonally disruptive period can help them be more tolerant and understanding. Communicate with your husband and others around you.

Once you know your own hormone cycle and symptoms, you will be better able to predict your difficult times of the month. Use your calendar to chart your cycle and to plan ahead for what might be coming. Talk to and warn your husband, family, or others close to you. For example, one woman told us of

> **Realize you are in a spiritual battle, but God's acceptance and love for you are unconditional and forever sure. You can never "out-symptom" His love for you!**

how, with her husband's support, she postponed a planned family trip to Disneyland. She knew that being out late, walking around all day in the heat, standing in long lines, and making her way through all the crowds of people would have just been too much for her at "day 18" of her cycle. It would have pushed her over the edge, and set her back a few days!

There might be times you lose control emotionally, overreact, or distance others with your rage. Make amends and ask for forgiveness and understanding, explain your struggle and take responsibility for your hormonal journey.

If possible, plan your dates and times for sex around your cycle. For example, a woman told us of how she had planned a weekend away with her husband to celebrate her birthday a few months in advance. The month before the event, after charting her projected cycle, she warned her husband of where she would be in her cycle while on the trip and prepared him that she most probably would not be feeling like having sex. They planned their weekend accordingly. She packed her flannels instead of negligees, and they had a very restful weekend reading and enjoying each other's company.

Change your method of birth control if it is a major source of difficulty. Adjust your daily schedule and ask for what you need in order to catch up on sleep, have a quiet time, relax, and exercise— whatever it takes. You have to decide that it is more important to your well-being and your partner's to accept the fact that hormones affect you. Work *with* yourself rather than *against* yourself. Work with your husband as much as possible to navigate through your cycles.

Points to Remember

1. The two most common health concerns of the women in our study were premenstrual syndrome (PMS) and menopause. Both of these are hormonally based and can impact sexual functioning. Many of the women in our study requested information to help them understand PMS and menopause.

2. Every woman needs to understand her hormonal cycle and how it affects her body and emotions. Journaling or charting the monthly symptoms is beneficial.

3. In our study 51% of women reported experiencing PMS. Of these women, 60% reported that their symptoms were moderate or severe.

4. Many of the women in our study expressed a concern about menopause. Menopause is a process that can span two to ten years or more and can begin as early as the forties (even the thirties).

5. Recognizing the subtle and obvious physical and emotional symptoms of the early stages of menopause can prepare a woman to make lifestyle adjustments and more effectively navigate this process.

6. Hormonal changes during menopause can impact sexual functioning by: altering sexual desire, creating vaginal discomfort and dryness, and changing orgasmic experience. A woman's attitude toward menopause and aging can greatly influence her emotional, physical, relational, and sexual health.

Chapter Eight

Marital Happiness and Sex

"His mouth is most sweet, yes, he is altogether lovely. This is my beloved, and this is my friend."

—Song of Solomon 5:16 NKJV

Most of us expect warm companionship, a lot of emotional support, and great sex when we get married. Unfortunately, these expectations are not always realized.

For some, sex in marriage delivers all it promises. For many it doesn't. Problems with sexual desire, arousal, and orgasm are common. It is extremely disappointing, after the first glow of marriage has subsided and children come along, to find that maintaining a strong and consistent interest in sex takes more hard work than couples bargained for.

We discovered through our study that there is a strong relationship between marital happiness and sexual satisfaction. It is our hope that, by examining what Christian women told us about their marriages and sex, we will be able to reveal keys to happiness and sexual satisfaction in marriage.

Many couples *can* and *do* find a great level of sexual compatibility, intimacy, understanding, and sexual fulfillment in their marriage. It takes hard work and a determined commitment to understand and overcome the unique differences between men and women in order to be compatible. This understanding is essential for every couple. Just learning sex techniques is not enough. The best-intended technique will fail if it is not under-girded with sensitivity, tolerance of differences, and understanding of the variability in sexual responsiveness.

Is Marriage Important to Sexual Satisfaction?

Does being married make a difference in being sexually satisfied? Perhaps we should go back even one step further and ask: Is it necessary to be married in order to have sex?

We live in an age when sex has been far removed from the marital context into which God placed it. Because so many these days question whether marriage is necessary at all, we need to first examine the importance of marriage to sex. It is sad but true that some Christians do not accept that sex is to be reserved for marriage.

An important characteristic of healthy adult sexuality is its capacity to focus on one sexual partner only. By this we don't mean focusing sexually on one partner at a time but on *one partner for a lifetime*. Does this sound radical? To some it might. Yet this is what God designed for us: one lifetime sexual partner.

> **An important characteristic of healthy adult sexuality is its capacity to focus on one sexual partner only.**

We know firsthand this is a broken world, one where living according to God's design for us can be extremely difficult. Many marriages fail. Not every divorced person is divorced out of his or her choosing. Thankfully, our God is a God of second chances. Where would any one of us be if He were not? If you have started your marital life over again with a new partner, God's standard for you is to share your sexuality only within this marriage.

Why do we state this so strongly? First, because it is biblical. Also because lifelong monogamy is still the best environment in which to mature your sexuality. We believe our research supports this. The evidence from many studies, including our own, indicates that the best and most fulfilling sex is achieved in marriage.

The most compelling evidence for this assertion comes from the personal stories of the women in our study—those who have been married to one partner, and those who have divorced or have been sexually promiscuous during their single years. Many have had multiple sex partners. For some, this was a part of their life before becoming a Christian. Others failed after becoming a Christian and have struggled to recover. Their life experience tells us that nothing good came out of being "sexually free." Read some of their stories:

> *"My greatest regret is that I had so many sexual partners earlier in my life. I didn't give myself to these affairs. Men used me, and I used them. What did I learn? Nothing. A total waste of time. I lost respect for myself sexually, and it is only now in my marriage that I am beginning to regain that respect."*

> *"My teen years were times of promiscuity. I thought sex was for everyone. 'Just enjoy yourself.' But I didn't. I was miserable. I became a Christian at seventeen and saw God work miracles in my life. Now I'm married and praise God every day for His healing and forgiveness."*

> *"I married at twenty-one as a virgin. After several years of marriage my husband and I both had sex with others, thinking it would help us in our marriage. It didn't. We recommitted our lives to the Lord, and now my orgasms are getting better and more satisfying. I am now the most satisfied I have ever been and believe this wouldn't have happened if we hadn't gotten our marriage back on the right track."*

By and large, Americans are faithful to one partner. According to the *Sex in America* study, more than 80% of Americans have had only one or zero sexual partners in the previous year. *Time* magazine agreed and stated that this is the experience of most Americans.[1] *Penthouse* rejected this and responded by asserting that the average male has five different sex partners a year. Perhaps the average reader of *Penthouse* does have five partners a year, but what has that got to do with the average American?

Marital Happiness

We are not implying that marriage is the only road to happiness and fulfillment in life. Many single men and women, whether they have or haven't been married, achieve a high level of fulfillment and happiness.

We devoted quite a few questions in our study to issues surrounding sexual satisfaction and marital happiness. Several issues concerned us: How are sexual satisfaction and marital happiness related? Is marital happiness possible even in the absence of a satisfying sexual relationship? What factors contribute to sexual satisfaction? And most important, what difference, if any, does being a Christian make to either sexual satisfaction or marital happiness?

The first question we posed regarding marriage was a very simple one: "If married, please circle the phrase that best describes your degree of marital happiness, all things considered." The answers are depicted in Figure 8.1.

The results were quite outstanding. Of all the married women in our study, 84% reported that they were happy to some degree in their marriages. Twenty-eight percent said they were extremely happy, 34% said they were very happy, and 21% said they were happy. Only 8% said they were fairly or extremely unhappy.

Of those women in the *Sex in America* study who reported having had sex at least once a week during the last year, 35% said they were sometimes fairly unhappy and 27% said they were unhappy most of the time.[2] This means that a total of 62% of women who are having sex regularly (the nearest we can come to marriage) are unhappy with life at least some of the time. While the comparison is not altogether equivalent in the married Christian women in our study, only 14% said they are unhappy in their marriage. This is surely a strong argument in favor of

MARITAL HAPPINESS
Figure 8.1

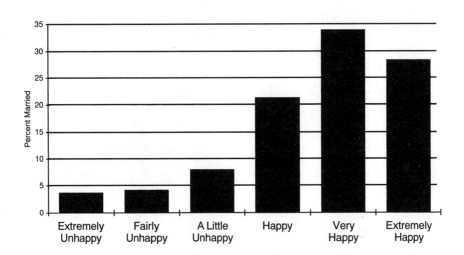

Christian marriages! The contrast is even greater where only 8% of Christian women said they were extremely unhappy or fairly unhappy with their marriages while 27% of the women surveyed in *Sex and America* said they were unhappy.

Even allowing for the inadequacy of the comparison, these statistics clearly indicate that our group is significantly happier than those surveyed in the *Sex in America* study. But before we rush to celebrate, we need to ask whether our sample was biased in any way. Did the women in our married sample desire to make their marriages look good?

We believe not, and our discussion on sexual satisfaction will show the reason for this. Our sample was not as positive about sexual satisfaction as they were about marital happiness.

Sexual Satisfaction

The sexual satisfaction question was worded as follows: "Circle the phrase that best describes the degree of sexual satisfaction, all things considered, of your sexual relationship." The results are shown in Figure 8.2.

SEXUAL SATISFACTION AMONG MARRIED WOMEN
Figure 8.2

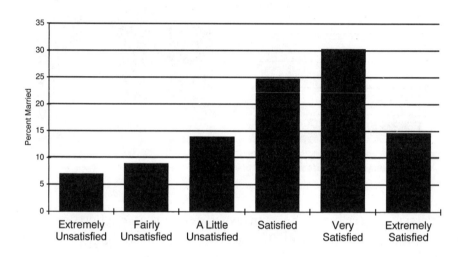

We discovered that 70% of the women in our study were sexually satisfied to some extent [satisfied (25%), very satisfied (30%), and extremely satisfied (15%)]. Only 9% were fairly unsatisfied, and 7% extremely unsatisfied.

It was interesting for us to note that 53% of wives reported they were satisfied with their frequency of sexual intercourse, while only 28% believed their husbands felt the same. Forty percent of wives reported wanting sex more often, while 70% reported that their husbands wanted sex more often.

Marital Happiness and Sexual Satisfaction

When we examined the relationship between marital happiness and sexual satisfaction, we found a very significant connection.

(See Figure 8.3.) Sixty-three percent of women who were sexually satisfied also reported a high degree of marital happiness. Only 6% of those who were unhappily married reported they were sexually satisfied.

THE ASSOCIATION BETWEEN WOMEN'S MARITAL HAPPINESS AND SEXUAL SATISFACTION
Figure 8.3

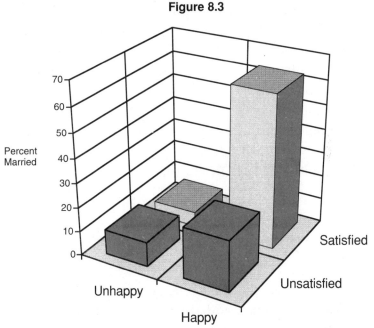

Interestingly, 21% of those women who were sexually unsatisfied were happily married. This means that it is possible to be unsatisfied in your sex life yet be happy in your marriage. Dr. Neil Warren also found this to be true in his survey of successful marriages. He writes: "While it seems clear that a mutually satisfying sexual relationship enhances every marriage, it is equally clear that great marriages can often be fashioned without great sex. But there is little doubt that if great sex for both partners can be obtained, it will contribute substantially to the management of marital stress and the attainment of marital goals."[3]

There may be many good reasons why a woman could be happily married but sexually unsatisfied. Illness, surgery, a husband's impotence, or other physical conditions can impact sexuality. On the other hand, perhaps the reasons require deeper exploration and therapeutic intervention.

We wondered whether length of marriage had anything to do with marital happiness. To our surprise, we found that there was no connection. Younger married couples were just as likely to be happy as older couples. What about the relationship between sexual satisfaction and length of marriage? The same story—there is no connection. Sexual satisfaction runs the whole gambit from young marriages to long-standing marriages. Furthermore, religious upbringing is not associated with either marital happiness or sexual satisfaction. You are just as likely to be happily married if you are brought up in a religious home as you are if you're not. It is your Christian commitment later in life that shapes your happiness or satisfaction.

Frequency and Duration of Sex

While husbands usually complain about the infrequency of sex, it seems that the major issue for women is the duration of sex. To what extent do frequency and duration of sex contribute to a woman's marital happiness and sexual satisfaction?

Our data show that most women have sex once a week. The next most common frequency is two to three times per week (30%). Only 14% have sex once a month. Thereafter the percentages drop dramatically (refer to Figure 8.4). This means that nearly 70% of women have sex one to three times per week.

Only 4% of the married women in our study reported that they never have sex, while 1% have it only once a year. The reasons for this infrequency came through clearly in the written responses. Some just plainly hated sex. They found nothing pleasurable in it. They felt relief when their husbands aged and lost interest also. Some women wanted to have sex, but their husbands weren't

HOW OFTEN DO MARRIED WOMEN HAVE SEX?
Figure 8.4

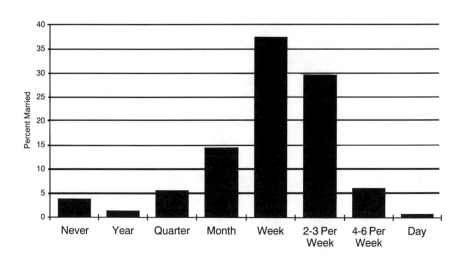

interested or were impotent for a variety of reasons. Some, while married, were emotionally separated from their husbands or said that the absence of sex was unavoidable.

These frequencies will probably come as a relief to many readers, judging by the comments we have received. Many expressed concern that they were not as sexually active as they thought others were. A lot of people feel that something is wrong with them when they don't have strong sexual feelings most of the time. On the other hand, Christians are not unresponsive, sexually inhibited, and unhappy as many believe them to be. We would say, according to the results of this study, that the majority of married Christian women are sexually satisfied.

How does the frequency of sex in our sample compare with other studies? Figure 8.5 shows comparisons with two groups from the *Sex in America* study: their total sample and Protestants only. The Protestant group is most similar to our sample. A slightly higher percentage of the Christian women in our study have sex a little more frequently than the other two groups.

STUDIES OF SEXUAL FREQUENCY
Figure 8.5

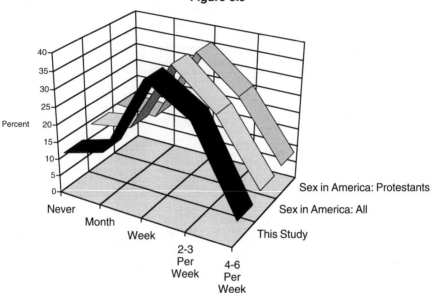

Does frequency of intercourse affect sexual satisfaction? Figure 8.6 shows the data, and this finding is once again very significant statistically. Frequency of intercourse and sexual satisfaction are extremely related.

We conclude from this that in some of these marriages, frequency of sexual intercourse increases sexual satisfaction. In others, the high level of satisfaction increases frequency. Therefore, if you want to

> **If you want to improve your sexual relationship, consider making love more frequently and making it more enjoyable for both of you.**

improve your sexual relationship, consider making love more frequently and making it more enjoyable for both of you.

What about duration of sexual intercourse? Nearly half of the women in our study reported that when they make love with their partner they usually take thirty minutes (see Figure 8.7). Twenty-five percent take fifteen minutes. It is almost impossible physically

SEXUAL FREQUENCY AND SEXUAL SATISFACTION
AMONG MARRIED WOMEN
Figure 8.6

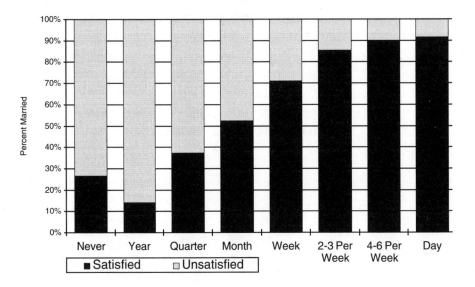

HOW LONG DO MARRIED WOMEN TAKE TO HAVE SEX?
Figure 8.7

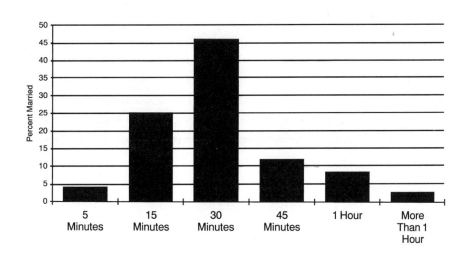

for a woman to reach orgasm in only fifteen minutes of lovemaking. A woman's body is designed for slower, longer lovemaking.

Figure 8.8 shows the association between the duration of sexual intercourse and sexual satisfaction. Sexual satisfaction is lowest for women when sexual duration is only five minutes (67%). Satisfaction steadily rises as the length of time increases, until at thirty minutes it is 73%, and at one hour or more it is 78%.

DURATION OF SEX AND SEXUAL SATISFACTION AMONG MARRIED WOMEN
Figure 8.8

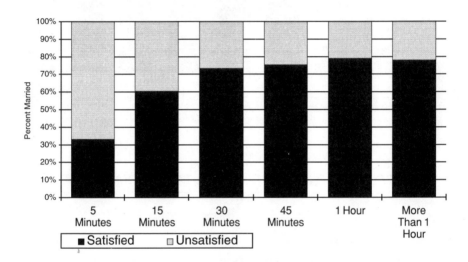

Our conclusion is that the optimum duration of lovemaking for a high level of sexual satisfaction is between thirty and forty-five minutes. Engaging in "sexual olympics" might be overdoing it; as one woman wrote: "We usually take two to three hours—too long for me!"

Sex and Communication

Satisfying sex is more than just sexual intercourse. A complete sexual experience embraces a continuum of expression. It begins with meaningful relating (communication), goes on to closeness (physical and emotional intimacy), then on to arousal (sensuality), and finally to intercourse (sex). It looks like this:

Relating ➡ Closeness ➡ Arousal ➡ Intercourse

Good sex and good communication go together. Many married couples make little progress toward achieving sexual harmony because they do not openly discuss their sexual feelings, preferences, or displeasure with each other, or with anyone else for that matter. Listen to what these women had to say about this:

> *"My husband and I have a hard time communicating about sex. For the most part I am satisfied, but I also think things could be better. When we discuss it he gets upset. It's a very touchy subject for him."*

> *"Sex is not just an act, but an all-day process through communication, touch, and time. At times we are both too tired, stressed, kids, and so on. And we communicate that to each other and go to sleep instead. Sex is a commitment—not just an act."*

> *"We have problems in communication. Words are spoken, but none are taken seriously. Feelings are conveyed, but none are validated despite the fact that my husband takes pride in his ability to express feelings. Sex is something we just do, like eating and sleeping. Next week we are going for marriage counseling."*

Not all of the comments were about communication failures. Some spoke of success:

> *"Communication is the key to a great sex life. God created men and women differently to give each other pleasure. If there are*

things you or your spouse like to try, you need to talk about it
and make sure you are both comfortable with it."

We asked our sample with whom they were able to discuss their sexual feelings.

Sixty-five percent of married women said they could talk to their partner, 23% said one friend, 12% said several friends, and 15% said no one. How does this compare with men? Sixty-four percent of the married men in the *Sexual Man* study also said they could talk to their partner. So we have very close agreement between Christian men and women regarding talking openly about sex with their partner. We have no data from non-Christian couples to compare this with.

Fifteen percent of the women in our study, nearly one in seven, reported that they had no one to talk to about sex (not a partner or a friend), and 6% said that they only had God to talk to. We need people, as well as God, to talk to about personal matters.

In marriage, the ability to communicate before, during, or after sex can prevent disappointment, resentment, and distrust. Both partners need to express what they like and don't like sexually, what satisfies them, and how frequently they desire sex in order to enhance their physical and emotional intimacy. These discoveries may require an unselfish response from both of you. Men, you might need to slow down a little. Women, you might need to

---

Communication Basics

1. Speak for yourself. Begin sentences with "I" and avoid using "you."
2. Talk about how you feel rather than only what you think. Use feeling words as much as possible. When you are speaking, don't hog the time. Take turns speaking and listening.
3. Listening is the most important part of communicating. Don't interrupt when your partner is speaking. Don't think about what you are going to say while your partner is talking. Really listen!
4. Repeat what you think you heard your partner saying periodically. Check to confirm that you heard accurately.
5. Affirm your partner by respecting what was shared. Partners don't have to agree to see one another's perspective.

learn to receive. Both may need to adjust their expectations in order to respond to each other.

Showing affection is one form of communication. How many couples share affection outside of their sexual relationship? Ninety-three percent of the women in our study said they did. Of the 7% who did not share affection, half were in unhappy marriages, and two-thirds of that number (63%) were sexually unsatisfied. Happy couples show affection to each other at times other than during sex and this contributes to both sexual satisfaction and marital happiness.

The communication basics outlined in the sidebar on page 170 are important skills for every aspect of marriage, including speaking openly about sex. We encourage you to set aside time to talk and listen to each other often. Keep your communication lines open.

Factors That Diminish Marital Happiness and Sexual Satisfaction

Health Problems

Many women informed us in their personal comments that medical and emotional problems affected their marriage or their sexual interest and responsiveness. Depression was the most common problem. Of these married women, 10% reported that they were having problems with depression. Our findings are confirmed by the National Institute for Mental Health (NIMH) estimates, which report the prevalence of depression as 10% of the adult population. Women are at twice the risk for depression as men. There is a one in five chance of developing depression during a lifetime, but only one out of three seek treatment.

Since women are at twice the risk for depression as men, it is not surprising that we found so many married women suffering from depression. Any of the following factors as well as many others can contribute to depression: abuse early in life, infertility, chronic physical problems, low self-esteem, a sense of helplessness, and an unhappy marriage.

How does depression influence sexual functioning? Occasionally depression increases sexual appetite, most often depression decreases desire. About 60% of depressed women lose interest in sex entirely.

How does depression affect marital happiness? In our study the level of marital happiness drops from 88% (women with no depression) to 70% (women who are depressed). This difference is statistically significant. It can be extremely difficult to live with a partner who is depressed, and it puts a strain on the marriage. An unhappy marriage, on the other hand, can also cause depression.

How does depression affect sexual satisfaction? The connection is as strong as for marital happiness and very significant statistically. Sexual satisfaction drops from 72% (no depression) to 52% (depressed). A depressed person usually has little interest in sex and has difficulty enjoying life in general. It is not surprising, then, that people who are depressed aren't sexually satisfied.

> **Depression can significantly reduce your level of both marital happiness and sexual satisfaction.**

Depression can significantly reduce your level of both marital happiness and sexual satisfaction.

There is another factor that links depression with sexual functioning. Some of the newer antidepressants (called SSRIs) have sexual side effects such as a delay in or inability to reach orgasm or decreased sexual desire. Appropriate adjustment of the dosage or a change to another medication can usually correct this problem. Discuss this with your doctor.

Two other health concerns mentioned frequently by the women in our study were premenstrual syndrome (PMS) and menopause. We have discussed these at length in chapter 7. Other health concerns affecting sexual functioning reported by the women in our study were: anxiety (6%), high blood pressure (6%), chronic pain (4%), low thyroid (2%), and chronic fatigue (2%).

Affairs

How common were affairs in our sample? About 11% of wives knew that their husbands had had one or more affairs. That is just over one in ten! Another 13% said they didn't know for sure if their husbands had ever had an affair. This is one woman's story:

> *"I believe that two factors from my past have had a negative impact on my sexuality: First, my father's involvement with pornography. It made me feel ashamed of becoming a woman. Second, my first husband had extramarital affairs so we divorced. This affected my ability to trust, but God is helping me work at my current marriage."*

What about wives? Twenty-five percent acknowledged having had an extramarital affair. However, many of these affairs occurred before the wives had become Christians. We know this because the women told us so. The memories of their past sexual behaviors were a source of great embarrassment and guilt for them, as reflected in these comments:

> *"I wish you had asked more questions about having an affair. I have carried the guilt of this with me for a long time—it would have been a helpful anonymous confession to get it all out."*

> *"I had an affair one night and told my husband about it. He said he could throw no stones, forgave me, and our marriage is better than ever. Thanks to the Lord! My husband has learned to be more attentive to me, and I have learned how much he loves me and what I really want in my life."*

The following comment highlights a reason women could be vulnerable to having an affair. Husbands, *please* read this comment carefully!

*"Sex is not as important to me as being loved and uncondi-
tionally accepted by my husband. I believe that if he were less
critical and more affirming of me, I would feel better about
myself and have more sexual desire for him. I am slightly overweight, and it is a huge issue for him. I have tried all sorts of
diets. He makes me feel ugly and unwanted. This kills my
desire, but he still wants me to satisfy him in bed every other day.
I do so out of duty to satisfy his libido. I am so frustrated I nearly
had an affair to prove I am desirable. If it were not for my
commitment to Christ, I would have!"*

Extramarital affairs happen, even among Christians. *Nothing
good* comes from an affair. This betrayal produces a profound sense
of abandonment. Trust is destroyed by such fundamental disloyalty.

We are not saying that a marriage cannot be restored after an
affair. We have worked with many marriages recovering from the
violation of an affair. When there is repentance, *a lot* of hard work,
and God's grace, a marriage can certainly be restored.

Because of the resulting devastation from an affair, we recommend improving marital happiness and sexual satisfaction as the
best form of prevention.

When marriage is successful, the outcome, as shown by much
research, is greater health, personal growth, and a high level of
personal fulfillment.[4] A successful marriage is also characterized by
higher levels of marital happiness and sexual satisfaction.

Points to Remember

1. Our data indicate a high level of marital happiness in
    Christian couples. Of the women we studied, 84% reported
    being happy, very happy, or extremely happy.

2. In our study, Christian women also reported a high level
    of sexual satisfaction (70%). The association between mari-
    tal happiness and sexual satisfaction is very strong.

3. Sexual satisfaction and frequency of lovemaking are related. Most of the women in our study had intercourse from one to three times a week and reported a high level of sexual satisfaction.

4. Duration of lovemaking is also associated with sexual satisfaction. The women who made love thirty minutes to one hour reported the highest levels of sexual satisfaction.

5. The health factors that impact both sexual satisfaction and marital happiness are: PMS, menopause, depression, anxiety, high blood pressure, chronic pain, low thyroid, and chronic fatigue.

6. The best form of marital enrichment and affair prevention is to learn how to talk and listen to each other, to be flexible and unselfish, and to grow spiritually and emotionally.

Chapter Nine

Female Sexual Trauma

"The watchmen who went about the city found me. They struck me, they wounded me . . . took my veil away from me."

—Song of Solomon 5:7 NKJV

Some of the most heart-wrenching comments received from the women in our study were about how their sexuality had been marred by sexual trauma. The following personal stories highlight just how traumatic sex can be for many:

"After being raped at age sixteen by a friend of the family at church, I became very promiscuous—had several partners in a short time. I had anorexia as well. I hated my body and felt extremely dirty. It seems that some of those feelings never go away—I just fill my schedule with so many activities that I'm always busy or tired. I feel guilty about how I reacted to the rape; I wish I had just told my parents, but I didn't want to see my father go to prison for murder. He (the guy who raped me) walked away without a care in the world, but I've had to spend the last twelve years reliving the nightmare of that day!"

"The loss of my father and the way I was molested during early childhood have had a huge negative impact on my sexuality. I associated sex with love. Because the only sex education I had was in school, I learned nothing about healthy love, desire, and

relationships. Many of the activities I participated in were a direct reflection of that. As an adult I now know the difference, but the impact is still there—it is always affecting me."

"I was molested for a year by a family friend staying with us. Shortly after, I became sexually active. My self-concept was skewed as I saw myself only as sexually important. My father was an alcoholic, and I turned sexually to other men to get the affection I wasn't getting from my father. Each time I gave myself to a man I felt overwhelming guilt and would immediately terminate all contact with that person thereafter. The problem is I still feel guilty during sex with my husband, like I don't deserve to enjoy it. I don't feel I am really able to talk about it with anyone (except on occasion with my husband). I don't know how to work through it, and I am afraid to try."

"I experienced severe emotional pain from being molested as a child. Now I experience extreme shame over my promiscuity during college and prior to marriage. Is there a correlation between women who were molested and women who become promiscuous?"

Sexual trauma—just the thought brings a chill to most women. But what is *trauma* in this context? The word originates from the Greek word for *wound*. A trauma, therefore, is "an injury (as in a wound) to living tissue caused by an external agent." Today, however, we use the term *trauma* for more than just physical hurt. Anything that damages us (physically or emotionally) is also considered to be a form of trauma. Sexual trauma, therefore, is anything that damages our sexuality.

We will discuss six types of sexual trauma: molestation, pornography, rape and sexual assault, body image distortions, abortion, and sexually transmitted diseases (STDs). Each of these is harmful to a woman's sexual feelings and responsiveness.

If you are a victim of sexual trauma, at the end of this chapter we provide some suggestions to help you as you seek healing.

Sexual Molestation

Sexual molestation is any sexual activity directed toward a child. It can range from a child being exposed to sexually explicit activity or inappropriate nudity, to being fondled and to vaginal or anal penetration. Some examples of what would be considered forms of molestation are:

1. An adult asking a child to undress in order to look at or touch the child

2. An adult touching a child's genitals

3. An adult showing a child his or her genitals

4. An adult having a child touch his or her genitals

5. Mouth to genital contact

6. Hand to genital contact

7. Penetration of anus or vagina with an object

8. Penile anal or vaginal penetration

9. Intercourse with a child

10. Taking sexual photographs of a child

No doubt many of our readers can add to this list from their personal experiences.

In summary, any activity that exposes a child to sexual stimulation that is inappropriate to the child's age, emotional development, and/or role in the family is sexually abusive to the child. A child is only a *child*, and children are not sexual objects. A child's sexuality is not yet fully formed. Premature exposure to any form of sexual activity can be frightening and traumatic, and it can harm the child both physically and emotionally. A child is not to be anyone's source of sexual gratification.

Sexual molestation of a child is about the most despicable form of criminal activity. Consequently, most civilized cultures impose severe penalties for any form of abuse. But why are we discussing such activity in a book about the sexuality of Christian women? Surely Christians are not guilty of such a heinous crime against innocent and defenseless children! Regrettably, this is not the case. Increasingly, there is evidence that molestation occurs among Christians. Christian leaders, teachers, parents, family members, and friends have been known to molest children. A recent report in *Christianity Today* indicates that volunteers in church work are the most frequent sexual abusers in the church context, representing 50% of the perpetrators.[1] Paid staff, including clergy, are next at 30%, and other children, 20%. So it is not a rare phenomenon for our subculture. The time has come for us to talk about it and raise our children's awareness of what constitutes molestation. Parents who don't prepare their children to recognize and ward off all forms of molestation are doing them a great disservice.

SEXUAL TRAUMAS AMONG CHRISTIAN WOMEN
Figure 9.1

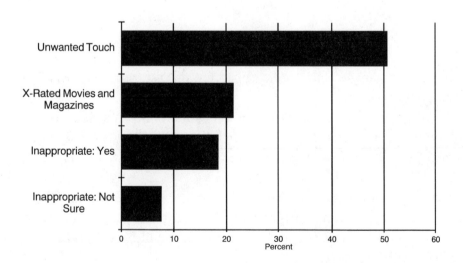

It doesn't matter whose research you look at, all credible research on child abuse turns up numbers we have difficulty believing. How common is child molestation? Currently, approximately one in three girls and one in five boys report having been sexually molested to some extent.

Usually, 75% to 95% of the time, the child knows the molester. Abusers can be fathers, stepfathers, mothers, stepmothers, brothers, stepbrothers, sisters, uncles, cousins, close friends, the next-door neighbor, your child's doctor or nurse, the school principal, the high school teacher, the pastor or youth pastor. They can be atheists, agnostics, or believers, rich or poor, educated or high school dropouts. All studies indicate that child sexual abuse occurs across every level of society. And unfortunately, it also happens in the church.

How common was sexual abuse in our sample of two thousand Christian women? Fifty percent reported that they had experienced unwanted touch. (See Figure 9.1.) Many wrote to us of the anguish they had experienced due to childhood molestation. A woman in her late forties wrote:

> *"My ideal sexual experience is simple: I would be free of my memories of sexual abuse as a child; I would not have reoccurrences of those memories that come frequently during sex with my husband; my husband would be fully understanding of the difficulty that sexual abuse has brought me. It takes the joy out of the sexual experience with him. I haven't felt free to share what happens in my head, why I freeze up at times, or tell him why I need space at times. If I felt he knew and understood, it would improve my sexual experience."*

And another said:

> *"Three months ago I found out that my daddy, whom I idolized all my life, had molested me. My trust in men, including my husband, has gone downhill from there. Also, my first boss, when I was*

seventeen, tried to rape me. My husband just doesn't have a clue
as to why these things from my past should still affect me today."

Three percent of those we surveyed can recall being molested as toddlers. Ten percent were molested as preschoolers. Unwanted sexual touch during grade school was reported by 23% and during the teens, 15%. (See Figure 9.2.) The most vulnerable ages for unwanted touching are preschool and grade school. The effects on sexuality are very clearly substantiated. One of these women wrote:

"I was abused at age five—and now I can't get the hang of
enjoying sex. How do you overcome past abuse so you can enjoy
sex with your husband?"

AGE DISTRIBUTION OF UNWANTED TOUCH
Figure 9.2

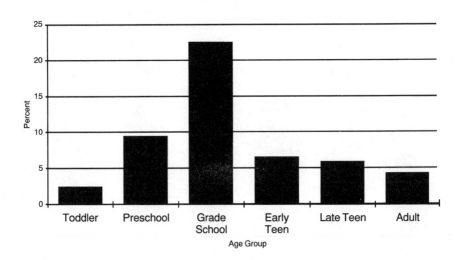

But not all sexual abuse involves touching. Nearly 20% of women believe that adults had been sexually inappropriate with them as children without even touching them. Sexually provocative behavior, inappropriate sexual jokes, and inappropriate nudity are all forms of child abuse.

While an adult behaving inappropriately with a child without touching seems less damaging, many of these children later exhibit the same problems and symptoms as children who were actually touched. And children who watched or knew of siblings being abused, even if they had not been abused themselves, often experienced the same symptoms later in life as those who were actually abused.

Pornography

Twenty-one percent of the women in our study reported that they had been exposed to pornographic material, magazines, or movies as a child. Of those exposed to pornography, 60% felt the exposure had been destructive to them. In our study, the age of exposure climbed slowly from age four with a peak between ages ten and twelve. It then dropped gradually thereafter.

It surprised us that women appear to be exposed to pornography at an earlier age than men, who are typically exposed between ages thirteen and fifteen. (See Figure 6.1 in Dr. Hart's *The Sexual Man.*) Fewer girls (23%) are exposed to pornography than boys (96%).

While men are strongly attracted to pornography, women generally are not. They certainly don't get as addicted to it as males. What is common, however, is how pornography impacts them secondhand when a husband gets hooked on it. Many women wrote complaining about how their husband's pornography upset them and inhibited their sexual arousal:

"Because my husband has problems with fantasy and porn, our sex life lacks frequency and causes me to be mostly concerned with how to interact with him."

"My husband had struggled many years with problems of lust and had another sexual partner. He also struggled with pornography—especially during our four pregnancies. This greatly affected my self-image and sexuality because I could

always sense his lust (even if it was not for me), and this would feed my own fears and pain."

Another woman wrote expressing concern for how her father's dependence on pornography impacted his children:

"I was addicted to violent sexual fantasies from age three on. I believe this started from looking through my father's pornographic magazines, which he left out in the open. This continued until I became a Christian at twenty-two and I was delivered through prayer. I would like others to know how devastating pornography can be to children's minds."

We are told again and again in the media that pornography is harmless and victimless. Yet, national experts on pornography have reached quite different conclusions:

1. Law enforcement personnel have testified that a disproportionate number of sex offenders have been found to have large quantities of pornography in their homes. "There is a correlation between pornographic material and sex offenses."[2]

2. Children and adolescents who participate in the production of pornography experience adverse and enduring effects.

3. Pornography that portrays sexual aggression as pleasurable for the victim increases the acceptance of the use of coercion in sexual relations.

4. In laboratory settings exposure to violent pornography increases punitive behavior toward women.[3]

Dr. Park Dietz, a criminal psychiatrist who served as a commissioner for the attorney general on the topic of pornography, summed up the realities associated with pornography eloquently:

"Pornography is a medical and public health problem because so much of it teaches false, misleading, and even dangerous information about human sexuality. A person who learned about human sexuality in the "adults only" pornography outlets of America would be a person who had never conceived of a man and woman marrying or even falling in love before having intercourse, who had never conceived of two people making love in privacy without guilt or fear of discovery, who had never conceived of tender foreplay, who had never conceived of vaginal intercourse with ejaculation during intromission, and who had never conceived of procreation as a purpose of sexual union."[4]

While some women can enjoy the stimulation of explicit erotica, especially romantic scenes, most women, quite rightly, decry it. Men are depicted as dominant and women are reduced to objects. In reality, women want to know they are more than just a sexual release.

Women feel threatened by their partner's preoccupation with pornography. These "other" women, even though they are only pictures, intrude into the marital relationship. It feels as though your husband is being unfaithful. Even more demeaning is the feeling that you are being compared with these women. And who can compete with airbrushed

> **Pornography demeans women. But it also demeans men.**

images that are touched up and unrealistic? The majority of wives can never compete with the lies portrayed in pornography.

The sexual acts portrayed are usually degrading to women and grossly immoral (multiple partners, bestiality, and so forth). These acts do not contribute to lifelong, committed relationships.

Finally, as shown in *The Sexual Man,* the prolonged use of pornography can significantly distort a male's sexuality. Very few of the men studied saw any good come of their exposure to or use of pornography.

What can a woman do to deal with her partner's dependence on pornography? Before you talk to your partner about how betrayed you feel, and how much his use of pornography intrudes into the relationship, learn and understand more about addiction to pornography. Prepare yourself for the long process of healing and overcoming this addiction together.

Try to understand how hard it is for men to break the porn habit. It is established very early in the majority of men and is very resistant to change. Nagging or rejection won't help. In the long run, your loving, firm request that he respect your feelings in this matter impacts his recovery.

Fantasy sex is not as satisfying in the long run as reality sex. Encourage your husband to work with you on making your own sex life more fulfilling. Also, build a support and prayer base for yourself so you are not alone in this struggle. Others praying with you can strengthen you when you feel helpless. If you can find other women who are also engaged in a similar battle with pornography, it will comfort you and give perspective.

If your husband's use of pornography is excessive and very demeaning to you, you have a right to demand that he get professional help for his problem. He cannot separate fantasy from reality and may well be addicted in the true sense of the word. It is no different from being married to an alcoholic—you may need to use the "tough love" approach. Whatever you choose to do, do it under the supervision of a wise pastor, counselor, or friend. It is very difficult to go through this on your own.

Rape and Sexual Assault

"Sex is the center of my life's problems. At sixteen I turned to the one person I could talk to, my boyfriend—and soon became pregnant. My parents forced me to go to an abortion 'doctor' in Tijuana. Immediately following the abortion the so-called doctor raped me. I was strapped down and coming out of a dose of anesthesia, unable to scream. It took twenty years and counseling to even talk about it."

Sexual assault is a sexual act done to a person against her (or his) will. This can range from undesired touch to nonconsensual penetration of any sort. *Rape* (in California) is defined as "genital penetration, however slight, under conditions of force, fear, coercion or incapacity to give consent."[5]

In 1993 there were 104,810 reported rapes in the United States.[6] Law enforcement officials know that rape is one of the most underreported of all crimes, primarily because of victims' fear of their attackers and embarrassment over what happened.

Sexual assault is *not* an act of sexual passion; it is a crime of violence and power. An assault is usually motivated by rage and anger, as well as the desire to dominate, control, humiliate, and degrade someone else. In at least 85% of cases, physical force and threats are used. Victims often become immobilized by fear, and 90% report fearing that they might be killed during the assault. Sixty to 80% of all rapes occur in a home by a friend, a neighbor, a relative, or an acquaintance of the victim. In 60% of rapes, the rapist is a date.

People of all ages, all physical appearances, all economic levels, all ethnic and educational backgrounds are victims of sexual assault. Men and boys can be sexually assaulted also, not just girls and women.

Perpetrators report that the feelings that drive the sexual assault are anger and hostility and have nothing to do with sexual arousal. Most admit afterward that they wanted to control, degrade, and feel their power over a woman.

Many rapists are married or in an ongoing sexual relationship with another partner. Most have histories of sexual abuse or sexual assault and act out their pain and anger with violence and assault. Although weapons are used in many sexual assaults, perpetrators are more likely to use threats, tricks, drugs, alcohol, and physical force.

Unfortunately, many women have experienced the betrayal of forced sex with their husband. Diana Russell reports that as many as one out of seven married women have been forced to have sex by their own husbands.[7] Evidence for this emerged in our study as well. One woman wrote:

"In twenty years of marriage my husband has used intimidation and coercion to get what he wants sexually. I've done things that have left me vomiting or scrubbing down in the shower. He doesn't fondle my breasts. He squeezes and twists my nipples to the point of pain. He considers sex his right and my duty—whatever he wants is okay. Period."

Another wrote:

"My first husband was a very violent man. I used sex to get him not to hit me. At night I would wake up to him having sex with me."

In every sense of the word, we consider such behaviors to be forms of rape. They are acts of sexual assault, not expressions of love. It is not surprising, therefore, that the consequences are as devastating as rape.

There is a fairly predictable emotional and behavioral pattern that follows being sexually assaulted. In phase one of the reaction the victim experiences intense emotions. She (or he) may feel depressed, cry frequently, be very moody, or become withdrawn. Many victims take excessive showers and have nightmares, flashbacks, and memory losses. Victims may feel fatigue or become hyperactive. They may have difficulty making decisions, sleeping, or concentrating, feel fear, guilt or anxiety, feel out of control, and believe they are going crazy. This phase may last a few days or up to six weeks. It ends when day-to-day functioning appears to have returned to normal.

Phase two lasts a few weeks to several years. The victim returns to school, work, and normal activities. She (or he) often says, "It's over; I've put it behind me." However, there is a lot of denial and rationalization of feeling tied to the assault. During this time victims frequently stop attending group or individual counseling and may choose to drop charges against the attacker. The victim's family and friends may feel relieved by this apparent satisfactory resolution of the assault.

For some this is the end of the issue. But for others, it is not. Phase three may come years later. Something happens to trigger a return of the intense emotions of phase one. Someone, for instance, may try to assault the victim again or may remind her (or him) of a previous abuser. The pain of phase one is revived. This phase may last for four years or longer. The victim becomes depressed and angry again, feels the need to talk about her (or his) feelings, and regains perspective on the impact of the original assault. The victim now needs to identify and work through unresolved problems such as damaged self-esteem, family struggles, and sexual problems.

Body Image Distortions

Despite all the information on health, fitness, and weight that tries to discredit our culture's emphasis on "thin is beautiful," most women believe they are ten to thirty pounds overweight. In a 1990 survey of over seven hundred women, 78% of the women polled saw themselves as overweight. That's nearly three times higher than the number of American women who actually are overweight according to medical findings. Less than 2% considered themselves underweight. Approximately one in five women consider themselves about right.[8]

About 25% of the women in that survey said that feeling fat sometimes caused them to avoid sex. In our study 27% of the women said that their weight affected their sexual desire, and 65% said other issues related to their bodies affected their sexual desire. (See chapter 4.)

A study at Princeton University indicates that "at puberty, girls' satisfaction with their bodies drops sharply, while boys remain reasonably content with the way their bodies are developing."[9] This problem seems to stay a lifetime! The following comments illustrate this phenomenon:

"I have a problem because of my teenage years—the premarital experiences and being exposed to the images of women in X-rated

*magazines—and now I am overweight. As a result I suffer from
low self-esteem and thus seem rigid when making love with my
husband.”*

*“While I am extremely fit, I suffer from low self-image because
I did not grow up to be the American ideal that is portrayed in
those glossy, airbrushed pages. Despite my husband’s comments
that he loves my body, I doubt it.”*

There is also a whole industry that feeds off this body image distortion. Walk up to any magazine rack and choose a handful of magazines. You will see titles like: “Snack More, Weigh Less”; “Look a
Size Smaller”; “Twenty-one Meals That Take Off Pounds”; “Look
Younger!”; “Fat to Firm in Five Weeks.” Women have a serious
problem with their body image. This is not to decry the importance
of health and fitness, but most women are overly concerned about
how they look, not how healthy they are. As one woman wrote:

*“If only I lost all the weight I gained from having the baby, then
I would feel sexier.”*

Her concern is not her health but her looks, and that is the
dilemma. If we aren’t hard enough on ourselves, some of us have
husbands, boyfriends, or family members who criticize our
appearance (not our lack of health). As one woman wrote:

*“I need to have my body accepted so that I can feel loved and
cared for by my husband. I want to feel safe.”*

Body image distortion can cause many of the traumas associated with inhibited sexuality including anorexia, bulimia, diet, and
exercise obsessions. In addition to inhibiting sexuality they are
also downright dangerous, as evidenced by how often models,
dancers, celebrities, and even ordinary teenagers are physically
harmed and often die from these disorders.

Quick fixes will not work. Just about every woman struggles with basic body image. However, serious body image distortions are difficult to eradicate and need the deeper exploration that only the Holy Spirit and professional treatment can provide.

God values you for who you are, not how you look. Your husband needs to join you in correcting our society's distortions of the "ideal body." This would not be so much of a problem if men understood this truth better, and if Christian men would lead the way in counteracting these cultural distortions.

> **God values you for who you are, not how you look.**

Abortion

Approximately 1.3 million women in the United States had an abortion in 1996. While initially many felt a sense of relief, long-term problems still persist. A national poll reports that at least 56% of women experience guilt over their decision.[10] One of the women in our study wrote:

> *"I believe the effects of my two abortions have grown over time. I had years of painful intercourse and decreased desire, but I never connected them to my abortions. When I rededicated my life to Christ and began to mature, then I recognized the abortions' effects."*

Postabortion distress is real. Symptoms can range from mild to full-blown post-traumatic stress disorder. There may be sleep problems, nightmares, repeated remembering of the abortion, avoidance of small children or pregnant mothers, a numbing or detachment from emotions associated with the abortion or with pregnancy and mothering, irritability, difficulty concentrating, decreased participation in activities previously enjoyed, eating problems, depression, and suicidal feelings.

Most of the women we surveyed reported experiencing symptoms the year following the abortion. Often symptoms surface long after the abortion. As one woman wrote to us:

> *"My abortion caused the breakup with my boyfriend of three and a half years because of the impact it had on me. I have recently begun to come to terms with what the abortion did to my life and that it was not something I really wanted to do. I have accepted Christ and am approaching my burden with the aid of Christ."*

Figure 9.3 presents the aftereffects of abortion both during the first year after the abortion and currently. Clearly guilt was the most significant immediate effect (52%) and with the passage of time drops by half. Symptoms changed after the first year, and many of the women seemed to have resolved their feelings and physical effects at the time they completed the questionnaire. Still, 26% continued to struggle with guilt feelings.

Sexually Transmitted Diseases (STDs)

It is estimated that there are thirty-three thousand new cases of sexually transmitted diseases every day in the United States. But 80% of those infected don't even know it. This leads to further acceleration and spreading of these diseases as more and more people change sex partners. There are currently more than twenty significant sexually transmitted diseases.[11] It is estimated that one in five Americans are infected with a viral STD, and bacterial STDs such as chlamydia, syphilis, and gonorrhea are also at very high levels. More than half of all STDs occur in those under age twenty-five.

Apparently many people still believe that if they get a sexually transmitted disease they will simply go to the doctor and

> **Women are more vulnerable to being infected with sexually transmitted diseases than men, and suffer more long-term damage than men do.**

EFFECTS OF ABORTION
Figure 9.3

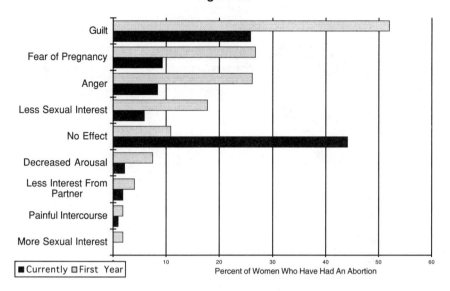

get a drug to fix the problem. But many STDs destroy future fertility and some STDs have been linked to cancer. There is no cure for AIDS or herpes. Gonorrhea and chlamydia can be treated by antibiotics but can leave scars that frequently require treatment in the future, and both can lead to infertility.

To what extent did the women in our study report STDs? Figure 9.4 shows the distribution. Thirteen percent of the women reported having contracted an STD at some time in their lives. This is a slightly lower percentage of women than in the *Sex in America* study.[12] There are probably many more women with STDs who don't know it because many STDs have very mild symptoms. (See Nine Most Common Sexually Transmitted Diseases sidebar.)

The three most common STDs reported in our study (nearly 4% each) were: genital warts, herpes, and chlamydia.

Sexually transmitted diseases can easily be passed on to children in childbirth. The only advice we can give you if you suspect an STD is to see your doctor and get medical treatment right away. Most of these diseases can be treated if caught early.

SEXUALLY TRANSMITTED DISEASES REPORTED
Figure 9.4

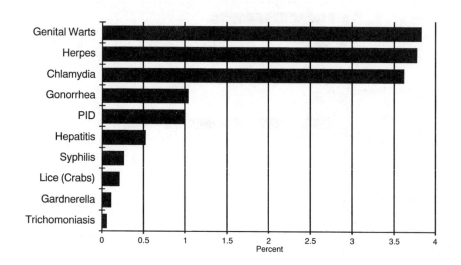

Is There Hope?

What hope is there for recovery from sexual trauma and the restoration of your sexuality? God wants to give us "beauty for ashes" (Isa. 61:3). Considering the destruction and overwhelming devastation caused by the trauma we are discussing, this promise of restoration that Jesus fulfills is the foundation of our hope.

Here are some suggestions for you as you begin your recovery.

1. Evaluate how your sexuality has been affected.

Sexual abuse has many effects and can express itself in a multitude of symptoms: depression, self-destructive behavior, sleeping disorders, and eating disorders.

Sexual abuse causes sexual problems as well. Some of the most common symptoms in women are: avoidance or fear of sex; negative reactions (such as anger, disgust, or guilt) with sexual touch; detachment during sex; disturbing sexual thoughts and images

Nine Most Common Sexually Transmitted Diseases

1. Vaginitis. Any vaginal infection or inflammation; it can be caused by yeast, trichomonas, or other bacteria. Vaginitis is not exclusively contracted through sexual contact. It is characterized by a change in vaginal discharge and can be accompanied by itching, burning when urinating, and pain during intercourse.

2. Chlamydia. Chlamydia is the most common of all the STDs. It is caused by a microparasite that infects the vagina, causing a vaginal discharge. Eighty percent of infected women have no symptoms until complications set in, such as pelvic inflammatory disease, which can lead to sterility.

3. Genital warts. Genital warts are caused by a virus similar to the one that causes common skin warts. It usually first appears as small bumps in the vagina, on the cervix, or around the anus with itching or burning. The symptoms do not show up until one to six months after having sex with an infected partner. They will not go away without treatment. There is a strong link between genital warts and cancer of the cervix.

4. Herpes. Herpes is caused by a virus. It is highly contagious. The infection appears as cold sores and fever blisters on the mouth, face, and lips, or sores and blisters around the genitals. Usually the first sign of infection (a kiss or touch will pass it on) is itching, burning, or tingling in the genitals, then the sores and blisters appear. Symptoms appear two to thirty days after sex; some people have no symptoms.

5. NGU (nongonococcal or nonspecific urethritis). NGU is caused by several organisms. Symptoms include a burning while urinating or vaginal discharge. But most women show no symptoms. Symptoms show up one to three weeks after having sex. NGU can lead to more serious infections and cause infertility.

6. Pubic lice (crabs). These are parasites that attach themselves to pubic hair. They can cause intense itching. They must be treated with a medicated shampoo (not regular washing).

7. Syphilis (the pox). A bacterial infection that causes heart disease, brain damage, blindness, and death. Sores show up one to twelve weeks after having sex. The sores go away, but the syphilis remains. Later a rash appears on your body, accompanied by flulike feelings.

8. Gonorrhea (clap or drip). Gonorrhea is a bacterial infection. Most women have no symptoms. If symptoms appear, it will be two to twenty-one days after having had sex. Symptoms include a thick yellow or white discharge from the vagina, burning, or pain when urinating or having a bowel movement. Gonorrhea can cause more serious infections that can result in infertility, heart problems, skin disease, arthritis, and blindness.

9. AIDS (acquired immune deficiency syndrome). Symptoms show up several months to several years after contact with HIV, the virus that causes AIDS. AIDS is spread by sharing IV needles and during sex (anal, oral, or regular intercourse). Symptoms include flulike feelings that don't go away, weight loss, diarrhea, white spots in the mouth, and purple bumps on the skin and inside the mouth, nose, or rectum.

during sex or at other times; compulsive sexual behaviors; avoidance or sabotaging intimate relationships; pain during intercourse; numbing of all feelings during sex; and loathing your body.

These symptoms can show up immediately after a sexual assault or long after the abuse. They can emerge slowly or appear suddenly. Usually they don't go away by ignoring them. There are no formulas, quick fixes, or easy answers—just intense therapeutic work and a ministry of prayer.

2. Resolve to pursue your sexual healing.

Sexual healing takes time and requires a lot of hard work. It can be emotionally and physically draining, and also very frustrating. It is, therefore, understandable why some women are afraid to pursue healing, whether through counseling or prayer. *When* to embark on the deeper journey of healing is your choice. We encourage you to begin the healing process slowly and gently.

3. Get help.

Getting help is the gateway to healing. Professional help from someone who is trained to work with sexual abuse survivors and sexual issues is the most effective and efficient way to get beyond your trauma.

In addition, join or start a support group. There are recovery organizations readily available, such as Adults Molested as Children and Co-Dependents Anonymous. Also there are recovery groups available through Christian counseling centers or churches. Ask your pastor regarding the various resources available in your area. Also, ask your family and friends to commit to praying and supporting you through your recovery.

4. Redeeming your sexual attitudes.

Sexual trauma distorts sexuality. So even when your emotions are fully recovered, you may still find that your attitudes interfere with your full functioning. When sexuality becomes distorted, we lose the true meaning of sex as God intended it. An example of how sexual attitudes can be distorted is reflected poignantly in the following comment:

> *"To me sex is filthy dirty. Sex is made for men to enjoy. Sex is used to get love, but you never get it. Sex is the only way to have a child. Sex is awful. I'd rather clean toilets. Sex is embarrassing."*

Wendy Maltz, a therapist who has worked extensively with sexual trauma victims, has contrasted healthy sexual attitudes with attitudes distorted by abuse.[13] Some of these differences are:

Unhealthy Sexual Attitudes	Healthy Sexual Attitudes
Sex is an obligation.	Sex is a choice.
Sex is addictive.	Sex is a natural drive.
Sex is hurtful.	Sex is nurturing, healing.
Sex is a condition for receiving love.	Sex is an expression of love.
Sex is secretive.	Sex is private.
Sex is exploitative.	Sex is respectful.
Sex benefits one person.	Sex is mutual.
Sex is unsafe.	Sex is safe.
Sex is power over someone.	Sex is empowering.
Sex is evil.	Sex is a gift from God.

We have emphasized frequently that the key sex organ is the brain because this is where sexual attitudes and beliefs reside. We can only reclaim the true meaning of sex by the "renewing" of our minds (see Rom. 12:2). To enjoy a healthy sex life, you must give high priority to undoing the damage caused by sexual trauma.

Points to Remember

1. All forms of sexual trauma can significantly damage a woman's sexuality.

2. The sexual molestation of a child is the most despicable and heinous of crimes against the innocent. Touching and physical violation of a child constitutes molestation. Jokes, innuendos, and sexual suggestiveness can also be damaging.

3. The Christian church is not free of the scourge of child molestation. We need to educate our children as to what constitutes molestation and give them the courage to speak out when it happens to them.

4. Pornography represents the most common form of sexual abuse of women today. It fosters many other types of sexual trauma by distorting sexuality in men.

5. Rape and sexual assault are crimes motivated by rage and anger (not sexual passion).

6. Body image distortions, abortion, and sexually transmitted diseases are all traumatic to a woman's sexuality, and help for these should be sought as soon as possible after they become evident.

7. It is God's purpose to redeem and restore every area of life that gets damaged. Our sexuality can be healed after sexual trauma.

Chapter Ten

Sexuality and the Single Life

"I charge you . . . do not stir up nor awaken love until it pleases."
—*Song of Solomon 8:4 NKJV*

The narrative responses we received from single women were poignant and moving. While many have adjusted to their singleness, there was a distinct tone of disappointment in some of their comments. This chapter tells their story.

The singles who participated in our study were diverse in their responses. There were those who were comfortable and content without sex in their lives. They neither desired it nor felt any sense of loss without it. Others deliberately chose a celibate lifestyle even though they had strong sexual feelings. They felt some greater purpose was being fulfilled, and believed that God had blessed them with the gift of celibacy.

Some women were frustrated about the lack of opportunity to express their sexuality through an intimate relationship with a man. They had not yet found the right man and prayed that one day they would. And there were those who revealed remarkable and graceful acceptance of being single. They were disappointed, yes, but accepted their singleness, focusing on growing in all areas of their life and serving others. As a result of having been deeply abused or emotionally hurt in previous sexual relationships, there were some who chose to be celibate.

The most profound information gleaned from our study on singles came from the narrative responses to our open-ended question: Any comments? We gave no guidelines and intentionally invited a wide range of responses. We wanted to hear whatever was on their minds. These responses speak for themselves, out of the hearts of single Christian women from across the country.

The most effective way to tell their story is simply to present their comments verbatim. Since we cannot print them all, we have arranged them along thematic lines and have chosen representative quotes. Our hope is that the reader will be inspired to avoid making the mistakes described in the quotes. In particular, pay attention to their comments on premarital sex.

These stories are all very special to us because they are full of wisdom and moved us deeply. Read for yourself:

"Since I am single and don't believe in sex outside of marriage, I have no sex in my life. It isn't that important to me. I have a very busy life and have always thought sex was overrated. Listening to all the married people I know, it seems always to bring more trouble than pleasure."

"It [sex] is something I would like to have as an expression of a loving, caring, committed partnership. While I have been celibate for the past six years, sex is still important for me. Sadly, so far the only choices presented to me are either a potentially painful, restrictive relationship, or celibacy. Neither is necessarily good, but we live in a world where women, more often than not, are given two or more painful choices and asked to choose out of a starvation diet with discernment. Can't win really!"

"I am content not being in a relationship and not having sex because I am not married. I take it [sex] very seriously and believe it is an important element in a healthy relationship. But it should never become the main focus in any relationship. Aside from physical pleasure, in the times I have had sex it has often

been an avenue of intimacy with a man whereby he will open up and be emotionally uninhibited. However, the spiritual consequences and morning after guilt aren't worth the brief moment of pleasure. My biggest challenge is finding a real Christian man who honors God's Word and respects my desire to wait for sex until we get married. A tall order!"

"Personally, as a single person it is difficult to come to terms with my own desires and the inability to explore those with a partner. Although I believe it is possible to live without being sexually active, I so much want to believe God intends it for everyone. Sex in a fallen world is a mystery still for many of us. I think that masturbation is a small gift to cope with such desires."

"Sex is a dilemma to me. It has become basically unimportant to me because I have chosen to sublimate it in my life. I believe sex is for marriage. I'm not married nor have ever been, so most expressions of my sexuality have been in illegitimate or even immoral situations. These escapades have resulted in stress, guilt, dishonesty, and ultimately the deterioration of the relationship. My sexual nature has often seemed to alienate me from myself, from my moral and relational self. I mostly try to ignore my sexual thoughts. I am not a prude, but I suppose I am a woman in denial!"

"I have been celibate for the past five and a half years while recovering from my painful past, including sexual promiscuity while trying to find myself. Finally, at age fifty, I dedicated my life to Jesus Christ. I, like many other women, have been looking for love in all the wrong places! I am now desirous of having a dedicated Christian partner to share my life, love, laughter, common goals, and sex with. In the past I made poor choices, but now I am trusting God to help me make better choices."

Trends in Singleness

More and more adults are spending a greater amount of their adult life as singles. While in 1954 only 17% of adults in the United States were single, today 49% of adult women are single.

There are several reasons for this trend. One reason is the rising age of marriage, which means many women are single for much longer. While 90% of us will eventually marry, the age of first marriage has risen considerably. The age at which people first marry is now the highest since 1890, when the United States government first started measuring marriages.[1] Other reasons for the rising age of marriage are: putting off marriage until they have completed college or career training, wanting to experience life first, and being afraid of making a lifelong commitment.

Is this a desirable trend? One woman in the study didn't think so and wrote the following:

> *"I believe that we have missed the mark in some ways as Christians by getting married later in life than we used to. It seems that in Bible times people got married as teenagers, when their sexual desire was strongest. These days people wait until they are older believing they have to be mature to make such an important decision—and also able to support themselves. This is great except when it comes to sex. To be obedient to God's Word it seems we have to suppress our sexual desires until we are married."*

Another, and more important, reason for the rising age of marriage is the loss of sexual morals. Marriage is no longer seen as the prerequisite for sexual activity. So the urge to establish a home and a secure sexual partner is no longer there. While this is very true for non-Christians, it is, unfortunately, also becoming true for some Christians.

For men in particular, marriage isn't a high priority. "Why buy a cow when you can get milk for free?" is a statement of marriage philosophy for many! Some observers see a definite trend. Men are postponing marriage because they would rather avoid commitment. They see no advantage to marriage when they can get all their sexual needs met without the burden of marital responsibility.

Singleness has also lost the social stigma it once had. While this is a plus in that American society is adjusting to the idea that many actually prefer being single, cohabitation has become the replacement for marriage. This is a problem, as we will see.

Many women are single again after years of marriage, due to the rise in the divorce rate. Some remarry, some don't, but single-parent homes are the fastest growing family group in our society.

The Struggle

Most Christian women, we believe, appreciate that the ideal goal is to stay sexually pure until marriage. Achieving this is a challenge. We don't want to downplay how difficult it is at times to stick to this ideal. Listen to how single women described the struggle:

"I am a single Christian woman and find it extremely difficult to abstain from sex. I'm in the prime of my sexual life. Abstaining from premarital sex seems almost impossible!"

"The most upsetting part of the questionnaire was that I was forced to face up to the fact that I've had three sex partners in the last six months—fifteen in my whole life. Although I feel closer in my walk with Christ, I realize that I am coming to grips with my age. I have a fear of being undesirable. I have not come to a place of being comfortably single."

"I have been sexually abstinent for seven years. I intend my next sexual partner to be my husband. However, waiting is not always easy, and I've often thought of having an affair just to satisfy my sexual drive. So far I'm winning the battle!"

"I am thirty-two and a virgin who continues to wait to have sex in marriage. I have difficulty knowing what to do with my sexual desires. I often just pray to God. My commitment to remain sexually pure until I get married is a tribute to my parents raising me in a godly home as well as nurturing a personal relationship with Jesus Christ."

A particularly difficult time sexually is the waiting period between engagement and marriage. The temptation is to believe that you are almost married, so what difference does it make? One young respondent expressed it this way:

"As a single Christian woman who is engaged to be married, I find my biggest spiritual struggle to be with my sexuality. I find it so difficult to hold back from sexual activities knowing that in only a few months it will be pure and right to express my love in ways that are not right at this time. But I am determined to wait and know that God will bless us for waiting."

Never Married Singles—Their Struggle

Where and how do never married single women get their romantic needs met? Figure 10.1 shows the results. The most common response was daydreaming (36%), followed closely by movies (29%), and my partner (27%). Only 7% reported that they have no need for romance.

We asked the women in our study who had never been married whether and at what age they first had intercourse. Nearly 75% of our respondents have had sexual intercourse.

Seventeen percent of singles reported that they were having sex. How regularly? Figure 10.2 shows the frequency with which they engaged in sex. The most common frequency for those never married singles who were having sex was similar to married women, between once and three times per week. Eighty-three percent said that they were not having sex.

HOW ARE ROMANTIC NEEDS OF SINGLES MET?
Figure 10.1

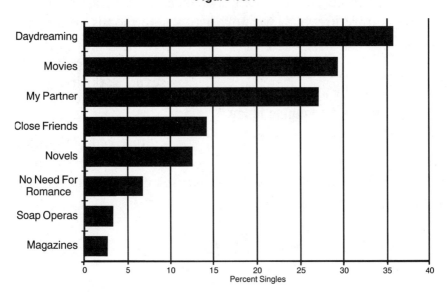

HOW OFTEN DO NEVER MARRIED SINGLES HAVE SEX?
Figure 10.2

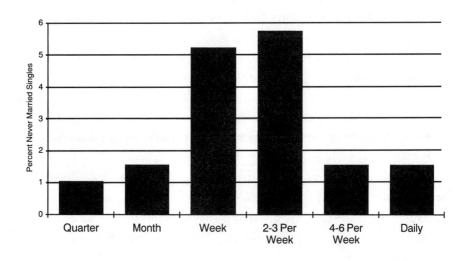

We share this information not to be critical of singles. Refraining from premarital sex is a challenge from start to finish.

The culture in which we now live, where morals are relative and an intrusion into our pleasure-seeking lifestyles, goes against pursuing the goal of sexual purity. The deterioration of the moral attitudes of our culture only intensifies the struggle for purity. Everything to do with sex is slowly becoming amoral. If you believe the media, sex is just a game and all can play it, making up their own rules.

> **Living a sexually abstinent lifestyle is a challenge for singles today.**

Divorced and Widowed Singles—Their Struggle

"After my divorce I was determined to experience other men—and I did—much to my great dismay and disappointment. That was before my commitment to Christ."

"I was married for eleven years and had sex every other day. It has been torture to try and remain celibate, but I believe it is the Lord's will for the unmarried. I don't like celibacy, but it has given me the opportunity to deepen my intimate relationship with God. Spiritual intimacy is very satisfying and peacefully safe. I am now able to wait patiently for the relationship God will lead me to."

If never married singles struggle with their sexual needs, imagine how much more those women who have become accustomed to having sex regularly must struggle.

How sexually active were divorced singles in our sample? Of the total divorced singles, 31% said they were currently having sex. Therefore about one in three divorced women are sexually active. This is twice the incidence of never married singles who are sexually active.

Unfortunately, we did not have enough widows who participated in our study for valid statistical analysis, so we cannot report if and to what extent they were different.

Waiting to Give "The Gift"

As we have said before, sexuality includes all of our attitudes and feelings about: being a woman, having a woman's body, flirting and relationships with the opposite sex, affection, and genital contact. Every woman begins to be aware of and explore her sexuality while she is a child and adolescent—and single. This exploration of sexuality includes the decision to wait or not wait to participate in genital sex. Waiting or not waiting to have sexual intercourse impacts marriage later on. If you are still a virgin and wondering if "waiting" has any value, pay careful attention to these stories:

"Since you can only give it once, I decided at an early age to give 'the gift' only to the man who would love me for the rest of my life. I was blessed to marry a man with the same goal, and now coming upon our one-year anniversary we cherish this gift. I am saddened, and even angered, by the lies society tells about premarital sex. It is stealing a beautiful experience from so many young people. Waiting was one of the best choices I have ever made in my life!"

"I had strong moral values to be a virgin when I was married. The only sexual experiences that I have had, from kissing to intimacy, have been with my husband. The best thing we ever did for ourselves was to not have intercourse before marriage!"

"The fact that my husband and I were both virgins when we met has played a big part in our high level of sexual satisfaction. We have no one to compare with or be compared against—and therefore to each other we are the best."

"My husband and I grew up believing that abstaining from sex was obeying God. When our honeymoon night came, we both agreed the excitement from waiting for each other and learning about each other's sexuality was very gratifying. We knew we were pure before God and each other, and felt God would bless us for following His commands for marriage."

We don't want to paint an impractical picture from just these few comments. There is no guarantee that just because you marry as a virgin all will be bliss. Important as it is, virginity by itself does not guarantee everlasting sexual ecstasy. Behind these stories are also marital challenges, and even sexual difficulties, that had to be overcome. However, again and again these women expressed their gratefulness for the wisdom that waiting is better than not waiting.

We did not receive a comment that hinted that waiting to have sex was detrimental to a subsequent marriage. The peace of mind in those who were obedient to what they believed to be God's way is overwhelmingly evident. In addition, those who waited could look forward to reaping the benefits of not having inherited a fear that some dormant disease would rise up from the ashes of their previous sexual involvement. They also didn't have to live in the shadow of comparisons with previous lovers.

Were married women the only ones to value abstinence before marriage? No. Many single women also expressed their commitment to waiting and gave reasons for their determination. One young woman wrote:

"I am young, not married, and have no serious boyfriend. I hope that when I do find the boyfriend I am looking for I will be able to stay sex-free until marriage. This is a major goal for me!"

Many of the single women in our study echoed the goal of staying sex-free until marriage. We need to keep raising this as a standard worth aspiring to. While it is God's design that sex be reserved for marriage, there are many other advantages to abstinence as well, as we will cover in this chapter. These advantages need to be promoted in our Christian communities.

Natural Consequences of Not Waiting

God designed creation to work a certain way, and when we violate this design there are definite, though sometimes unforeseen, consequences. It is a fact of human existence that we reap what we sow. God planned this law into our sexual behavior as well.

God's boundary of reserving sex for marriage is intended for our own good. He instructs us over and over in the Bible to keep ourselves pure and to avoid sexual immorality (see Col. 3:5; 1 Cor. 10:8; Eph. 5:3; 1 Thess. 4:3). These boundaries are designed to protect us from the negative consequences of sex outside of marriage and to provide us with true, healthy, and long-lasting intimacy in marriage. One woman wrote:

> *"I wish I had known Jesus in my childhood years or teenage years. I could have known His plan for sex and love and one partner. The Lord has such a plan, and there are natural consequences for going outside that plan. They are emotional, mental, and physical."*

The painful consequences for those women who weren't able or chose not to wait to have sex seemed to cluster into four categories:

1. Regret, guilt, and emotional distress

2. Unplanned pregnancies, abortion, or adoption

3. Marital and sexual problems

4. Sexually transmitted diseases

Let us allow the personal stories of the women in this study to illustrate each of these consequences.

1. Regret, guilt, and emotional distress

"I have had over six hundred partners in my lifetime—and I regret every one of them!"

"Having sex before marriage with someone different caused me tremendous guilt when I married my husband. We did not have sex before our marriage, but my past was a barrier for me to overcome. Now, after my first baby, I have almost no desire."

"I truly wish that I had never had sex before marriage. I became a Christian soon after getting married. My virginity would have been the greatest gift I could have given to my husband."

"All through high school I was determined to keep myself specifically for marriage. After we became engaged, my husband and I had intercourse close to the wedding date. We both regretted it after we were married and wish we had waited."

"My husband and I had sex once before we got married. We carried guilt for a long time about sex before marriage. It is sad that we had to find out the hard way that the greatest blessing comes when you wait. This is why God wants us to save sex for marriage."

"As a married adult, I now wish I had had less sexual partners in my life, that I didn't give myself away so easily. I attribute my having done this to my lack of respect for myself sexually."

"At sixteen I was forced to have sex with a boy I went out with. After that, I felt like it didn't matter anymore. I felt ruined! Over the next few years I had several different partners, leaving me feeling guilty each time."

Years later, these women still see their sexual choices outside of marriage as a mistake that produced regret, guilt, and sadness. Their stories reaffirm the idea that sexual sin is different from other sins. When we engage in sex outside of marriage, we violate our entire selves: mind, body, emotions, and spirit. Sex outside of marriage is disobedience not just to God's laws but to the integrity of our whole being.

Sex unites two into one. So, when we have sex, our body is saying, "We are becoming one," but the reality is that if you are not married you cannot "become one" in the deepest sense of its meaning. The sexual act is incongruent, causing a division within yourself. This internal confusion creates emotional and relational turmoil. Only in marriage can we have intercourse and remain whole.

> **The problem with sex outside of marriage is that it does not allow us to say with our whole being what we are saying with our bodies.**

2. Unwanted pregnancies, abortion, and adoption

One of the serious consequences of sex outside of marriage is the risk of pregnancy, which can result in forced marriage, single parenthood, abortion, or adoption. No birth control method is flawless. It's a challenge to avoid pregnancy even when you are married. It is naive to think pregnancy can be avoided outside of marriage. Passion can make us careless, and our birth control method can fail.

Listen to what these women said:

> *"I've had several abortions previously. My husband and I struggled with passion when we were engaged and managed not to have sex until our wedding night. After we married, my passion and desire for sex virtually came to a halt. In spite of multiple layers of healing regarding my abortions, I believe they are still a blockage to my relationship with the Lord and with my husband."*

> *"The breakup with my boyfriend of 3 1/2 years was caused by the impact my abortion had on me. I have recently begun to come to terms with the impact it had on my life and that it was not*

*something I really wanted to do. I have accepted Christ into my
life and am approaching my burden with His aid."*

*"It is sad that I feel I have to stay in the closet because I gave up
a son to be adopted. To talk about it seems less socially acceptable
and less understood than if I said I had an abortion. I gave him
up because I loved him and felt it was best for him. But I still feel
guilt and fear and am physically and emotionally shut down. My
emotional state of mind very much affects my physical drive."*

Dr. Hart recalls a patient he saw at the beginning of his career as
a clinical psychologist. It is one of his saddest cases. As a teenager she
became pregnant in a casual relationship. Her parents insisted she
give the baby up for adoption. Years later, she was married and in a
deep depression. Her marriage was disintegrating, and her career was
already destroyed.

What caused this depression? She had discovered she couldn't
have any more children. She became obsessed over the child she
had given up for adoption, a boy, and tracked him down, spending
hours every day waiting in a park near where the boy lived so she
could watch him play. She never approached him. But the pain
of not being able to love her own child was destroying her.
Through therapy and prayer she was able to achieve a measure
of healing.

God's plan for sex prevents the situations that can devastate us.

3. Marital and sexual problems

*"I believe that the greatest factor contributing to our sexual
relationship is that we both had a lot of premarital sex, which has
distracted from the joy of experiencing sex exclusively with each
other. Tremendous guilt and lack of interest pervaded our honeymoon. I have struggled with being jealous of his previous lovers.
It is only now after eight years that I believe we are beginning to
get past that."*

"I strongly believe that if I had waited until marriage to have sexual intercourse my marital relationship would be more satisfying and fulfilling."

"When I married my husband, he was a virgin, and I wasn't. I am still frustrated to this day that I compare him with my previous lovers and want him to do things I did in previous relationships. I am plagued with guilt because of my premarital sex."

"I have been married for a few years now and am fairly happy. However, I can't forget a previous lover I had. I miss him very much. I often think of him when my husband and I are making love, wishing I could be with him again. I know it's wrong. I won't act on my feelings, but I can't get him out of my mind."

These women, along with others, confirm that many of their current marital difficulties are the result of premarital sexual activities. Apart from their ongoing guilt, they fear being compared to other women and comparing their husband to previous lovers. They were jealous of their partner's previous sexual partners and hate the flashbacks to earlier sexual experiences. The emotional connections with previous lovers interfere with their current sex lives and attempts to build intimacy.

It seems to us that our culture has not sufficiently communicated these devastating effects. Hopefully, readers will choose to benefit from the experiences these women shared.

4. Sexually transmitted diseases

One of the many devastating consequences of being involved sexually before marriage is the inevitability of contracting a sexually transmitted disease (STD). We have already discussed STDs in our chapter on sexual trauma (chapter 9). In this chapter, we want to provide a brief overview of the problem as it affects adult singles.

STDs are the most common reportable communicable diseases in the United States, which has the highest STD rate of any developed country in the world. One reason for this is the early age of sexual intercourse. By the twelfth grade, 70% of Americans have had intercourse, with 40% having had multiple partners. And the greatest paradox of all about our culture is that it is very concerned about STDs, but not as concerned about preventing premarital sex.

The dramatic spread of STDs has even greater implications. Treatment-resistant strains are emerging all the time. AIDS is, of course, the most feared, but it pales in significance when the entire group of STDs is considered. According to the Medical Institute for Sexual Health (MISH), nearly five million Americans visit a public STD clinic each year, with many others seeing either a private doctor or none at all. One-third of all sexually active teens are already infected with chlamydia.

One very strong medical reason for abstinence in the teenage years is that teenage girls are more likely to become infected with an STD than an older woman. Researchers estimate that a sexually active fifteen-year-old has a one in eight chance of developing pelvic inflammatory disease (PID), while a twenty-four-year-old has a one in eighty chance.

> **One very strong medical reason for abstinence in the teenage years is that teenage girls are more likely to become infected with an STD than an older woman.**

How frequent were STDs in our sample? See chapter 9, Figure 9.4. In our sample, 10% of sexually active singles reported having an STD within the past year, 30% within their lifetime. There was a clear association between number of partners and percentage of women contracting an STD. Only one case of HIV and one of syphilis was reported.

We encourage singles to consider very carefully the risks involved in having sex outside of marriage, especially with multiple partners. It can ruin your chances of marriage or safe, healthy childbearing if you acquire an STD. Catherine tells of one woman in counseling who had an STD. When she finally told the man she loved and was hoping to marry, he decided that the consequences for their marriage were too difficult for him to live with. He withdrew from the relationship.

"But can't I take precautions to avoid catching something?" There are no foolproof, absolutely safe methods of prevention. Condoms break, leak, and slip off. Lovers lie about whether or not they have an STD and about the number of previous partners. Herpes can be dormant for years before breaking out. The risks are enormous.

Redeeming Sexual Purity

Whether one is single by accident or choice, divorced or widowed, there is one common struggle: How do you remain sexually responsible to your own convictions as well as to what you believe to be God's expectations? As we have learned from the personal stories of these women, this is not an easy struggle. You need help from outside yourself. What follows is a summary of our recommendations for those who want to make sexual purity a serious goal.

All sexual intercourse outside of marriage is, in biblical terms, immoral (Heb. 12:4; 1 Thess. 4:3). We hope that our readers understand this, but we are not so naive as to think that all who read this book will agree with us. Our advice that follows is based on the assumption that sex is to be enjoyed within marriage alone. If it is not palatable to all our readers then we hope that you will be gracious enough to read what follows. Perhaps you will find something helpful in this closing section.

Virginity Isn't a Dirty Word

We assert that sexual purity is God's design for us. What really is the greatest motivator that will keep you from doing what you know you shouldn't be doing or that you desire not to do?

Are conservative Christians the only ones who believe in abstinence until marriage? No, they are not. Even non-Christians are figuring out that *abstinence* isn't a dirty word. Virginity has been rediscovered as a better alternative while unmarried. Let us cite an example.

Congress, desperate to deal with the alarming rise in teenage pregnancy, is making a major shift in sex education. They are betting on a new abstinence program, and they're putting their money where their mouth is. Last year's welfare law guaranteed $250 million in abstinence education grants. The other programs that offer birth control information haven't worked. These programs do not help reduce teen pregnancy. So Congress is taking this new approach, advertising with big billboards that read: *Virgin—Teach Your Kids It's Not a Dirty Word.*

Therefore, abstinence is now becoming acceptable as a solution to some of our most pressing social problems. But it is also the solution to our most urgent personal dilemmas. Many of you are probably saying: "But I've already blown it. My sex life is a mess. I've gone too far." We want to make it clear: There is never a point where one cannot start over again. Life in Christ offers "new beginnings." "Therefore, if anyone is in Christ, he [or she] is a new creation; old things have passed away; behold, all things have become new" (2 Cor. 5:17 NKJV). *Becoming a "new creation" means that your sexual past is behind you, like all your sins and failings.*

For those of our readers who are still virgins and wondering how this discussion affects them, let us say that you need to take steps now to protect yourself for the temptations that lie ahead. Our suggestions are as valid for you as for any other singles.

How can you redeem your sexuality? Here, in summary, are our suggestions:

1. **Make your relationship with Jesus Christ the most important one in your life, and determine to live according to His ways.**

Some of the women in this study reported very traumatic past sexual experiences before they became Christians. It was their relationship with Jesus and a commitment to His ways that were the turning point in their recovery. Their faith now keeps them sexually pure. Listen to these testimonies:

"I wish I would have waited to have sex and that I had had a close relationship with our Lord. Now I believe everybody should wait until they get married. I have had problems from starting so young—and by not always having the Lord in my life."

"My lifestyle changed after I became a Christian. I never felt loved until I met Jesus. I was so upset when I realized that my abortions were murder—I think I wore out God confessing guilt before I realized His forgiveness. The Scriptures on purity and marriage mean so much to me. God gave us sex to bond in marriage."

"My teenage years were times of promiscuity. I became a Christian at seventeen and saw God work miracles to change me. I am convinced that if the Lord had not intervened at that time, I would have continued a very destructive path sexually. Praise God for His healing and forgiveness."

"Before I became a Christian I had many partners, and my sex drive was almost all-consuming. After five years with Jesus those old feelings and patterns subsided. My husband and I both had bad experiences sexually before we met the Lord, and we are very grateful for each other. He is the first human I've ever been able to be intimate with."

There are many others who have a relationship with Jesus or have been in the Christian church for a while who are still struggling with sexual immorality for a variety of reasons. It is important that we all come to terms with God's design for our lives.

Although His plan might be difficult to follow, ultimately it is the best for us. We did not encounter any women in our study who complained that following God's way ruined their lives. Quite the contrary!

Right choices can be difficult. But from reading the stories of so many women, we are convinced that the struggle to choose self-control and trusting God's way more than your own immediate desires seem nothing compared to the regret and consequences of choosing to go your own way and fulfill your own desires. It is important to remember the bigger picture.

2. Claim the grace and forgiveness of God to cleanse and heal your past experiences.

Don't live in the past. Don't allow your past to haunt you. Don't punish yourself for any of your failures. Self-punishment invalidates the work of Christ on the cross. You can't accept God's forgiveness and keep punishing yourself at the same time. It's one or the other.

Many women in the study shared how they have received God's forgiveness and are learning to forgive themselves.

> *"I continue to struggle with guilt because of having premarital sex and one affair. I often wonder if my husband thinks about it and still looks down on me for it. I know God has forgiven me, but I am having trouble forgiving myself, even though those experiences happened ten and sixteen years ago."*

> *"I am ashamed of my behavior in the past, and it was hard to see myself reflected while doing this survey. Praise God He has washed me clean!"*

No matter what you have done in the past (even as recent as today), God has provided a sacrifice so you can be forgiven. Once you repent, you are cleansed and redeemed. This is the glory of the Christian walk. Receiving God's forgiveness and healing brings hope and the incentive for a new beginning. It is not merely "turning over a new leaf" but being cleansed and free from the past, receiving power to overcome your struggle.

There are those of you who didn't have a choice in staying sexually pure—sex was forced on you! As one woman wrote after being forced to have sex, she felt ruined. *So what the heck,* she thought, *it doesn't matter anymore. I might as well just keep going.* You are never ruined beyond hope—not if you belong to God and come to Him.

3. Practice virginity now.

You will never be able to take back your past sexual actions and experiences. However, with confidence you can be cleansed and your sexual purity restored. Remember that in a new relationship you have the opportunity to choose to be sexually pure. One of the blessings of the grace of God is that you can have a new beginning in your life, even regarding your virginity. With God's forgiveness undergirding you, you have the possibility of entering marriage in the new purity that God promises to you.

> **One of the blessings of the grace of God is that you can have a new beginning in your life, even regarding your virginity.**

"I've always felt very moral, but lost my virginity while I was drunk. All three one-time events were while I was drunk, and my one-year sexual relationship started with drinking. This saddens my heart. I know better now and trust Jesus Christ to make me pure as snow for my 'someday' husband."

"The change in my sexuality and self-worth occurred after age nineteen. I began to work through the guilt and shame from previous sexual relationships and to grow in my faith in God. I'm so glad that I abstained from sex from then on until I got married."

"I now believe that you should not have sex until you are married. When I had sex with my boyfriend of two years I tried to stop. He was a bad influence and pushed and pushed. I ended up getting pregnant, so we had to get married. He was an alcoholic and finally left. I recently remarried. We did everything right (no sex), and it has turned out wonderful."

4. Practice chastity now.

Just as you can reclaim your virginity by "starting over again," so you can reclaim your commitment to sexual abstinence now.

Unfortunately, the exquisitely radiant word *chastity* has lost its appeal and is mocked in our society today. Just ask teenage girls what their friends have to say about it. *Chastity* needs to be defined. It needs to be resurrected because it is at the heart of what it means to be sexually pure.

Chastity is the absence of genital interaction. It is purity in conduct and intention. It is not the absence of sexuality, or sexual feelings. These remain intact. It is also not just for priests or nuns. Chastity is to be the goal of all who are not married and, at times, those who are married.

Chastity is not the suppression of sexuality. Your body and your hormones will want to do their thing and there is little you can do to stop them. The whole concept of chastity only makes sense in the presence of a raging sex drive. If you have no drive whatsoever, *chastity* is not the right term. You can only pledge to control that which is trying to dominate you. To be chaste one has to be sexually responsive in the first place.

Sexual sin, as with all sin, is all about the choices we make. Chastity, then, is a set of choices that one determines to make. For nuns and priests it is a vow they take. There is no reason why it cannot be a vow for us also. The choices we must make all relate to how we will express our sexuality. Chastity may be temporary, as when a spouse is seriously ill or absent on a trip for a period of time. It is also temporary for the teenager who wants to wait until she marries and give herself as a gift to her husband. Or it may be permanent, as when a woman decides that marriage is not her chosen lifestyle.

Chastity is voluntary. It is an act of one's will, and it will only work if you freely choose it. The decision may be motivated by moral or biblical reasons, but it can also have a personal or altruistic rationale. Dr. Hart knows a missionary who chose a celibate life in order to fulfill her calling to go to the mission field. The man dating her had no interest in missionary work, so what else could she do? She chose to be true to her calling.

If you decide to set aside genital sexuality until you are ready for marriage then you cannot engage in other activities that lead to sex either. No French kissing, genital fondling, oral sex, or "fooling around" to test how far you can go. You cannot court temptation and try to believe you are living a chaste life. Listen to what one single woman in the study had to say about how early sexual activity only set her up for later frustration:

> *"I am single—a thirty-six-year-old virgin with a strong sex drive. I became a Christian at sixteen and am thankful that my early conversion has protected me from immoral sexual activity. I have felt great sexual frustration as a single Christian. I have Christian single friends who struggle with this as well. Perhaps earlier sexual experiences, masturbation, and heavy petting as a younger teenager opened the door to this struggle."*

5. God has a plan of prevention.

It is important for us to take steps to prevent foolish mistakes. Here are our suggestions for developing your "sexual wisdom" so that you won't make these mistakes:

Work hard at developing self-control. There is nothing that can replace good, old-fashioned self-control when it comes to sexual temptation. If you *put yourself* in a compromising situation don't be surprised if God doesn't send an earthquake to shake up that compromising situation. He expects you to use common sense and exercise self-control.

"Anything, but don't tell me self-control!" you say? Ah, you want a magic pill—the easy way out! God doesn't dispense magic pills. He gives us His Spirit, which empowers us to have self-control.

So what do we mean by self-control? God gives us our sexual drive and also states the boundaries to express it in. The emphasis is not on trying to control *ourselves* but on allowing the Holy Spirit to control us. Mark Abbot, in an article entitled *Monks and Maniacs Need Not Apply*, states: "Biblical self-control is not winding ourselves up in knots or trying to make ourselves do something or avoid something. Biblical self-control is being an open channel for the Spirit's power to work in us."

> The emphasis is not on trying to control *ourselves*, but on allowing the Holy Spirit to control us.

Understand Nongenital Intimacy. We close this chapter by pointing out that all of us, not just singles, need to differentiate our intimacy needs from our sexual needs. These two basic needs easily get confused.

God has given us a desire for emotional closeness. We need community and intimacy about as much as we need air and water. The drive for intimacy is good. How we try to get this need met is not always good. Too often the sex drive becomes confused with the need for emotional closeness. As Dr. James Dobson once said when Dr Hart was taping a radio program with him about *The Sexual Man,* "men give intimacy to get sex, and women give sex to get intimacy."

Women in our study wrote and told us they wanted emotional closeness, and they usually could only get it through sexual interaction. One woman described her confusion this way:

"Twelve partners is eleven too many! I would say God's guidelines for us regarding chastity and sex only in marriage are a true guideline, just like a manual for correct use of any elec-

tronic appliance. I knew I was looking for emotional closeness by experimenting sexually. By the time I had figured out what I was doing it had already become painful. I paid a high cost for just a little intimacy.”

Another wrote:

“I keep looking for love in all the wrong places. Something happened to misdirect my love sensors!”

She went on to explain that ever since she can remember, she searched for emotional closeness by experimenting with sex. Like so many, she erroneously connected her need for intimacy with sexual closeness and thought that sooner or later the perfect sex partner would come along and meet all her intimacy needs.

Dr. Hart has a friend who is a priest in the Catholic church. As an unmarried priest he has, of course, had to struggle with sexuality. His calling expects chastity at all levels, from the physical to the emotional, in behavior as well as in thought. This priest says that the discipline of celibacy is not a matter of repressing or denying sexuality. Sexuality doesn't go away for a celibate, and it is healthy to acknowledge it, embrace it, and even express it appropriately. But the struggle is trying to separate sexuality from genitality. What this means is that there is much that is good that surrounds sex, but this needs to be separated from the act of sex, which is really only genital satisfaction.

It is important for all of us to try and find nonsexual ways to meet our need for physical and emotional closeness. You can have real intimacy without connecting it to your genitals. And this closeness doesn't have to be with the opposite sex, or even involve having sex at all.

Points to Remember

1. The single population of adult women is higher than it has ever been in history and is rising. Some choose singleness

because they have not found the right partner, others because of divorce, others because they are delaying marriage until they are older, and others because they prefer singleness.

2. Many singles struggle in the area of sexuality. Most Christian women have the goal of staying sexually pure but find it difficult.

3. Many women regret their premarital sexual experiences because it left an emotional residue of regret and guilt that interfered with their marital and sexual fulfillment.

4. Premarital sexual activity can also result in other traumatic consequences, such as unwanted pregnancies and sexually transmitted diseases (STDs).

5. When we separate our need for emotional closeness from our sexual needs and find ways to fulfill emotional intimacy apart from sex, we are less likely to cross the sexual purity boundary.

6. No matter how extensive their previous sexual involvement, the women in our study encouragingly reported that they were able to redeem their sexuality through God's grace and forgiveness.

Chapter Eleven

Sex Education for Girls

"I would lead you and bring you into the house of my mother, she who used to instruct me . . ."

—Song of Solomon 8:2 NKJV

"How do I explain sex in a healthy, positive, Christian way to my daughters?"

"I want to know more about female sexuality—how to be approachable to my two daughters and lead them correctly and honestly."

"How can I and other mothers bring up our daughters in the real world, honestly?"

"I want to encourage my sons and daughters to wait to have sex until they are married to avoid all the emotional mud I am still dealing with—thirty partners, twenty-nine prior to marriage."

Recently Debra was speaking to a group of mothers on the topic "How to Talk to Your Kids About Sex." One of the mothers expressed her frustration and discomfort by jokingly saying, "I wish we could all just bring our kids to you, and you could tell them what they need to know. You're so comfortable talking about this!" Debra laughed ruefully.

Earlier the same week she sat with her two children and read through a children's book about sexuality, and all three of them felt uncomfortable! She told these mothers some of her own experiences and suggested they all pass their children one mother to the right, allowing that mother to talk to a different child about sexuality. At least some of the time we may feel more comfortable educating someone else's child about sexuality than our own!

But the reality is this: You *are now*, and *always will be*, the greatest influence on your child's developing sexuality. You have at least two reasons to dive in and get going in this area (or if you have already begun, to keep going!). First, if you don't teach your children about sex, somebody else will. And that somebody may give them the wrong information in the wrong setting at the wrong time. Second, God has given *you* the responsibility to train your kids about their sexuality.

> **You are *now*, and *always will be*, the greatest influence on your child's developing sexuality.**

Why do we believe that God wants parents to train their children regarding sex? Beginning in the Old Testament, God gave parents the responsibility of passing on faith in God and correct behavior to their children. He said this: "Love the LORD your God with all your heart and with all your soul and with all your strength. These commandments that I give you today are to be upon your hearts. Impress them on your children. Talk about them when you sit at home and when you walk along the road, when you lie down and when you get up. Tie them as symbols on your hands and bind them on your foreheads. Write them on the doorframes of your houses and on your gates" (Deut. 6:5–9 NIV).

Building character in our children is the primary goal for every parent. Character means moral excellence and firmness. It is not enough to tell children the right facts at the right time (or some of the right facts at some of the right times). It is not enough to discuss "abstinence until marriage" with your child. Your child needs to learn how to handle powerful urges that will go with her (or him) *throughout* their lifetime. The goal is not just to teach them how to keep themselves sexually pure up to the point of marriage. It is to train them to live in purity all of their lives.

How Do Girls Learn About Sexuality?

We asked the women in our study several questions about how they first learned about sex and sexuality. Less than half of the women in our study said that their parents had discussed sexuality with them while growing up. And of those who said their parents did discuss sexuality, 36% were instructed by their mothers, 7% by both parents, and 2% by their fathers.

We have heard horror stories from friends and clients who told us they knew nothing about menstruation until they actually began their first menstrual period. So we asked women how they learned about the menstrual cycle. Eleven percent said they knew nothing about menstruation until the day they first began menstruating, 29% learned about it at school, and only 40% learned about it from a parent. Many also wrote to tell us that a grandmother, an aunt, or another relative had explained menstruation to them, not a parent.

When we asked how they had learned about sexual intercourse, we were dismayed to learn that, most frequently, women had learned about it from friends (26%). Same-age friends are usually an incomplete and inadequate source of sexual information. The next most common answer was school (21%) and then a parent (20%). (See Figure 11.1.) Almost 10% of the women in our study learned about sexual intercourse the first time they had sex. Imagine, one in ten women learn about intercourse when they first experience it! Clearly parents are failing to teach their daughters about the basics of sexuality.

When we asked what women found most helpful in learning about sexuality, they reported that a private talk was the best (15%). Nine percent said a book about sexuality was the most

HOW WOMEN FIRST LEARNED ABOUT SEXUAL INTERCOURSE
Figure 11.1

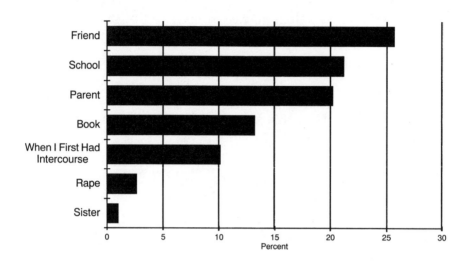

helpful, and about 8% said sex education at school helped them the most. (See Figure 11.2.) Tragically, several women reported that they first learned about sexuality through sexual molestation of some sort.

The Parents' Influence

The most powerful way parents teach and communicate is by modeling. A girl's mother is an example of how to be a woman, and the father's reaction to his wife communicates to the daughter how acceptable this is to men. A father's attitude toward his wife, the way he treats her consistently at home, and the approval he shows of how she conducts her life—all have an influence on a daughter's self-concept and development. It is important for Dad to give verbal encouragement and appropriate affection to his wife, and also to his daughter.

As girls develop physically and emotionally, they need their parents' love and approval in order to accept and enjoy the

MOST HELPFUL FORM OF SEX EDUCATION
Figure 11.2

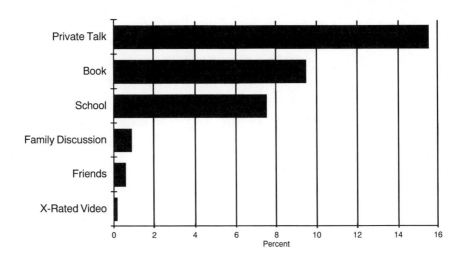

developmental changes they are going through. Often dads feel awkward as their little girl develops a woman's body. Many men withdraw at this point, emotionally or physically or both. Girls sense this withdrawal and feel confused about what it means. They can misinterpret this to mean that they are unacceptable, unattractive, or unlovable.

Many women wrote to us of how, during their teen years, they tried to find this missing love, acceptance, and approval through sex with boys. As one woman said, she was "looking for love in all the wrong places."

Here are some of the other stories women shared regarding their fathers' impact on their sexual development:

"My sexuality has been negatively affected by my father's lack of physical and verbal show of affection. He showed me he loved me by his actions (working, putting food on the table), but he never told me and rarely ever (maybe one or two times) hugged or kissed me. I honestly believe I was raped because I went looking

for affection in other men. I would flirt and once I knew they were giving me attention I would back off. But that one time, it didn't work."

"My father was an alcoholic, and I married another child of an alcoholic. My first sexual experiences were based out of my need to feel wanted, to feel worthy, and to fill a void that stemmed from low self-esteem. As a physically attractive young girl it was easy to gain the affection of boys. This gave me a feeling of importance for a while, but it resulted in a lot of problems for me."

Love-hungry girls are at high risk for early sexual experiences. They also develop a distorted view of God and His love. The sad result, as many women have shared throughout this book, is that seeking love through sex is ultimately disappointing. It is a bottomless pit that can never be satisfied because they never get the real love and acceptance that is missing from their child-hood. Some get a fleeting, temporary sense of being desired, but it is short-lived.

Girls also need encouragement to develop a personal relation-ship with Jesus. Teach and model God's love and acceptance. Many wrote to us of how coming to the Lord and applying His ways to their lives saved them from further confusion and harm during their teen years.

One woman put it so well:

"When I was young I was desperate for emotional closeness and acceptance, and I tried to find it through getting attention from boys. This caused me to be promiscuous from ages fourteen to nineteen. As a result, I suffered many heartaches, an abor-tion, and STDs (a painful price to pay!). In my late teens, Jesus came into my life. I learned to trust in God's love for me, and to be secure in who I was in His eyes. I really believe having Jesus in my life and living His ways turned my life around and saved

me from further harm. I tried to keep myself for marriage, and I am now married and have a loving, fulfilling marriage. I now understand that no one person can meet all your needs and how God designed sexual intimacy for marriage. The Lord has been faithful to heal me emotionally."

How Can I Train My Child in Sexuality?

There are three facets to training your children in healthy sexuality: example, facts, and correct timing.

1. By example

One of the most important influences in the formation of your child's sexuality is your example. How do you interact with the opposite sex? How do you react when the topic of sex arises? How do you handle sexual humor? How do you express yourself physically toward the opposite sex in private and in public? What television shows do you watch? What comments do you make while you are watching? How do you treat your husband (or, if you are a man, how do you treat your wife)?

Children "catch" a lot of their values. They are consciously and unconsciously watching and learning from us all the time. Our influence may be positive or negative. Women wrote to us about the examples they grew up with. Some women wrote to us about the negative influences of their family:

"My mom shared with me about her sex relations as a teen, and I believe this had a negative impact on me. Deep down I felt it was okay for me to mess up because she did. I've often judged gray areas by my mom's life. Because of this, I'm not going to tell my kids what they don't need to know."

"My grandfather always had private affairs. As a teenager I found out my father cheated on my mother for years. I now

*find myself in affairs. I have accepted Christ in my life and
have changed my habits, yet it really scares me how this has
happened."*

It is important to honestly reflect on how you are doing as an
example to your children. Perhaps you are flirtatious with your
boss, the repairman, or a leader in your church. When one of
your children brings up something sexual, you may shush them,
avoid the question, or speak angrily to them. You may treat your
spouse with contempt or disgust. A women speaker once said:
"You can't teach what you don't know, and you can't lead where
you won't go."

Training your children sexually can be challenging if you have
unfinished business from your own childhood, gaps in your own
training, or some current sexual sin in your own life. Resolving
these issues will have an impact on your ability to lead your children into a healthy experience of their own sexuality.

2. With facts

The facts about sex are the easiest part of the sexual training
process! You need to know your material before you begin discussing the basic facts. Fortunately there are some excellent materials available both to educate yourself and to help you to educate
your child. You will need to know about sexual parts, their correct
names (don't use slang or baby talk), and their functions (this may
actually help you in your own sexuality!). Your local Christian
bookstore can supply you with such books. (See Appendix 1 for
resources.)

Always look over a book carefully before purchasing it, and
read it thoroughly yourself before actually reading it with your
child. Why? There are a lot of materials available that contain
information you may not agree with and do not want to teach
your child. Some will try to push alternative lifestyles or values or
don't emphasize Christian morality. So choose carefully.

3. Correct timing

Timing takes into account *which* facts should be presented at *what* stage in your child's development. Many experts say that children are naturally inquisitive, and you can allow their questions to direct your conversations. We do not believe this is true for every child, and maybe not for most children! Many children don't ask—so you will wait years if you let them set the pace. Also, life gets busy. Parents don't realize that questions are *not* being asked, and conversations about sexuality are just *not* happening.

Most of us have good intentions about ensuring our children get the sexual information they need. However, we are usually behind in our estimation of when to present this information by several years! (We tend to run two to five years behind!) Connie Marshner, in her book *Decent Exposure,* makes the point, "Kids need intellectual arguments to defend their virtue. They need their parents to provide these arguments. What often happens instead is that parents shield kids from information that might become useful ammunition to them, mistakenly thinking they are protecting their innocence."[1]

Also keep in mind that your children are being exposed to some form of sexuality all the time. Television and movies have an incredible influence. Advertisers use bodies (particularly female bodies) to sell everything from cars to cameras. One writer estimates that children see ten thousand implied acts of intercourse on television each year. And for those

> **Keep in mind that your children are being exposed to some form of sexuality all the time.**

of us who believe we closely monitor what is shown on television, what about the movies our children see?

Debra spoke to a nine-year-old boy recently who said his favorite all-time movie was *The Three Musketeers.* One of the key characters in this story is a woman who uses her body and all her sensual skills to entrap and murder political enemies. And the key villain in the movie is a religious leader who is both evil and sexually driven. What conscious and unconscious messages do our children get from such movies?

Even if you are able to protect your child from the media and to follow the developmental model for sex education that we present, there will be times when you will be caught off guard and have to jump ahead with information before you had planned on it. When you send your child off to school in the morning, or off to soccer practice in the afternoon, you have no idea what sexual information he or she will pick up from other children. Please tell your children not to talk about sex with their friends either. Encourage them to only talk to you about sex. This protects them from getting faulty information and protects other children from being given information they are not ready for.

Preparing Yourself to Talk About Sex

Decide now that you are going to become an "approachable" parent—someone your children can feel free to ask about anything. Show them that you are approachable, that they can come to you and ask about sex and God and what matters in life. This will require that you formulate your own biblical sexual values.

Develop a plan for how you will train your children in Christian sexuality and sex, and develop it long before you think you will need to implement it. You never know when your child will ask you a question. Set aside time for sexual talks and make the most of daily teachable moments. Also, occasionally remind your children that if they have anything they want to ask, you are available to them.

> **Develop a plan for sex education . . . long before you think you will need to implement it. You never know when your child will ask you a question.**

Buy age-appropriate books or videotapes and go over them with your child. As your child hits prepuberty and again during puberty, plan specific times (like a weekend away with just you and your child) in order to discuss sexual matters.

One talk, or even an annual talk, isn't enough. Try to keep the communication lines open at all times, and take advantage of questions that arise. At the same time, don't flood your children with information. Ask if your answer satisfies them or if there is anything more they would like to have explained.

Unless you are particularly open and relaxed about sexual matters and have a child who is very inquisitive, don't expect that all these talks will go smoothly or that you will both feel comfortable. Children have their own sense of privacy and also their own developing opinions about sexuality. Most children (approximately ages five to twelve) express surprise and/or disgust when they figure out or are told about sexual intercourse and reproduction.

A ten-year-old daughter approached her mother and asked about sexual intercourse. After receiving an explanation she asked, "You and Daddy do this?" With outward calmness the mother replied, "Yes."

"And how many times have you done this?" the child wanted to know. "Oh, hundreds of times," the mother responded, again with outward calmness.

"Mom, that's gross!" her daughter exclaimed with a shocked look.

This kind of reaction is common when children first hear about sexuality and human reproduction.

How to Talk About Sex

In addition to the facts about sexuality and the timing of presenting these fact, *the way* that girls are told about sex makes a big impact.

Here are three contrasting examples of this:

"My parents taught me the sacredness of sex within marriage—as created by God. God has blessed me and given me the commitment and desire and patience to save myself for my husband. I can't wait!"

"My parents told me that if I ever had sex before marriage I would be a slut and no decent man should have to stay married to me once they found out. I really believe that if I had had more positive, unconditional love from my parents, and if they had spent more time explaining why God doesn't want us to be involved with anyone until marriage, I most probably would have waited and saved myself."

"I was brought up with the idea that sex was sinful and anything to do with sex was gross. The thought of sex before marriage totally horrified me, and much of that came through in our marriage. I recently found out that my mother was molested a few times in her late teens—and that's why she let me know how dirty sex was."

Be positive whenever you talk about sexuality. Use every opportunity to reinforce that God made you and your body parts, that sex is good, that sexuality is a gift from God, and that God designed the gift of sex for marriage. Using scare tactics or manipulating with guilt and shame are not effective ways of educating children about sex, or of motivating them to stay pure. If you don't have a positive attitude toward sexuality, reach out for help beyond yourself. Look into some of the resources we recommend in Appendix 1. If you are truly unable to approach the topic of sexuality by yourself, arrange for someone who can give a healthy Christian perspective to talk to your child.

> **Be positive whenever you talk about sexuality. Reinforce that . . . sex is good, that sexuality is a gift from God, and that God designed the gift of sex for marriage.**

When and What to Share With Your Child

Many parents wonder when the appropriate age is to begin talking to children about sex. How much do you tell them when they are young?

Does it all happen in a one-time sit-down talk or in little bits and pieces along the way? Sex education should be an ongoing process, taking your child through each stage of her or his development.

As we mentioned earlier, there is a developmental "appropriateness" of when to explain certain facts to your child. It is important that you protect your child's innocence by not sharing too many facts too soon. A child becomes ready for more detailed information as they grow. Most sex education resources are outlined by ages to assist parents with the facts to share for each developmental stage. An example of this is a four-book series entitled *God's Design for Sex.*[2] Information is presented according to a child's age, with separate books for each stage.

As a child gets older, there are books that they can read themselves. You can help by encouraging them to discuss the material with you. In addition to these helpful educational resources, use everyday situations that arise to talk about the topic. Role-play to help them work through how they will respond when sexual situations come up. This strengthens their character and teaches them personal responsibility, which are both a part of healthy sexuality.

At what age should you actually begin talking to children about sex and sexuality? Here are our suggestions of what to say at each stage of a child's life:

Infancy (Ages Birth to Three)

Sex education should begin in infancy, as you talk and name body parts while bathing or dressing your child. It is helpful to teach them the proper name for body parts, including genitals. This helps us as parents to get used to saying the words aloud, and it teaches kids from the beginning that all their parts have respectful names and every part is good.

If you choose to give pet names for body parts, be certain they know the proper names as well. Otherwise, it sends a message to the child that certain body parts are so difficult to talk about that we have to give them nicknames. We've never heard of pet names for ears or eyelashes—only for a penis or a vulva. Many girls grow up knowing their genitals, anus, and urethra as "unmentionables" or as the area "down there." We need to make sure we stress to our children that all our body parts have dignity and special functions made by God.

Ages Three to Five

The facts about sex. Building on the basics of body parts, children can be introduced to simple basics of human reproduction such as the growth of a baby inside a mother's body and the birth process. Stress the importance of genitals being private and not letting anyone touch them. Children are naturally curious and will begin exploring themselves and their world and asking questions.

During this stage of exploration, it is common for children to be curious about the differences between girls and boys. Perhaps they want to touch or look at each other's bottoms, genitals, or nipples. Children may also touch or fondle themselves openly while on the couch watching television. If this occurs, respond as calmly as possible, and do not shame them. Every situation is an opportunity to teach the basic facts and instill values. Reinforce that genitals are private, and they are not to show their genitals to someone else, fondle their genitals in front of someone else, or ask to see or fondle someone else's genitals.

God's design. During this stage it is also important to lay a spiritual foundation for the child's understanding of being a *girl* or a *boy* created by God's design. Your daughter should learn that she is created by God, in His image, as a girl. She is a special gift from God.

Ages Six to Eight

The facts about sex. A child can now be introduced to the changes the body goes through to become a woman or a man.

Explain in simple terms the basic nature of sexual intercourse between a wife and a husband. It is important to be the first to introduce your daughter to the facts about sexual intercourse from a biblical perspective, before they are exposed to sexual material from other kids at school, around the neighborhood, or on television. It is crucial to lay a positive, biblical foundation. Again, at this stage children will be curious about themselves and about the topic of sex, and they may ask questions. Be prepared, and make the most of every opportunity to instruct them with facts about God's design for our sexuality.

God's design. During this stage it is important to lay the foundation for biblical morality. Cover all the essentials, such as God's design for the family through a husband and wife coming together in marriage and that intercourse is reserved for marriage.

Ages Nine to Eleven

The facts about sex. It is now appropriate to explain sexual intercourse in more detail. Begin to teach a sense of responsibility for keeping pure (physically, mentally, emotionally, and spiritually). Look for opportunities in everyday life to address how your child should respond to the opposite sex.

In girls, puberty will begin during this stage. You need to provide details about all the changes they will go through.

God's design. At this stage you can expand on information introduced previously. For example, sex is a gift from God, He designed our bodies and how they fit together, He designed our hormones and our physical development, and sex is good. We hear so many negative messages about sex and so many misuses of it, we need to remind ourselves and teach our children that sex is intrinsically good.

Start preparing your children for the attitudes toward sexuality they will encounter in the world. As we stated earlier, it is impossible to protect your child from all the destructive messages they will encounter. However, you can begin addressing issues such as teenage pregnancy and sexually transmitted diseases. As your child begins to understand God's created design and plan for sexuality she will be strengthened in her moral choices.

Ages Twelve to Fourteen

The facts about sex. Prepare your child for the variety of feelings, emotions, frustrations, and social pressures of adolescence. By now menstruation usually begins (some girls begin as early as age ten). Be honest with your child about sexual arousal, encouraging them to talk about what they are experiencing in their minds and bodies, as well as the beliefs and attitudes they are encountering.

At this age, there are many books available for your child to read alone. We encourage you to read the same book and then talk openly with them about it. This can be difficult for both parent and child. Teens are often embarrassed to talk with their parents as they are hit with sex hormones and begin exploring and questioning their sexual feelings. If you have been openly talking about sex through each stage, it will be more comfortable for you to talk about these topics as your child gets older.

Don't wait until this developmental stage to begin teaching, and don't simply give them a book to read and then consider your job as done. Sexual development and sex education are a process that cannot be covered by a book read at puberty.

God's design. Continue to build on the foundation of God's view of sexuality and the beautiful intentions of His creative order for women and men. As your child develops through puberty, he or she needs to learn to respect their own body, keep themselves pure sexually, and reserve the gift of sex for marriage.

Puberty, Teens, and Sex

"As a parent now, and in retrospect of my teen years, I understand the importance of protection, supervision, and communi-

cation, which educates a child to make informed decisions when out of the parents' presence. The age-appropriate communication should consist of specific biblical principles addressing every stage of a child's development followed by nonperverted open examples of God's kind of love, affection, and admiration. This gives inspiration and develops desires toward a life filled with integrity. I am determined that my children will never suffer the cruelties that I did."

One of the issues we have not come to terms with as a culture is the phenomenon of the dropping age of puberty. The age of puberty for both girls and boys in our Western culture is the lowest it has ever been in history—and it continues to drop.

Just over 150 years ago, the average age of puberty in girls was about 17 years. Records show that in Germany the average age in 1795 was 16.6 years. By 1920 it had dropped to 14.5 years. In the United States the average age in the early 1930s was 13.5 years, but it had dropped below 13 by the mid-1960s. A full discussion of this phenomenon and its ramifications can be found in Dr. Hart's book *The Sexual Man.*

The average age of first menstruation reported by the women in our study was 13.4 years. The distribution of age for puberty is depicted in Figure 11.3. The majority of men in *The Sexual Man* study reached puberty between ages 12 and 13. The most common frequency for boys was age 12 (32%) followed by age 13 (28%).

How does this drop in the age of puberty affect our children? They will have a longer period of waiting between the time they are physically mature for sex and the time they are emotionally and spiritually mature enough for marriage and child rearing. Girls may be capable of sex now at twelve or thirteen, but

> **The dilemma we face as a culture, therefore, is that while our children are now physically capable of sex they are definitely not emotionally mature enough to handle it responsibly.**

they are not mature enough for mothering, nor are their bodies for bearing children.

The dilemma we face as a culture, therefore, is that while our children are now physically capable of sex they are definitely not emotionally mature enough to handle it responsibly. Improved health care and nutrition may have accelerated physical development, but they do nothing for the emotions and the maturing of the brain. The two have not kept pace with each other.

If we could slow down the dropping puberty age, or better still, raise it back up in some way that was not harmful to our children's health, we would be better off.

AGE OF FIRST MENSTRUAL PERIOD
Figure 11.3

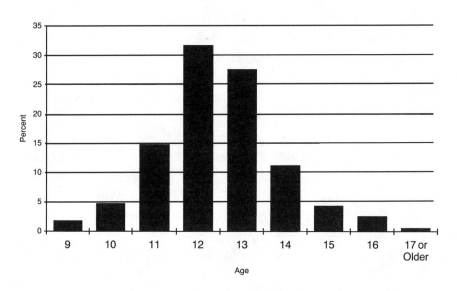

Reclaiming Abstinence

The only approach that will protect our children is abstinence! We need to teach our children that *virgin* isn't a dirty word. We need to teach our girls how not to give in to pressure from boys and how to delay getting physically involved too soon. "There will be plenty of time to date girls after you finish high school," Dr. Hart's grandmother used to preach at him. She was right. None of his high school girlfriends were permanent!

Abstinence alone is not enough. In this chapter we have emphasized the importance of sharing the facts about sex with your children, with special consideration for the timing of that process. In addition, we've strongly advocated the teaching of children about God's design and the training of your children to have strong values and character in all aspects of sexuality. It is not enough to teach them about sex, you must train them in responsible biblical sexuality.

The long period of waiting creates the potential for premature involvement, emotionally and sexually. Girls often become preoccupied with romantic fantasies, how boys perceive them, how to attract boys, and intense relationships with boys. Boys, on the other hand, can become preoccupied with erotic fantasies often through pornography and masturbation. Sex becomes an end in itself, rather than a means for building a solid marital relationship. Healthy, biblically based sex education can help to prevent these distortions during the extended period of sexual development.

Consequences of Neglecting Sex Education

In the United States, the percentage of girls, ages fifteen to nineteen, who reported having sexual intercourse increased from 29% in 1970 to 52% in 1988. In 1996, *Science Magazine* reported that by the twelfth grade 70% had had sexual intercourse, and almost 40% had had four or more partners. "Each year more than 1 million unmarried teens become pregnant and more than 3 million adolescents contract an STD. . . . STDs can result in infertility, sterility, pregnancy complications, birth defects, chronic pain, cancer and even death."[3] Teenagers are actually more susceptible to contracting an STD when exposed than adults are. And women are more vulnerable than men because medically, it is twice as easy for a man to infect a woman with an STD than for a woman to infect a man.[4]

But teenage sexuality leaves more scars than physical ones. Early sexual involvement and multiple partners also lead to emotional scarring. Many of the women in our study wrote about their experiences:

> *"I had eight sex partners before marriage. Looking back I can say that the only great sex was (is) with my husband. We have grown sexually to know each other. I am doing my best to ensure that my girls (fourteen and sixteen) save themselves for the Christian man they marry."*

> *"Neither my mom nor dad or anyone else in school ever talked to me or gave me reasons not to have sex before marriage. I'm grieved that no one offered that as an option to me—in fact the opposite was encouraged."*

> *"I had twenty-six partners prior to marriage. I believe that if my parents had been more involved in my adolescence I would not have needed so much sexual attention."*

Part of the message of standard sex education in the United States is that teenagers are going to have sex anyway, so just teach them how to do it safely. Many teenagers genuinely believe they have a right to have sex—that sex is uncontrollable—and it never crosses their minds that they have a choice. Yet recent studies continue to show that adolescents, even those who are sexually active already, "want to learn how to say no to sex without hurting the other person's feelings."[5] Other studies show that those children whose parents talk to them about sexuality and maintain open communication with them about both the facts of sex and the values of sex are more likely to postpone becoming sexually active. This is in direct contrast to studies that show that teenagers who have had sex education in public schools are more likely to have sex by age fifteen or sixteen than teenagers who did not have sex education in school.[6]

Proponents of "value-free comprehensive sexuality education" (which is the approach usually taught in sex education classes in the United States) use as a model the Swedish sex education program. However, this model *didn't* reduce adolescent pregnancies, STDs, or teenage sexual activity. Sadly, many of us leave the sex education of our children to the so-called experts (school), who have based their program on a faulty model.

Consequences of Dating Too Soon

One of the striking findings of our study is shown in Figure 11.4. The time between the first date and sexual intercourse has dramatically declined for the girls of today who have sex before marriage.

TIME BETWEEN FIRST DATE AND FIRST SEXUAL INTERCOURSE
Figure 11.4

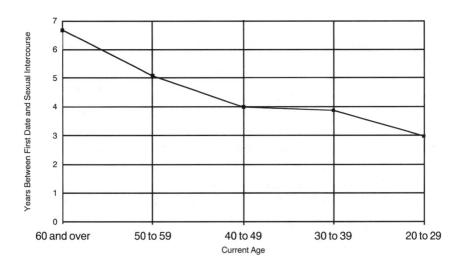

We asked women at what age they began dating, kissing, petting, and having intercourse. In contrast to an average of six years between first date and first intercourse for the women in our sample over sixty, there were only three years between first date and first intercourse for women ages twenty to twenty-nine. Women who began to date earlier had sexual intercourse earlier. This must be considered

> **The earlier a girl starts dating, the earlier she is likely to have sexual intercourse.**

when allowing your children to date (or attend boy/girl sleep-overs) at an early age. We have had many clients (of all ages and stages of singleness) tell us that sexual intercourse is expected within the first few dates. One woman wrote to tell us about her experience:

> *"My sexual experiences outside of marriage were a result of dating too early. I had very low self-esteem because of my sexual permissiveness, but I wanted desperately to be loved. When I met God and accepted His personal gift of salvation, I then began the emotional healing and the establishment of healthy self-esteem."*

Can we expect our children to listen to us and delay becoming involved sexually? Many experts say it is impossible to convince adolescents to delay intercourse. However, many of the women in our study reported that it was becoming a Christian that helped them to wait until marriage to have intercourse. *It is possible* to educate our children in the realities of sexuality and God's standards. Women wrote to us celebrating the effects that early training and their own decisions had produced in their sexual lives:

> *"I had strong moral values to be a virgin before I was married. The only sexual experiences from kissing to intimacy that I have had have been with my husband. The best thing we ever did was to not have intercourse before marriage."*

"I decided at an early age to give 'the gift' I could only give once to the man who would love me for the rest of my life. I was blessed to marry a man with the same goal. Now, coming up on our first-year anniversary, we cherish this gift. I am saddened and angered by the lies society tells us about premarital sex and the beautiful experience it is stealing from so many young people. Waiting was one of the best choices I ever made!"

But what do we do for our children while they struggle with desire and wait for their opportunity to express their sexuality? A complete program of developmental sex education, as we presented earlier, including learning the discipline of waiting, is essential. We discussed waiting more completely in chapter 10. The new national program designed to curb the exploding teenage pregnancy rate is an excellent contribution (especially if it includes congressional support and federal funds).

Be involved in your daughter's life, including her sexual education. Be willing to learn the information and model the attitudes she needs. There is no person who loves your child the way you do, or who knows her as well as you do. Demonstrate your love by staying involved.

Points to Remember

1. Many parents are failing in their sex education responsibilities. Only 40% of girls first learned about menstruation from a parent. Only 20% of girls first learned about intercourse from a parent.

2. Both mother *and* father impact their daughter's sexual and emotional development. If girls don't get the love, acceptance, and approval from their parents that they need, they are more vulnerable to try to meet these needs through sex.

3. Healthy Christian character is the best lifetime protection against our culture's distorted sexual messages.

4. Sex education should start in infancy and continue throughout adolescence. Timely instruction includes facts of healthy sexuality, as well as God's design for our sexuality.

5. Our data shows very clearly that the earlier a girl starts dating, the sooner she is likely to start having intercourse. Parents should be careful, therefore, to delay early serious dating, ensure that girls know all the facts about sexuality including the negative consequences of premarital sex, and are equipped and empowered to say no to sexual advances.

Chapter Twelve

Bridging the Gender Gap

"You have ravished my heart with one look of your eyes. . . . How much better than wine is your love."

—*Song of Solomon 4:9–10 NKJV*

Some things never change. The sun always rises in the east, time always moves forward, and men will always be different from women.

One of our primary goals for this study was to find out what Christian women think and feel about sex and how they express their sexuality. Over two thousand women told us their stories with honesty and forthrightness, sharing intimate details beyond what we expected.

Having worked through this entire book and digested so much information, one could be left with an overwhelming sense of just how different we are as sexes. You might ask: What difference does this information about female sexuality make? How can we apply it to our lives as Christian men and women?

We want to say that our differences, great as they may be, can be transcended. In fact, they have to be transcended. God didn't make us the way we are so that we can wallow in the mire of our differences. Every couple needs to find a way to rise above the influential effects of estrogen/progesterone and testosterone. The only way to do this is to ensure that men understand women and women understand men. An impossible task, you say? We hope not.

Secrets of Eve is as much for men as it is for women. It is as difficult for women to comprehend the "testosterone fog" (as discussed in *The Sexual Man*) as it is for men to grasp the "estrogen/progesterone mist."

> It is as difficult for women to comprehend the "testosterone fog" as it is for men to grasp the "estrogen/progesterone mist."

A part of our goal in writing this book was to help women to understand themselves and to help men understand the women they love.

It is our hope that men will read this book, especially this chapter.

Male and Female Differences

Never before in human history have we needed to bridge the gap between the sexes as much as we do today. The changing family structures, role definition not being as clear as it once was, and a variety of other political, cultural, and social factors have intensified this gap. These sweeping social changes, both subtle and obvious, have caused us to deny that male/female differences exist.

But God made us different as sexes—not superior or inferior, just different. This is God's design. It is not an accident nor did it come about by chance. We were formed by God to play in exquisite harmony—to be a duet, not a solo or to be in unison. The sexual responses of men and women are not intended to be identical. Their beauty lies in the differences brought out by their harmony, not by their sameness. Our diversity has been the source of much frustration and a lot of misery as well because we have failed to really understand and cooperate with His intended plan for us as women and men.

No wonder one woman, speaking for many we are sure, wrote:

> *"I think all women want to know more about the differences between males and females. We boast about being a sexually*

sophisticated society, but we, as women, are about as ignorant of our differences from men as they are of their differences from us."

Far too many women—single, dating, or married—are troubled by the fear that the differences they perceive between themselves and the men they are trying to relate to are substantial enough to be an obstacle to real intimacy. Need they be concerned? Not at all. The differences that you feel and see are there by design. Learn to play the best harmony you can with these differences.

Being different as male and female does not make the sexual experience of one more important than that of another. For God's harmony to be played out in healthy marital relationships, one person should not be given priority above the other. With great tolerance and understanding for each other, couples can work out a blending of their differences. We then can "become one," the Hebrew way of describing the uniting of bodies, spirits, and emotions. The musical term for this is *consonance*. It refers to a pause or harmonious chord that provides a feeling of satisfaction and resolution. "Ahhhhh . . ."

As we reflect on the many ways this harmony has been achieved by the participants in our study, we hope to reveal the secrets of their success through their stories and quotes.

What about those who are single or celibate? God has created all of us as sexual beings. How will our comments relate to them? The tensions that arise between nonmarried women and men in dating, in the workplace, and in friendships still exist and need to be understood. If you intend to marry, then you will definitely benefit from knowing as much as you can about how to bridge the gap between the sexes.

Just How Different Are Women from Men?

The development of our sex organs is an analogy for understanding our sexuality as women and men. The genitals in both the female and the male fetus develop out of the same tissue. But under the influence of a different genetic pattern and hormones, a woman's genitals turn out to look and function differently from a man's.

Although as adults we all have the same basic hormones, we have them in differing amounts. These hormones (greater amounts of testosterone in men, greater amounts of estrogen/progesterone in women), together with our different genetic patterns and anatomy, produce distinct expressions of sexuality in women and in men.

But the million-dollar question is: How on earth can we come to understand each other and be united with such differences? From our study we want to highlight six key differences between women and men.

1. We differ in how we think about sex.

That men and women don't think alike is pretty much common sense, though many couples at the height of a conflict often forget this crucial point. We might differ in our patterns of thinking as well as basic logic, but we also differ in how often we think about sex. Men, your wives think about sex a lot less than you do. Women, your husbands think about sex more often than you do. This is perfectly normal—expect it and accept it. Neither of you is right or wrong; this is just how you are.

Why is this important? Because women have sex with their partners just a little less often than they think about sex. In other words, if you think of sex about once per week, you are probably engaging in sex about once per week or a little less. Most men think about sex at least once per day, and some even more than once per hour. Men have sex far less often than they think about sex.

Most of the women in our study were satisfied with how often they were having sex. In contrast, most reported that their spouses were not satisfied (men wanted to have sex more often). Couples often lock in conflict over this issue; the husband accuses the wife of never thinking about sex and even attacks her by saying, "You probably could go forever without having sex!" Maybe. It is normal for a woman not to think about sex or want it as frequently as a man. It is normal for a man to think about sex more frequently and want it more often. You're different. Both of you need to accept and adjust to this difference.

> **The challenge for all of us is how to bring our different sexual styles together in a harmonious way.**

The challenge for all of us is how to bring our different sexual styles together in a harmonious way. If you fight about who sings which notes or insist that you sing in unison rather than in blended harmony, you will probably stop singing with each other altogether.

2. We differ in what we want from and enjoy about sex.

When we asked women what they liked the most about sex, the overwhelming majority chose physical closeness or emotional closeness. This even took precedence over orgasm.

Men, on the other hand, most enjoy the pleasure and release of orgasm. As one man put it: "I've concluded that in sex women are more interested in the foreplay and afterplay, while men, or at least this man, is more interested in what happens between those two events."[1] Compare this male's comment to the one hundred thousand women who wrote to Ann Landers in response to the question, "Would you be content to be held close and treated tenderly and forget about 'the act' [of sexual intercourse]?" Seventy-two percent (that's almost three out of four women) said yes to this question.[2] Need we say more to make this point?

In several places throughout this book we suggested ways in which couples can fulfill a woman's desire for closeness. Love is the most powerful enhancer of sexual desire that there is. To have great sex in your relationship you must have great loving.

> **Love is the most powerful enhancer of sexual desire that there is.**

And if you want to restore lost love feelings in your partner, start establishing closeness by holding her—both emotionally and physically. It is an accepted therapeutic fact that if you behave toward someone as if you love them, you will soon begin to feel that love.

There are a host of ways you can develop closeness. Here are some suggestions:

- Spend more time together by yourselves (without the kids).
- Focus on your partner's positive traits.
- Say "I love you" often—your partner isn't a mind reader.
- Decrease criticism and increase praise.
- Treat your partner with respect.
- Really try to listen and understand where your partner is coming from.

3. We differ in our energy resources for sex.

The energy/sex connection differs between women and men. When a woman is drained and tired, sex is usually the last thing she wants. When a man is drained, tired, or frustrated, many times sex is what he wants most before keeling over from exhaustion. One of the reasons for this is that orgasm serves as a tranquilizer for a lot of men. It relieves their stress and frustration. It also can be the most pleasurable experience he had that day!

Women today juggle multiple demands, often without as much cooperation and participation from their husbands as they need.[3] As shown in chapter 6 on the energy crisis, depletion of energy is particularly acute for mothers with children living at home. So, if you want to have a sex life after children arrive, the three essential pieces of equipment are: a dead bolt (or heavier) lock on the bedroom door, a tough shell so that you can rigidly demand and enforce a realistic bedtime for all, and a special form of deafness that switches on when you know the kids are calling for you just to get attention! Seriously, couples at the child-rearing stage of life have to be creative if they are going to have any sort of sex life.

This is especially true for two-career families. Responsibility for the cooking, grocery shopping, bill paying, housecleaning, and child care cannot fall completely on the wife. Household maintenance (everything involved in keeping your family operating) must be discussed periodically and divvied up between you.

4. We differ in our concerns about body image.

Women carry this burden to a much greater degree than most men. Body image is a big issue, and men don't seem to understand how much this affects women.

Most women are not truly accepting of and comfortable with their bodies. How can they be? They get the constant message that how they look matters a lot, starting from the time when they are little girls. Weight matters. Measurements matter. Shape matters. There is no escaping the comparisons with models, movie stars, and the occasional insensitive male who cracks jokes about breasts or any other part of the female anatomy.

Our study shows that a woman's sexual desire is definitely affected by how she feels about her body. If she gains a few pounds she stops feeling sexy and sexual desire goes out the window. And if her partner criticizes her weight or makes comments about how "So-and-so looks great in her bikini," she becomes even more self-conscious. How can a woman possibly enjoy sex and abandon herself to orgasm when she has to be so focused on what angle she should hold her body and whether or not her stomach is sticking out?

Our message is to both men and women. Men, please be more understanding of your partner's concern that her body is not acceptable to you. Women, try to be less self-conscious. We know several women whose husbands are quite accepting of their bodies but who continue to criticize themselves.

Song of Solomon portrays lovers rich in the skill of caressing their partner's soul with their words. They praise each other's bodies freely and liberally. They admire each other physically, and they say so. They speak their admiration of each other's attractiveness while they make love. They speak positively about each other to the people around them. They initiate lovemaking with compliments. "Arise, come, my darling; my beautiful one, come with me. . . . Show me your face, let me hear your voice; for your voice is sweet, and your face is lovely" (Song of Solomon 2:13–14 NIV). Read the Song of Solomon as a couple and learn from its wisdom.

5. We differ in how often we want to have sex.

Our study and *Sex in America* found that most American married couples (Christian and non-Christian) have sex between once per month and three times per week. This directly disproves the myth that "everybody is having sex more than I am." Everybody else is not having sex every day or several times a day.

Women need to try to understand how important sex is to most men. How frequently does your husband *really* want to have sex? Men often ask for it more than they really want to have it because they know they have to initiate several times prior to hearing a yes. If you truly understand that sex is one of your partner's favorite things to do—and he wants to share it with you—would you be motivated to have sex more often?

Men need to understand that most women must feel loved and connected in order to want to have sex. Also, if she declines sex for the moment, because of timing, energy, or not feeling connected, she is not rejecting *you*. If you understand that she needs to feel loved, appreciated, and connected, would you be

> **Men need to understand that most women must feel loved and connected in order to want to have sex.**

motivated to give her this, and be willing to wait until a better time for her to have sex?

We need to take into account the reality of life, and the importance of variety in our lovemaking. There will be times for "fast-food sex" (when you are busy), "meat-and-potatoes sex" (your standard sexual routine), "gourmet sex" (when you have more time and on special occasions),[4] and "dessert sex" (when you feel like a treat, exploring or laughing). This variety helps meet each of your needs within realistic time constraints.

6. We differ in how we connect sexually.

Men and women connect differently. Women first want to talk and feel close and then (if the time is right) have sex. Men frequently use sex as a means of achieving closeness.

This difference can be very frustrating for couples. He wants to connect with her and get more in touch with his feelings of love and tenderness. His answer is to have sex. She wants to feel connected with him in order to prepare herself for sex. Her answer is talking together or a romantic evening. She feels frustrated and used if there hasn't been talking, affection, or sharing prior to the initiating of sex.

Men need to understand that to most women sex is not the vehicle for achieving closeness, it is the expression of being close. Women, on the other hand, you need to understand that when your partner is feeling distant, sex may be the way for him to connect with you again. Sex can be the way for opening up a man's loving feelings toward you when he is distracted. If you are both insistent on your own way, you cannot bridge this gap.

Stop Comparing

We need to stop focusing on gender comparisons in order to bridge the gender gap.

To be honest, we think that women compare their sexuality to men more than men do to women. We read it again and again in the narrative responses:

> *"I'm not like my husband. He always seems to be ready for sex. It takes me hours to get ready. Sometimes I have to force myself to get going. Is this normal?"*

By and large, women tend to take their cues and judge their normality by contrasting it with the men's instant sexual readiness and the distorted images of our culture, when in reality, a woman's sexual feelings are like a dimmer switch. They turn on slowly, and they may or may not go to full brightness depending on the circumstances. For most men a conventional on-and-off switch controls their sexual response.

Seldom do we come across men who say:

> *"Gee whiz, my wife is phenomenally ready for sex at every drop of the hat. She needs no preparation, gets over any disappointment I caused her, can forget about the kids, her mother's illness, the pile of laundry, or the host of other chores waiting to be done, and jumps into bed with me. I wish I could be like her."*

Men don't measure their sexuality against women's sexuality. Not most men, anyway. And as we have emphasized throughout this book, this doesn't make female sexuality any less important, only different.

Women are often unaware of the complexity of their sexuality. We have tried to explore this complexity with an open mind. We hope you have had an open mind in receiving what we have said.

A woman's sexuality is affected by many subtle influences. Herein lies much potential for conflict between the sexes. More so than men, women are influenced by factors beyond mere physiology: her energy level, how she feels about her body, the emotional closeness of her marriage, and her comfort or discomfort with her own sexuality. Both men and women need to understand these influences and how to respond to them.

Conclusion

We opened this book by emphasizing that the stories of the women we studied are unique, yet universal. Female sexuality is awesome and mysterious, not only to men, but to many women as well.

In our study we have attempted to discover the "secrets" about Christian female sexuality. What are Christian women's attitudes about sex and sexuality? How do Christian women feel about sex? How do they express their sexuality? What has shaped their current sexual experience?

We trust that in sharing this knowledge we have validated that our differences as women and men are part of God's design. A better understanding of female and male sexuality will help to bridge the gap between the sexes.

And what should the church's response be to this? Hopefully our study has raised enough issues to warrant an overhaul of how we help people develop a truly Christian understanding of sexuality, an understanding not distorted by toxic beliefs and attitudes. We need improved programs and resources for helping parents to model and teach their children healthy and balanced sexuality. We need programs for teenagers that will teach virtue and chastity. We need settings in which young married couples can get the help that will set them on the right

> **There is no other social group more balanced, moral, and concerned for the well-being of the total person than the church today.**

track toward a satisfying sexual relationship and a happy marital life. We need to give clear and unambiguous messages and support to widowed, divorced, and never married singles about appropriate sexual behavior. And, above all, we need to reassert the validity of God's design for our sexuality.

If the church doesn't provide this help, who will? There is no other social group more balanced, moral, and concerned for the well-being of the total person than the church today.

Our closing prayer is that all who read this book will be helped to understand God's awesome design for our sexual lives. Hopefully, the fellowship of these women's stories will strengthen our resolve to celebrate God's design for our sexuality and live within the boundaries He has given us.

Points to Remember

1. Women and men will always be different, but these differences can be transcended through understanding and persistence.

2. Women and men are different in how they think about sex, what they enjoy from sex, the amount of sex they want, the need for connection prior to sex, and the way lack of energy and distorted body image inhibit sexual interest.

3. Women need to celebrate the uniqueness of their own sexuality and stop comparing themselves with male sexuality.

4. Our study explores Christian female sexuality in the hope that women and men can bridge the gender gap through what we have learned.

Appendix I

Additional Resources

We recommend the following books, magazines, videos, and tapes for further understanding in the following areas:
(Note: * indicates a non-Christian author.)

General

Christians in a Sex Crazed Culture, Bill Hybels (Victor Books, 1989).

Bonding-Relationships in the Image of God, Donald Joy (Word, 1985).

Money, Sex and Power, Richard Foster (Harper and Row, 1985).

Sex for Christians, Lewis Smedes (Eerdmans, 1976).

Women

His Needs, Her Needs, Willard F. Harley (Revell, 1986).

How to Beat Burnout, Frank B. Minirth, M.D. (Moody, 1986).

Hormones

Menopause Manager—Safe Path for a Natural Change, Joseph L. Mayo, M.D. and MaryAnn Mayo (Fleming Revell, 1998).

Emotional Phases of a Woman's Life, Jean Lush (Revell, 1987).

What Do You Need to Know About Menopause? Paul Reiser and Teri Reiser (Vine Books, 1994).

The Silent Passage, Gail Sheehy (Random House, 1992).

The Menopause Self Help Book, Dr. Susan Lark (Celestial Arts, 1992).

Coming of Age, Lois Mowday Rabey (Thomas Nelson, 1995).

Pre-Marital

Before You Say I Do, Wes Roberts and Norman Wright (Harvest House, 1978).

Finding the Love of Your Life, Neil Clark Warren (Focus on the Family Publishing, 1992). Distributed by Word Books.

Intended for Pleasure, Ed Wheat and Gayle Wheat (Revell, 1981).

Before the Wedding Night, Ed Wheat, M.D. (2 Audio tapes). Available from Spiritual Counsel, Inc. (1-800-643-3477).

Love for a Lifetime, Dr. James Dobson (Multnoma, 1987).

Marriage

Communication: Key to Your Marriage, H. Norman Wright (Regal Books, 1975).

Intended for Pleasure, Ed Wheat and Gayle Wheat (Revell, 1981).

Love-Life for Every Married Couple, Ed Wheat, M.D. and Gloria Okes Perkins (Harper, 1991).

Pillow Talk, The Intimate Marriage from A to Z, Karen Linamen (Revell, 1996).

* *How to Make Love to the Same Person for the Rest of Your Life and Still Love It,* Dagmar O'Connor (Bantam Books, 1985).

Restoring the Pleasure, Clifford Penner and Joyce Penner (Word, 1993).

A Celebration of Sex, Douglas Rosenau (Thomas Nelson, 1994).

* *The Fragile Bond,* Gus Napier (Harper and Row, 1988).

Healing for Sexual Trauma

Free to Love Again: Coming to Terms with Sexual Regret, Dick Purnell (Here's Life Publishers, 1989).

Re-bonding: Preventing and Restoring Damaged Relationships, Donald Joy (Word Publishers, 1986).

The Wounded Heart, Dr. Dan Allender (NavPress, 1990).

Pain and Pretending, Rich Buhler (Thomas Nelson, 1988).

Pursuing Sexual Wholeness, Andrew Comiskey (Creation House Publishers, 1989).

Love Must Be Tough, Dr. James Dobson (Word, 1983).

A Door of Hope, Jan Frank (Here's Life Publishers, 1987).

An Affair of the Mind, Laurie Mills (Focus on the Family Publishing, 1996).

The Broken Image, L. Payne (Crossway, 1981).

Sex and Singleness

Single Adult Passages, Carolyn Koons and Michael Anthony (Baker Book House, 1991).

Wide My World, Narrow My Bed, Luci Swindoll (Multnomah, 1982).

Too Close/Too Soon, Bobbie Reed and Jim Talley (Thomas Nelson, 1982).

Passion and Purity, Elisabeth Elliot (Fleming, Revell, 1984).

Sex Education

Mom's a Bird, Dad's a Bee, Mary Ann Mayo (Harvest House, 1991).

Decent Exposure, Connie Marshner (Focus on the Family Publishing, 1988).

"Teaching Your Children About Sex" tape series, Dennis Rainey. Available from Family Life Today Ministries, Little Rock, AR (1-800-358-6329).

Medical Institute for Sexual Health (MISH). National Guidelines for Sexuality and Character Education (1-800-892-9484).

Sex Respect, Kathleen Sullivan. Committee on the Status of Women, 1850 E. Ridgewood Lane, Glenview, IL 60025.

Best Friends, Elayne Bennett and Phyllis Magrab. Georgetown University Child Development Center (1-202-822-9266).

God's Design for Sex (four-book series) (NavPress).

Why Wait: What You Need to Know About the Teen Sexuality Crisis, Josh McDowell (Here's Life Publishers, 1987).

A Gift for All Ages, Clifford Penner and Joyce Penner (Word, 1986).

Teenagers and Sex

Love, Sex and the Whole Person, Tim Stafford (Zondervan with Campus Life Books, 1991).

"No! The Positive Answer," video featuring Josh McDowell (Word, 1987).

Worth the Wait: Love, Sex and Keeping the Dream Alive, Tim Stafford (Tyndale with Campus Life Books, 1988).

Men

His Needs, Her Needs, Willard F. Harley (Revell, 1986).

If Only He Knew, Gary Smalley (Zondervan, 1979).

The Sexual Man, Archibald Hart, Ph.D. (Word, 1994).

Men and Sex, Clifford Penner and Joyce Penner (Thomas Nelson, 1997).

Focus on the Family Booklets

1-800-A-FAMILY (1-800-232-6459)

Depression: Help for Those Who Hurt, Archibald D. Hart, Ph.D.

Cultivating Affection in Your Marriage, Willard F. Harley Jr., Ph.D.

Premenstrual Syndrome: Advice from a Doctor, Marvin E. Eastlund, M.D.

Husbands and Wives: Unlocking the Gateway to Intimacy, Gary Smalley and John Trent, Ph.D.

Five Tips for Parents of Teens.

His Needs, Her Needs: Finding Fulfillment in Your Marriage, Willard Harley Jr., Ph.D.

Fatigue and the Homemaker.

Understanding Menopause.

Sex and Communication in Marriage, Dr. Kevin Leman.

Tough Love for Singles.

Help For Pregnant Teens, Linda Roggow and Carolyn Owens.

Why Wait for Marriage? Tim Stafford.

Questions Women Ask About Middle Age, Menopause and Maturity, Joe McIlhaney, M.D.

The Power of the Picture: How Pornography Harms, Dr. Jerry Kirk.

Help for Postabortion Women, Terri K.Reisser, M.S., and Paul C. Reisser, M.D.

Crisis Pregnancy Centers: How You and Your Church Can Help, Pamela Pearson Wong.

The Facts of Life: Teaching Your Children About Sex, Lenore Buth.

The Living Way Ministries Resources

Audio and video tapes on sexuality, featuring Dr. Jack Hayford. 1-800-776-8180
Internet address 75462.1407@compuserve.com.

Resource Information available on CompuServe in the Christian Interactive Network Forum (GOCIN).

Appendix 2

The National Survey of Christian Female Sexuality

This appendix outlines the research strategy we used in gathering the information about the sexuality of Christian women. We are presenting it in the appendix because not all our readers will want to be bothered with the technical aspects of our study. We feel, however, that it is necessary to outline our research strategy here for the benefit of those who would like to know how we gathered our data.

First, let us acknowledge three apparent limitations in our study.

Limitation 1. Our sample does not represent women from all religious groups. It isn't meant to be all-inclusive, neither is it meant to be comparative. Our goal was *not* to compare women from one group with women from another. Our data also does not represent women across the whole spectrum of Christian churches. Our primary target was women from the evangelical end of the church spectrum. This group is characterized as having a strong commitment to the integrity of Scripture in matters of faith and conduct and an emphasis on salvation through the grace of God by faith.

Limitation 2. We funded this study out of our own private resources. This has the advantage that we are not beholden to any special-interest group. We are free to arrive at whatever conclusion we deem appropriate. Even our publisher has no idea what our conclusions will be.

Limitation 3. It is one that has dogged every researcher since the beginning of the scientific era: sampling limitations. A random sample drawn from a random selection of the groups you want to study with a guarantee that everyone approached would participate, is every researcher's dream. And that's all it is—a dream. In our case this study would have taken many more years and a small fortune in research money to even begin to make a dent in such an ideal.

From the beginning we knew that we would have sampling problems to overcome. Many researchers have argued that it is *not* the size of one's sample but the percentage of subjects who respond that is important. For instance, if you ask one hundred people of a certain group to complete a questionnaire and 90% respond, you are better able to generalize to that population than if you had asked one thousand and only ninety had agreed to participate.

Rather than trying to select a truly random sample from a local area, we decided to approach a variety of church groups from around the country that were representative of our target population. If we could cast the net as widely as possible and try to achieve a high percentage of returns from within each group approached, we could come as close as possible to the representative sample (not random sample) we needed.

What about the possibility that our subjects, given the nature of the topic, would distort the truth? Our simple answer to this legitimate concern lies in the very nature of the women we were targeting: They have no reason not to tell the truth. They are by the very nature of their religiousness motivated to be honest. We found evidence for this again and again in the written comments we received to our open-ended questions. Many provided comments that confirmed their determination to "tell it as it is." We were pleasantly surprised to see that the timing for this study was right on target.

The Questionnaire

Sex surveys abound, so we had no difficulty getting ideas for our own. We drew on many, from the documents of hard-nosed scientists to the authors of popular magazine sex surveys. Since we were clear that the focus of our study was sexuality and not sexual practice as such, we quickly eliminated many of the popular questions that asked about sexual behaviors. We added questions that were informed by our combined clinical judgments.

Some questions from Dr. Hart's study of men (reported in *The Sexual Man)*[1] were added so we could make some male/female comparisons. Similarly, some questions similar to those from the *Sex in America* study were added so we could compare our findings with that study. There were a few points about female sexuality that we hypothesized would be the same in both studies. Comparisons would help to validate the adequacy of our sampling techniques as well as highlight significant differences between the general population and our particular subgroup of Christian women.

It was our firm belief that women would not just want to say yes or no to a bunch of forced choices but would desire to elaborate on their responses. We believed they would want to explain their feelings and describe their disappointments or accomplishments. *Quality* of response, not just facts, would be important to our sample. And we were right. Our subjects loved having the freedom to elaborate with written comments. Many told us so.

The questionnaire covered four sections. First, background information such as age, marital status, medical and social history, and religious upbringing and current practice. The second section covered early sexual experiences, sex education, first sexual experiences, and abuse of any sort. The third section examined current sexual experiences, attitudes toward masturbation, orgasmic responsiveness, and emotional and physical factors associated with female sexuality. This section also covered hormonal effects as well as the impact of mastectomy, hysterectomy, PMS, and abortion on a woman's sexuality. The fourth section was the narrative section, where subjects were encouraged to describe their "ideal" sexual experience, write about what sex means to them, and ask questions about female sexuality.

While these written comments are not as amenable to statistical analysis as are the quantitative responses, they have proven invaluable in communicating the depth of feelings associated with sexuality.

Getting Our Sample

As previously indicated, our sampling strategy followed several principles. First, because we could not randomly sample subjects, we tried to maximize the percentage of returns from a particular church group. Furthermore, because we could not systematically sample every region of the country, we tried to get subjects from as many church groups from across the country as possible. By ensuring a large enough sample from each region, we could at least test the results for differences between each region. If no regional differences were found, we could confidently assert that our findings were generally applicable.

Each of us regularly gets invitations to speak at church groups. Dr. Hart, in particular, speaks at least twice a month at church and pastors' groups around the country. These engagements provided us with the necessary opportunities to recruit Christian women to participate in our study.

The seminars at which women were recruited seldom focused on female sexuality per se, as we did not want to influence how women responded by our presentations. Where sexual topics were addressed we were careful not to make statements that would bias the answers. Our universal message was: "Please be as honest as you can. No one will know who you are. Don't even discuss your answers with your husband as this might just influence how you would respond." We heard that this caused a crisis in quite a few Christian marriages around the country—nothing serious! It's just that husbands are notoriously inquisitive as to what their wives think about their own sexuality. We advised the women to tell their husbands to read the book!

Who Are the Women in Our Study?

In this final section we want to provide basic demographic data. This is important because it helps to describe the *composition* of our sample.

Figure A.1 gives the age distribution for the two thousand women, breaking it down into five-year increments. Figure A.2 shows how our age distribution compares to the United States census.

AGE DISTRIBUTION OF SAMPLE
Figure A.1

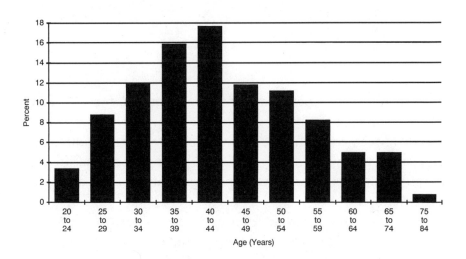

How do we compare? We have slightly more women than the United States census in the forty to forty-nine age range but less in the under twenty-four range. However, we think that this is representative of the church population we sampled. Many women in the eighteen to twenty-four age range were away at college when we gathered our data, and we did not target college churches in our study.

COMPARISON OF AGE DISTRIBUTION WITH U.S. CENSUS
Figure A.2

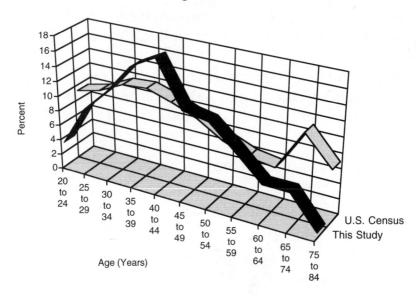

Also, the higher percentage of women in the forty to forty-nine age range is probably due to the influence of the church-growth movement, which has impacted the thirties and forties age-groups. Many churches who have been intentional in their church growth activities report a preponderance of this age-group in their churches.

While our sample shows a lower percentage of women in the sixty-nine age range, we had a larger sample of elderly women to analyze than did the *Sex in America* study.

The marital status of our sample is depicted in Figure A.3. By far the married group predominates (63%), followed by those who have been divorced and are now remarried (16%), then those not previously married (10%), divorced and now single (8%), and those widowed (2%) and separated (1%). Currently married women make up 79% of our sample.

How does this compare with the United States census? We are higher for currently marrieds (78% versus 58%) and lower for never marrieds (10% versus 27%).

MARITAL STATUS OF SAMPLE
Figure A.3

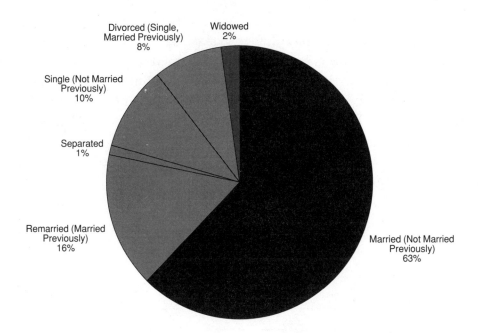

Are these differences significant? This probably needs further study, but our opinion at this point is that our sample, while not representative of the age distribution of the total United States adult population, *is* representative of the average churchgoing groups we studied. Many churches have a higher percentage of currently marrieds and a lower percentage of never marrieds than we see in the general population.

Our study shows a higher percentage of Asians (5% compared to less than 1% for the United States) and a lower percentage of African Americans (1.5% compared to 11.7% for the United States). Because of this deficiency, we are not able to draw any conclusions about how ethnic background shapes sexuality.

A comparison of the educational backgrounds of our sample with the United States census shows that our sample is more educated than the general population since we found a higher proportion who have a college education. They also are more likely to have a graduate degree.

Even though our sample was better educated than the general population, our analysis of the influence of education did not show any significant effects for either sexual satisfaction or marital happiness. Women who are more educated tended to be only slightly happier and more sexually satisfied, but the significance was small.

The length of Christian commitment for our sample is depicted in Figure A.4. Unexpectedly, the curve was not smooth. One dip appears at the thirty-five to thirty-nine year age range.

The length of marriage for the currently married group is shown in Figure A.5. Again the curve shows an even distribution.

LENGTH OF CHRISTIAN COMMITMENT
Figure A.4

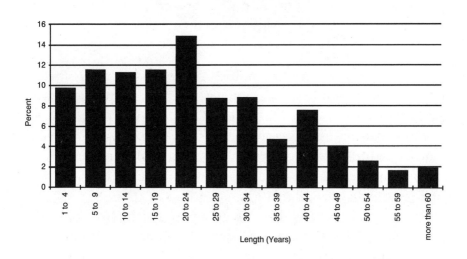

Length (Years)

Conclusion

This, then, describes the women in our study. But statistics cannot reveal the deeper stories of these women. They tell us nothing about their hopes and aspirations, or their disappointments and failures. We relied heavily on their personal comments to fill in the gaps and put real people with the facts and figures we reported.

We don't doubt for one moment that the women in our study

LENGTH OF CURRENT MARRIAGE
Figure A.5

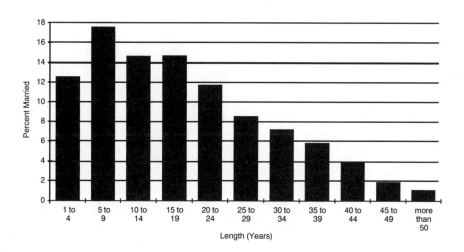

wanted to share their deepest feelings from their innermost being. There was little need to withhold information about painful experiences or avoid owning up to their struggles. Many were confused about sexuality. There was hardly a questionnaire returned that did not pose a question or two to us about this confusion. The answers to these questions are addressed throughout the book.

Appendix 3

QUESTIONNAIRE

The purpose of this national survey is to find the truth about what Christian heterosexual women are thinking and experiencing. WE APPRECIATE YOUR HELP. By completing this survey you will contribute greatly to this important research topic. You are not required to identify yourself so your confidentiality will be assured. Please answer the questions that apply to you currently as honestly as possible and return it in an unmarked envelope to the address given on the last page. Thank you.

Research team: Debra Taylor, M.A., Catherine Weber, Ph.D., Archibald Hart, Ph.D.

I. BACKGROUND INFORMATION

1. Date of Birth: Date_____ / Month_____ / Year 19_____
2. My ethnic background is (circle one): Asian / Black; African American/ Hispanic; Latino / Native-American / Caucasian /Other_____
3. Please circle your current status: Single / Married / Divorced / Separated / Remarried / Widowed
4. If married, date of current marriage? Month_____ / Year 19_____
5. If married, circle the phrase that best describes your degree of marital happiness, all things considered: Extremely unhappy / Fairly unhappy/ A little unhappy / Happy / Very happy / Extremely happy
6. Have you been married previously? Yes / No
7. How many times? _____
8. Length(s) of previous marriages _____
9. If divorced, were matters of sex a factor in the breakup? Yes / No

10. How many partners have you lived with without being married?
 _____(zero if none)
11. Did living with the most recent partner before marriage lead to:
 Marriage / Divorce / The relationship breakup /
 Current marital difficulties / Sexual problems
12. How many children do you have? _____ (zero if none)
13. How many are stepchildren?_____
14. How many children are living with you?_____
15. What percentage of the time? _____
16. Circle highest level of education attained.
 High School/ A.A. / B.A. / B.S. / M.A. / M.S. / Ph.D. /
 Other _____
17. Occupation _____
18. Spouse's occupation _____
19. I have the following medical problems: (Circle All That Apply)
 Diabetes / Chronic Fatigue Syndrome / Fibromyalgia /
 High Blood Pressure / Cancer / Atherosclerosis / Chronic Pain /
 Previous Heart Attack / Depression / Anxiety / Other _____
20. What prescription medication(s) do you take? _____
 _____
21. My spouse has the following medical problems: (Circle All That Apply)
 Diabetes / Chronic Fatigue Syndrome / Fibromyalgia /
 High Blood Pressure / Cancer / Atherosclerosis / Chronic Pain /
 Previous Heart Attack / Depression / Anxiety / Impotence /
 Other _____
22. I was raised (ages 0–18 years) in a strongly religious home (circle one):
 Not at all / Part of my youth / All of my youth
23. Growing up, did your parents or family attend church or synagogue?
 Yes / No
 If Yes: Family attended / One parent and children attended /
 One parent attended / Other _____
24. Do you consider yourself a committed Christian? Yes/ No
 If yes, for how long? _____(months), _____(years)
25. What denomination or religious group do you belong to? _____
26. How frequently do you attend your church? (circle one) More than
 once per week / Once per week / One to three times per month /
 Once or twice a year / Never
27. Does your current partner share your faith? Yes / No
 If yes, is he: More committed / Has same commitment /
 Less committed / Not committed at all

28. While you were growing up did your parents: Divorce/ Separate/ Distance emotionally
    If they divorced, what was your age when they divorced?
    _____ months _____years
29. Who did you spend most of the time with? Mother/ Father/ Grandparent / Other _____
29a. If they separated, what was your age (or ages) when they separated?
    _____ months _____years

II. EARLY SEXUAL EXPERIENCE

30. How did you first learn about the menstrual cycle? School / Friend / Parent / Book / I began without being told about it / Other_____
31. At about what age did you first menstruate? _____
32. How did you first learn about sexual intercourse? School /Friend / Parent /Book /Rape/ When I first had sexual intercourse / Other_____
33. Did either (or both) parent(s) discuss sexuality with you? Yes / No
    Who?: Mother / Father / Both Parents / Other_____
34. If your parent(s) explained sexuality to you, how was sexuality explained? (Circle all that apply) Private talk / Gave me a book / Family discussion / Allowed to attend sex education at school / Watched an X-rated video with me / Other_____
34a. Which one of the above was the most helpful to you? Private talk / A book / Family discussion / X-rated video / Sex education in school/ Other_____
35. In your childhood, was affection expressed in your home:
    (Circle those that apply)
    between your parents? Frequently / Occasionally / Rarely / Never
    between your father and you? Frequently / Occasionally / Rarely / Never
    between your mother and you? Frequently / Occasionally / Rarely / Never
    between your father and your sibling(s)? Frequently / Occasionally / Rarely / Never
    between your mother and your sibling(s)? Frequently / Occasionally / Rarely / Never
36. How was affection expressed? (circle all that apply) Hugs / Kiss on the cheek / Kiss on the lips / Praise / Other_____
37. What is the earliest age you recall having sexual feelings? _____ years
38. At what age did you begin dating? _____ years

39. At what age, and with whom, did you first experience each of the following sexual experiences?
Kissing: Age_____ male / female / both
French kissing: Age_____ male / female / both
Fondling breasts: Age_____ male / female / both
Fondling genitals: Age_____ male / female / both
Oral sex: Age_____ male / female / both
Sexual Intercourse: Age_____ male / female / both

40. Were these early sexual experiences with: (circle all that apply)
A younger child than you / An older child than you /
About the same age as you / An adolescent / An adult / A relative /
Other _____

41. What was your first experience with sexual intercourse like? (circle all that apply) Pleasant / Unpleasant / Painful / Forced / Guilty /
Ecstatic / Have never had intercourse / Other _____

42. At what age did you first masturbate? (zero if never masturbated) ____

43. How did you first discover masturbation? (Circle all that apply):
Read about it/ Saw it in a movie / Child showed me /
Adult showed me /Adult had me stimulate them /
Someone told me about it / Accidentally "discovered" it /
Other_____

44. Were you exposed to X-rated pornographic magazines or movies as a child? Yes / No
If yes, age(s) of exposure:_____

45. I believe that the effect of this early exposure to X-rated material has, in the long run, been (circle one): Beneficial / Neutral / Destructive /
Not exposed / Other_____

46. Have you ever been touched sexually by someone you did not want to touch you? Yes / No

47. If yes, at what age(s)? (Circle all that apply) Infancy (0–1) /
Toddler (13 mos. to 3 yrs.) / Preschool (4–6 yrs.) /
Grade School (7–11 yrs.) / Other_____

48. If yes, by whom were you touched? (Circle all that apply): Uncle /
Grandfather / Father / Stepfather / Brother / Mother /
Grandmother / Stepmother / Sister / Aunt / Female Cousin /
Male Cousin / Pastor / Other_____

49. As a child (age 0–15 years), were family members or other adults sexually inappropriate with you without touching you?
(i.e., inappropriate nudity, sexually suggestive in clothing or words,

sexually provocative gestures, etc.)
Yes / No / Not Sure / Other_____

III. PRESENT SEXUAL EXPERIENCE

50. Circle the phrase that best describes the degree of sexual satisfaction, all things considered, of your sexual relationship:
Extremely unsatisfied / Fairly unsatisfied / A little unsatisfied / Satisfied / Very satisfied / Extremely satisfied

51. At present, my sex drive is: Very strong / Strong / Moderate / Low / Feel no sex drive

52. My thoughts turn to sex about once every (circle one): Year / Quarter (every 3 months) / Month / Week / 2–3 times per week / Day / Hour / Never

53. Currently, my partner and I have sex about once every: (circle one) Year / Every 3 months / Month / Week / 2–3 times per week / 4–6 times per week / Day / Never / Other _____

54. I would like to have sex with my partner: (circle one) More often / Less often / I am satisfied with the frequency of our sexual relations.

55. My partner would like to have sex with me: (circle one) More often / Less often / He is satisfied with the frequency. / Don't know

56. When my partner and I have sex, we usually take: More than one hour / One hour / Forty-five minutes / Thirty minutes / Fifteen minutes / Five minutes

57. When my partner and I have sex, I would prefer to take:
More than one hour / One hour / Forty-five minutes / Thirty minutes / Fifteen minutes / Five minutes

58. When my partner and I have sex, he would prefer to take:
More than one hour / One hour / Forty-five minutes / Thirty minutes / Fifteen minutes / Five minutes / Don't know

59. In order to become aroused and reach orgasm, I need:
Five minutes or less of stimulation / 15 minutes of stimulation / 30 minutes of stimulation / 45 minutes of stimulation / One hour or more of stimulation / Other _____

60. I find it sexually stimulating to fantasize about having sex with someone other than my partner. Yes / No

61. I currently masturbate about _____ times per month or _____ per year (zero if you don't).

62. I believe the reason(s) I masturbate are that I (Circle all that apply):

Have a strong sex drive / Have an addiction to it / Just a habit /
No other sexual outlet / Merely enjoy it / Don't masturbate /
Spouse not interested in sex / Spouse doesn't stimulate me to orgasm /
Don't know / Other_____

63. I reach orgasm during lovemaking with my partner (circle one):
Always / 75% of time / 50% of time / 25% of time /
10% of time / Never

64. I cannot reach orgasm during intercourse unless I am stimulated
(circle all that apply): Manually (with my hand or my partner's hand) /
Orally (with partner's mouth or tongue) / Other _____

65. I can reach orgasm during intercourse without direct clitoral
stimulation (i.e., through intercourse alone). Yes / No

66. What I like most about sex with my partner is: (circle all that apply)
Physical closeness / Emotional closeness / Physical release /
Time together / Romance / Affirmation (loving words, praise) /
Other _____

67. What I like least about sex with my partner is: (circle all that apply)
The mess / Inconvenience / Partner's smell /
The words partner uses (demeaning, dirty words) /
Intercourse hurts / Sexual practices my partner insists on /
Sexual positions partner insists on / Other _____

68. I get my romantic needs met by: (circle all that apply)
No need for romance / My partner / Close friends / Movies /
Novels / Soap operas / Magazines / Daydreaming / Other _____

69. Do you and your partner share affection (kissing, hand-holding,
hugging, notes to each other) separate from your sexual relationship?
Yes/ No

70. When I want to express love to my partner, my preference is to:
Hug him / Cook his favorite meal / Go out for a romantic evening /
Buy him a gift / Send him a note or card / Call him at work /
Make love / Lie down with our arms around each other for a little
while / Other _____

71. I experience a strong sexual desire for someone other than my partner
(circle one): Very often / Often / Sometimes / Rarely / Never

72. I am sexually attracted to other women: Never / Slightly /
Sometimes / Often / Exclusively

73. I am able to discuss my personal sexual feelings or activities with:
(circle all that apply) Partner / One friend / Several friends / Parent /
Pastor / God / No one / Other_____

74. My spouse has been involved in an affair: (Circle all that apply) Once/

Twice / Three times / More than three times / Never been involved / Currently involved in an affair / Don't know / Other _____

74a. I have been involved in an affair: (Circle all that apply) Once / Twice / Three times / More than three times / Never been involved / Currently involved in an affair / Other _____

75. I have difficulty in the following sexual areas: (Circle all that apply) Feeling sexual desire / Becoming aroused / Reaching orgasm / Finding energy for sex / No difficulty

76. I consider this difficulty (question 75) to be: Severe / Moderate / Mild / No difficulty

77. My sexual desire is affected by: My menstrual cycle / Going through menopause / How I feel about my body/ How much I weigh / How fit I feel / Other _____

78. Have you had a hysterectomy? Yes / No

78a. If yes, how long ago? _____

79. Do you think that your hysterectomy caused any of the following? (circle all that apply): Less sexual interest / More interest / Less sexual sensation during lovemaking / Vaginal dryness/ Less intense orgasm / Partner reports discomfort during intercourse/ No effect / Other_____

80. Have you had problems with infertility? Yes / No

81. If yes, how has this impacted your sexuality? _____

82. Have you had a mastectomy? Yes / No

82a. How long ago?_____

83. Do you think that your mastectomy caused any of the following during the first year after surgery? (circle all that apply): Less sexual interest / More interest / Partner less interested / Don't feel "sexy" / Decreased arousal / No effect / Other_____

84. Are there any current sexual effects from your mastectomy? (circle all that apply): Less sexual interest / More interest / Partner less interested / Don't feel "sexy" / Decreased arousal / No effect / Other _____

85. If you experience premenstrual tension (PMS), how severe are your symptoms? Mild / Moderate / Severe/ Other _____

86. Do you think your PMS causes any of the following sexual effects? (circle all that apply): Less sexual interest / More interest / Less interest from partner / Decreased arousal / Increased marital conflict / No effect / Other _____

87. If you experience menopausal symptoms, how severe are your symptoms? Mild / Moderate / Severe / Other _____

88. Do you think your menopausal symptoms cause any of the following sexual effects? (circle all that apply): Less sexual interest / More interest / Less interest from partner / Decreased arousal / Increased marital conflict / No effect / Other _____

89. Have you ever had an abortion? Yes / No

89a. How many? (zero if none)_____

90. If yes, how long ago was the last abortion? _____months _____years

91. Do you think your abortion caused any of the following during the first year after your procedure? (circle all that apply): Less sexual interest / More interest / Less interest from partner / Painful intercourse / Decreased arousal / Fear of pregnancy / Guilt / Anger / No effect / Other_____

92. Are there any current sexual effects from your abortion? (circle all that apply): Less sexual interest / More interest / Less interest from partner / Painful intercourse / Decreased arousal / Fear of pregnancy / Guilt / Anger / No effect / Other _____

93. Which of the following sexually transmitted diseases (STDs) have you ever had? (circle all that apply): Gonorrhea / Syphilis / Herpes / Chlamydia / Genital warts / Hepatitis / AIDS/ HIV / Vaginitis / Pelvic inflammatory disease (PID) / Other _____

94. Which of the following have you had in the past 12 months? Gonorrhea/ Syphilis/ Herpes/ Chlamydia/ Genital warts/ Hepatitis/ AIDS/ HIV/ Vaginitis/ Pelvic inflammatory disease (PID)/ Other _____

95. For which of the following have you received counseling? Infertility / Hysterectomy / Mastectomy / Abortion / PMS / Menopause / STDs / Sexual dysfunction / Medical problems / Other_____

96. Who did you go to for help about the above problem(s)? Psychiatrist / Psychologist / Private doctor / Medical clinic / Marriage counselor / Clergy or pastor / Other _____

97. Length of counseling? _____ months _____ years

97a. Number of sessions? _____

98. How did counseling improve your sexuality? Greatly / Moderately / A little / Not at all / Other _____

99. How many sexual partners have you had in the past year? _____

100. Approximately how many sexual partners have you had throughout your lifetime? _____

Narrative response: Any comments? Add extra pages if necessary.

Thank you for completing this questionnaire. Please return it to:
Dr. Archibald D. Hart, 180 N. Oakland Avenue, Pasadena, CA 91101

Glossary

The following may not be complete or adequate definitions for the key words used in this book, but they do reflect the meaning that we intend to convey.

Abstinence – voluntarily going without sexual intercourse or anything that could directly lead to sex.

AIDS (Acquired Immune Deficiency Syndrome) – a viral disease communicated through body fluids.

Anorgasmia – the inability to achieve an orgasm.

Chastity – refraining from sexual intercourse, or the thoughts, desires or actions that lead to sexual intercourse.

Chlamydia – a sexually transmitted disease caused by a micro-parasite that infects the vagina, usually causing no symptoms until serious complications set in.

Chronic fatigue syndrome – a form of severe, longstanding, and periodic fatigue with diverse causes.

Clitoris – a small, sensitive organ at the upper end of the female vulva capable of erectile response similar to the male's penis.

Fatigue – physical and mental exhaustion.

Genital warts – a sexually transmitted disease caused by a virus that produces warts or bumps in the vagina, on the cervix, or around the anus.

Gonorrhea (also called "clap" or "drip") – a sexually transmitted disease caused by bacteria that can result in discharge, infertility, heart problems, and blindness.

Herpes – a sexually transmitted disease caused by a virus and causing blisters or sores on the face, in the mouth, or around the genitals.

Intercourse – the sexual joining of two individuals; inserting the penis into the vagina during lovemaking.

Libido – the sexual urge, desire, or instinct.

Masturbation – to manipulate one's own genitals for sexual gratification.

Menopause – the entire transitional period that includes two to ten years prior to the last manstrual cycle, the last menstrual cycle, and a year or more after.

NGU (nongonococcal or nonspecific urethritis) – a sexually transmitted disease caused by several organisms. Symptoms may be silent and lead to serious infections or infertility.

Orgasm – a series of pelvic and clitoral muscle contractions that mark the climax of sexual excitement.

Perimenopause – early stage of menopause (two to ten years before the final menstrual period).

Pornography – writing, pictures, or movies displaying overt nudity or sexual activity and intended to cause sexual excitement.

Premenstrual syndrome (PMS) – a state of increased tension, depression, agitation, or anxiety that occurs two to ten days prior to beginning monthly menstrual bleeding.

Pubic lice (also called "crabs") – a sexually transmitted disease in which parasites attach themselves to pubic hair, causing intense itching.

Purity (sexual) – sexuality that is free of distortion and follows God's standards for its expression. (See "Chastity".)

Rape – the crime of forcible sex with a girl or woman without her consent. When a male has sex with a girl below the minimum age stipulated by a given state, it is called "statutory rape."

Sex – the act of intercourse or other genital satisfaction.

Sexuality – a broad term embracing all that it means to be a sexual being.

Sexually Transmitted Disease (STD) – a disease that is uniquely transmitted mainly, though not exclusively, through genital contact or intercourse.

Sexual trauma – any act or experience that damages sexuality or sexual responsiveness.

Syphilis (also called "the pox") – a sexually transmitted bacterial infection that causes brain damage, heart disease, blindness, and eventually death.

Vaginitis – infection and inflammation of the vagina, causing irritation and discharge.

Virgin – a woman who has never had sexual intercourse.

Notes

Preface

1. Archibald D. Hart, *The Sexual Man* (Dallas: Word, 1994).

Chapter 1

1. Robert T. Michael et al., *Sex in America—A Definitive Survey* (New York: Little, Brown, 1994), 15.
2. Ibid., 286.

Chapter 2

1. Patricia Long, "Why am I So Tired?" *Health* (October 1995): 37–38.
2. Ibid.
3. "Lately, many doctors are cautioning against all anal sex, pointing to the impossibility of knowing anyone's complete sexual history and the irrevocability of AIDS. For patients who still choose to have anal sex, doctors counsel using not one but two condoms." Priscilla Grant, "Am I Normal?" *SELF* (May 1997): 220.
4. Dr. James Dobson, *Solid Answers* (Wheaton, Ill.: Tyndale, 1997), 286.
5. Hart, *Sexual Man*, 137.

Chapter 3

1. Holly Phillips, *What Does She WANT From Me, Anyway?* (Grand Rapids, Mich.: Zondervan, 1997), 136.

2. Ibid.

3. *Webster's Seventh New Collegiate Dictionary,* s.v. "romance."

4. Michael et al., *Sex in America,* 126.

Chapter 4

1. Helen Singer Kaplan, *Disorders of Desire* (New York: Simon & Schuster, 1979).

2. Hart, *Sexual Man,* 130.

3. Michael et al., *Sex in America,* 114.

4. *U.S. News and World Report,* 6 July 1992, 61–66.

5. Leiblum and Rosen, *Sexual Desire Disorders* (New York, Guilford, 1988), 2.

6. Michael et al., *Sex in America,* 126.

7. Helen Singer Kaplan, *The Sexual Desire Disorders* (New York: Burnner/Mazel, 1995), 142.

8. Kaplan, 1995, 19.

9. Archibald D. Hart, *Adrenaline and Stress* (Dallas, TX: Word, 1991).

10. Kaplan, 1995, 72.

11. Kaplan, 1995, 72–73.

Chapter 5

1. Barbara Seaman quoted in *The Hite Report,* by Shere Hite (New York: Bantum Doubleday Bell, 1981), 183.

2. Julia Heiman, "Evaluating Sexual Disfunctions", *Primary Care of Women,* D. P. Lemcke, J. Pattison, L. A. Marshall, D. S. Cowley, eds., (Norwalk, Appleton, and Lang, 1995), 127.

3. Shere Hite, *The Hite Report* (New York: Bantum Doubleday Dell, 1981), 186.

4. Samuel Janus and Cynthia Janus, *The Janus Report* (New York: John Wiley and Sons, 1993), 381.

Chapter 6

1. Clifford Penner and Joyce Penner, *The Gift of Sex* (Dallas: Word, 1981).

2. Juliet B. Schor, *The Overworked American* (New York: BasicBooks, 1991), 21.

3. Internet reference: http:/www.hugme.com/med/me/cdc-cfs.html.

4. Internet reference: http://cybertowers.com/selfhelp/articles/health/cfs2.html.

5. Barbara Killinger, *Workaholics: The Respectable Addiction—A Family Survival Guide* (New York: Fireside, 1991), 121.

Chapter 7

1. Health Report, *Time,* 14 July 1997.

Chapter 8

1. *Time,* 17 October 1994, 68.

2. Michael et al., *Sex in America,* 130.

3. Neil Warren, *The Triumphant Marriage Workbook* (Colorado Springs, Colo.: Focus on the Family Publishing, 1992), 50.

4. Richard Stuart, *Helping Couples Change* (New York: Guilford Press, 1980), 1–20.

Chapter 9

1. "News: Sexual Abuse in Churches Not Limited to Clergy," *Christianity Today,* 6 October 1997, 90.

2. The Attorney General's Commission on Pornography, *The Final Report of the Attorney General's Commission on Pornography,* (Nashville, Tenn.: Rutledge Hill Press, 1986) 268–270.

3. Consensus of leading researchers gathered by the Surgeon General to report to the Pornography Commission, as reported in *The Final Report,* xviii.

4. "Statement of Park Elliott Dietz, M.D., M.P.H., Ph.D.," in *The Final Report,* 489.

5. Ventura County Coalition Against Family and Sexual Violence, printed handout on sexual assault, 1997.

6. *The World Almanac and Book of Facts 1996* (Mahwah, N.J.: Funk and Wagnalls, 1995), 958.

7. Diana Russell, *Rape in Marriage* (New York: MacMillan and Company, 1982), 4.

8. Susan Jacoby, "The Body Image Blues," *Family Circle,* 1 February 1990, 41–44.

9. Anne McCammon, "Beating the Blues at Last," *New Woman,* (February 1990), 64–69.

10. George Skelton, "Many in Survey Who Had Abortion Cite Guilt Feelings," *Los Angeles Times,* 19 March 1989.

11. Medical Institute for Medical Health (MISH), Austin, Texas.

12. Michael et al., *Sex in America,* 187.

13. Wendy Maltz, *The Sexual Healing Journey* (New York: Harper Perennial, 1992), 85–107.

Chapter 10

1. Gilbert D. Nass and Mary Pat Fisher, *Sexuality Today* (Boston: Jones and Bartlett, 1994), 185.

Chapter 11

1. Connie Marshner, *Decent Exposure* (Brentwood, Tenn: Wolgemuth & Hyatt, 1988).

2. *God's Design for Sex.* A four-book series (Colorado Springs, Colo.: Navpress, 1995).

3. Medical Institute for Medical Health (MISH), Austin, Texas.

4. Michael, et al., *Sex in America,* 186–187.

5. M. Howard and J. McCabe, "Helping Teenagers Postpone Involvement," *Family Planning Perspectives,* vol. 22, #1, 1990, 21–25.

6. D. Dawson, "The Effects of Sex Education on Adolescent Behavior," *Family Planning Perspectives,* vol. 18, #4, July/August 1986, 151, 166.

Chapter 12

1. Bernie Zilbergeld, *The New Male Sexuality* (Boston: Little, Brown, 1992), 167.

2. "What 100,000 Women Told Ann Landers," *Reader's Digest* (August 1985): 44–46.

3. Arlie Hochschild, *The Second Shift* (New York: The Penguin Group, 1989), 1–10.

4. John Gray, *Mars and Venus in the Bedroom* (New York: HarperCollins, 1995).

Appendix 2: The National Survey of Christian Female Sexuality

1. Hart, *Sexual Man.*

Index